Quality Management

Dr. Sarika Gupta
MBA Ph.D
DGI G.Noida

Gaurav Gupta
Cvent India Pvt Ltd

KHANNA BOOK PUBLISHING CO. (P) LTD.
::: Publisher of Engineering and Computer Books :::

Head Office : 4C/4344, Ansari Road, Darya Ganj, New Delhi-110002
Phone: 011-23244447/48 Fax: 011-23244447
Regd. Office : 1694-95, Nai Sarak, Delhi-110006
Phone: 011-23283211 Fax: 011-23256658
E-Mail : sales@khannapublishers.com, contact@khannabooks.com
Website : www.khannapublishers.com

QUALITY MANAGEMENT
Dr. Sarika Gupta, Gaurav Gupta

ISBN : 978-93-82609-45-2

First Edition : 2015

Published by:
KHANNA BOOK PUBLISHING CO. (P) LTD.
4C/4344, Ansari Road, Daryaganj, New Delhi-110 002
Phone: 011-2324 44 47-48
E-mail: sales@khannapublishers.com
Website: www.khannapublishers.com

Cover Design & Layout by
Akriti Print & Graphics, Delhi

Printed in India by
S.P.S. Printers & Binders, Delhi

Preface

The Book itself is an acknowledgement to the intensity, drive and Technical competence of many individuals, who have contributed to it.

The Book starts with a development of the theory in each area and then provides a contextualization which considers what the theory might mean for organizational practice. Due to the complexity of many of the issues addressed, it is possible to write much more on any single topic but I have tried to cover most of the key points in order to provide a foundation, and further literature linked from the text allows the reader to investigate any topic in more depth if they wish. Finally, at the end of each chapter there are a number of questions for you to develop your thinking in the area.

Dr. Sarika Gupta

Contents

Introduction 1

INTRODUCTION

Quality is perceived differently by different people. Yet, everyone understands what is meant by "quality." In a manufactured product, the customer as a user recognizes the quality of fit, finish, appearance, function, and performance. The quality of service may be rated based on the degree of satisfaction by the customer receiving the service. The relevant dictionary meaning of quality is "the degree of excellence."

However, this definition is relative in nature. The ultimate test in this evaluation process lies with the consumer. The customer's needs must be translated into measurable characteristics in a product or service. Once the specifications are developed, ways to measure and monitor the characteristics need to be found. This provides the basis for continuous improvement in the product or service. The ultimate aim is to ensure that the customer will be satisfied to pay for the product or service. This should result in a reasonable profit for the producer or the service provider. The relationship with a customer is a lasting one. The reliability of a product plays an important role in developing this relationship.This figure shows Quality—

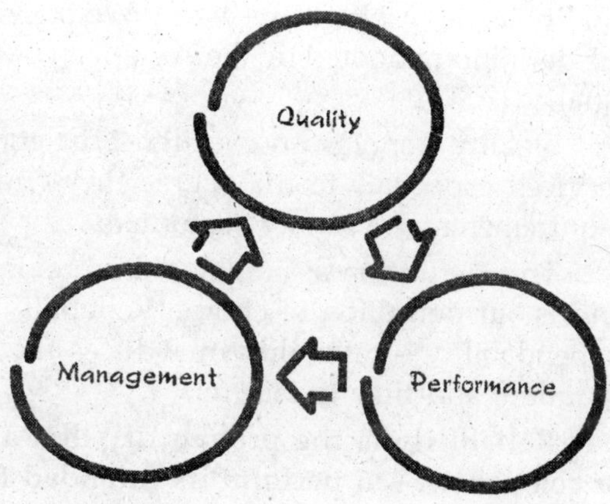

1.1 WHAT IS QUALITY

According to the American Society for Quality, "quality" can be defined in the following ways:

- Based on customer's perceptions of a product/service's design and how well the design matches the original specifications.
- The ability of a product/service to satisfy stated or implied needs.
- Achieved by conforming to established requirements within an organization.

1.2 QUALITY AND RELIABILITY DEFINED

There are many definitions of quality available in the literature. A definition attributed to quality guru Crosby states the following:

1.3 QUALITY IS CONFORMANCE TO REQUIREMENTS

The preceding definition assumes that the specifications and requirements have already been developed. The next thing to look for is conformance to these requirements.

Another frequently used definition comes from Juran:

1.4 QUALITY IS FITNESS FOR USE

This definition stresses the importance of the customer who will use the product. W. Edwards Deming defined quality as follows:

Good quality means a predictable degree of uniformity and dependability with a quality standard suited to the customer.

The underlying philosophy of all definitions is the same – consistency of conformance and performance, and keeping the customer in mind. Another definition that is widely accepted is **Quality is the degree to which performance meets expectations.**

This definition provides a means to assess quality using a relative measure. We provide here the definition adopted by the American Society for Quality (ASQ):

Quality denotes an excellence in goods and services, especially to the degree they conform to requirements and satisfy customers.

This definition assimilates the previous ones and is our definition of choice. Reliability implies dependability – reliability introduces the concept of failure and time to failure:

Reliability is the probability that a system or component can perform its intended function for a specified interval under stated conditions.

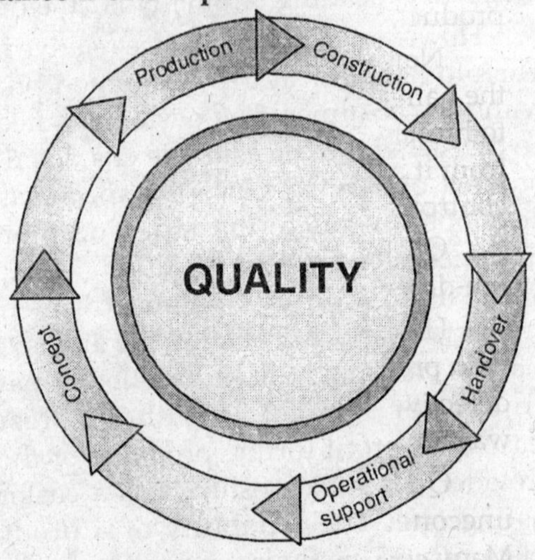

Applied throughout the entire project lifecycle

Quality and reliability go hand in hand. The customer expects a product of good quality that performs reliably.

This diagram shows all the component of Quality:

1.5 WHY IS QUALITY IMPORTANT

Business success may simply be the extent to which your organization can produce a higher-quality product or service than your competitors are able to do at a competitive price. When quality is the key to a company's success, quality management systems allow organizations to keep up with and meet current quality levels, meet the consumer's requirement for quality, retain employees through competitive compensation programs, and keep up with the latest technology.

1.6 THE ORIGINS OF THE QUALITY MOVEMENT

To investigate how the quality movement started, we need to understand its origins in industry. It is from industry that the language, concepts and the methodology of TQM are derived.

There has always been a need to ensure that products conform to their specification and give customer satisfaction and value for money.

Achieving consistent quality allows consumers to have confidence in a product and its producers. The marks of gold- and silversmiths are evidence of this long-standing concern.

Quality assurance became an issue with the advent of industrialization. Prior to this craftsmen set and maintained their own standards, on which their reputations and livelihoods depended. They established guilds that regulated quality and developed apprenticeship programmes that ensured that there was proper training and regulation in the craft. The advent of mass-production changed the emphasis completely. No longer were individuals responsible for making whole products. Instead the manufacturing process broke down work into narrow and repetitive tasks. Importantly for our discussion, it took away from the worker the possibility of self-checking quality.

One essential feature of a craft, the responsibility of the worker for the quality of the product, was lost when goods were mass-produced.

New production methods, associated with the scientific approach to management and the name of F W Taylor, at the turn of the twentieth century, reduced many in the workforce to human components in the process of manufacture. A strict division of labour developed from it and necessitated the expansion of a system of detailed inspection known as quality control.

Quality control and inspection are processes that ensure that only products that meet a pre-determined specification leave the factory gate.

However, quality control is an after-the-event process. It is divorced from the people who produce the product. Inspection and quality BASICS 5 control are designed to detect defective products. They are necessary processes under mass production, but they are often wasteful and expensive, involving considerable amounts of scrap and reworking.

Quality control and inspection in the past 20 years have increasingly been seen as uneconomic and wasteful, as they do not assure that the workforce care about quality. Many companies are replacing or augmenting them with methods of quality assurance and quality improvement that seek to build quality into the production process by returning to workers their responsibility for quality.

Notions of quality improvement and quality assurance began to emerge after the Second World War. However, in Britain and the United States they only began to attract attention on a large scale in the 1980s as companies started to ask questions about why the Japanese were at the time capturing larger and larger shares of world markets in a wide range of manufactured products. Questions were asked about their success, and whether it is bound up with their national culture and their novel quality management techniques. To find the origin of this new quality movement we need to start the search in the United States in the late 1920s.

1.7 HISTORY OF QUALITY

The quality movement can trace its roots back to medieval Europe, where craftsmen began organizing into unions called guilds in the late 13th century.

Until the early 19th century, manufacturing in the industrialized world tended to follow this craftsmanship model. The factory system, with its emphasis on product inspection, started in Great Britain in the mid-1750s and grew into the Industrial Revolution in the early 1800s.

In the early 20th century, manufacturers began to include quality processes in quality practices.

After the United States entered World War II, quality became a critical component of the war effort: Bullets manufactured in one state, for example, had to work consistently in rifles made in another. The armed forces initially inspected virtually every unit of product; then to simplify and speed up this process without compromising safety, the military began to use sampling techniques for inspection, aided by the publication of military-specification standards and training courses in Walter Shewhart's statistical process control techniques.

The birth of total quality in the United States came as a direct response to the quality revolution in Japan following World War II. The Japanese welcomed the input of Americans Joseph M. Juran and W. Edwards Deming and rather than concentrating on inspection, focused on improving all organizational processes through the people who used them.

By the 1970s, U.S. industrial sectors such as automobiles and electronics had been broadsided by Japan's high-quality competition. The U.S. response, emphasizing not only statistics but approaches that embraced the entire organization, became known as total quality management (TQM).

By the last decade of the 20th century, TQM was considered a fad by many business leaders. But while the use of the term TQM has faded somewhat, particularly in the United States, its practices continue.

In the few years since the turn of the century, the quality movement seems to have matured beyond Total Quality. New quality systems have evolved from the foundations of Deming, Juran and the early Japanese practitioners of quality, and quality has moved beyond manufacturing into service, healthcare, education and government sectors.

1.8 ASPECTS OF QUALITY

Quality denotes an excellence in goods and services, especially to the degree they conform to requirements and satisfy customers.

There are five aspects of quality in a business context:

1. Producing - providing something.
2. Checking - confirming that something has been done correctly.
3. Quality Control - controlling a process to ensure that the outcomes are predictable.
4. Quality Management – directing an organisation so that it optimises its performance through analysis and improvement.
5. Quality Assurance – obtaining confidence that a product or service will be satisfactory. (Normally performed by a purchaser)

1.9 CHARACTERISTIC OF QUALITY

Quality in business, engineering and manufacturing has a pragmatic interpretation as the non-inferiority or superiority of something; it is also defined as fitness for purpose. Quality is a perceptual, conditional and somewhat subjective attribute and may be understood differently by different people. Consumers may focus on the **specification quality** of a product/service, or how it compares to competitors in the marketplace. Some characteristic of Quality is as described

1. **Functionality:**
   - the system should detect errors and specify what they are, thereby enabling the user to correct them;
   - the system should not specify non-errors;
   - the system should be able to handle combinations of errors to some extent.

The present study focuses on this characteristic, since this is the one that has to do with NLP.

2. **Usability:**
   - the user interface should have a form that makes the system easy and efficient to use, e.g.
     - dialogue;
     - windows-based;
     - text replacement;
     - marked-up copy.
3. **Reliability:**
   - the system should not crash or loop;
   - the system should always specify the same grammar error in the same context the same way.

This characteristic will not be tested explicitly.

In addition to the characteristics proposed by ISO 9126, we suggest:

4. **Customisability:**
   - the system should allow the user a certain control over the functionality.

Customisability could be said to be part of functionality, but in our opinion it is a separate characteristic.

1.10 CONTINUOUS QUALITY IMPROVEMENT (CQI)

Continuous quality improvement came into existence in manufacturing as a different approach to quality and quality systems. It does not focus as much on creating a corporate quality culture, but

more on the process of quality improvement by the deployment of teams or groups who are rewarded when goals and quality levels are reached. CQI allows individuals involved in the day-to-day operations to change and improve processes and work flows as they see fit.

CQI implementation attempts to develop a quality system that is never satisfied; it strives for constant innovation to improve work processes and systems by reducing time-consuming, low value-added activities. The time and resource savings can now be devoted to planning and coordination.

CQI has been adapted in several different industries. For example, in health care and other service sectors, it has taken on the acronym FOCUS-PDCA work:

Find a process to improve.

Organize to improve a process.

Clarify what is known.

Understand variation.

Select a process improvement.

Then move through the process improvement plan:

Plan—create a time line, including all resources, activities, dates, and personnel training.

Do—implement the plan and collect data.

Check—analyze the results of the plan.

Act—act on what was learned and determine the next steps.

The FOCUS-PDCA acronym is an easy system for management to communicate to teams, and it helps them stay organized and on track with the end result in mind. The system has proven to be very successful for the CQI team approach.

1.11 ELEMENTS OF A QUALITY SYSTEM

There are several elements to a quality system, and each organization is going to have a unique system. The most important elements of a quality system include participative management, quality system design, customers, purchasing, education and training, statistics, auditing, and technology.

1.12 PARTICIPATIVE MANAGEMENT

The entire quality process, once started, will be an ongoing dynamic part of the organization, just like any other department such as marketing or accounting. It will also need the continuous focus of management.

The implementation and management of a successful quality system involves many different aspects that must be addressed on a continuous basis.

Vision and Values. The starting point for the management and leadership process is the formation of a well-defined vision and value statement. This statement will be used to establish the importance of the quality system and build motivation for the changes that need to take place, whether the organization plans to exceed customer expectations, commit to a defined level of customer satisfaction, or commit to zero defects. The exact form of the vision and values is not as important as the fact that it is articulated and known by everyone involved.

This vision and value statement is going to be a driving force to help mold the culture that is needed throughout the organization in the drive for quality. It is not the words of the value statement that produce quality products and services; it is the people and processes that determine if there is going to be a change in quality. The vision and value will be very important statements to set agendas for all other processes used to manage the quality system.

Developing the Plan. The plan for the quality system is going to be different for every organization, but there are similar characteristics:

- There should be clear and measurable goals.
- There are financial resources available for quality.
- The quality plan is consistent with the organization's vision and values.

The plan for the quality system might also include pilot projects that would entail setting up small quality projects within the organization.

This will allow management to understand how well the quality system is accepted, learn from mistakes, and have greater confidence in launching an organization-wide quality system. The plan should provide some flexibility for employee empowerment, because, as has been demonstrated, the most successful quality systems allow employees at all levels to provide input.

Communication. Change, especially a movement toward higher quality, is challenging to communicate effectively, yet the communication process is essential for the company's leaders to move the organization forward. Communication is the vital link between management, employees, consumers, and stakeholders. These communication lines also bring about a sense of camaraderie between all individuals involved and help sustain the drive for the successful completion of long-term quality goals.

Communication systems also must allow for employees to give feedback and provide possible solutions to issues the company must face. Management needs to allow for this in both formal and informal ways, such as employee feedback slips and feedback roundtable meetings.

The responsibility for fostering a culture that values communication lies with senior management. They alone have to ensure that goals and objectives are communicated to all. They are also responsible for setting up the system for feedback from the employees.

Rewards and Acknowledgment. Rewards, compensation, and acknowledgment for achievements in quality are very effective ways to motivate employees. They tell employees at the end of the day exactly what management is trying to accomplish. Rewards, compensation, and acknowledgment may also be seen as a form of communication—they are tangible methods that senior management uses to let employees know that quality is important. This could come in the form of individual rewards or team rewards. Rewards, compensation, and acknowledgment take many forms, and it is up to management to ensure that this type of program is in line with the goals and objectives of the quality system and the goals and objectives of the organization. Organizations have found that the best and most cost-effective reward, compensation, and acknowledgment programs are geared to meeting specific criteria. These programs motivate managers who in turn motivate their employees to strive toward predefined goals.

1.13 QUALITY CONTROL

Quality control, or QC is a process by which entities review the quality of all factors involved in production. This approach places an emphasis on three aspects. Elements such as controls, job management, defined and well managed processes, performance and integrity criteria, and identification of records

1. Elements such as controls, job management, defined and well managed processes, performance and integrity criteria, and identification of records
2. Competence, such as knowledge, skills, experience, and qualifications
3. Soft elements, such as personnel, integrity, confidence, organizational culture, motivation, team spirit, and quality relationships.

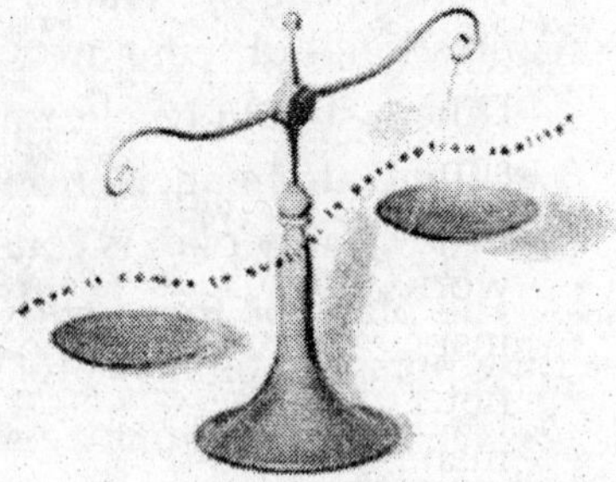

Quality Control

1.14 QUALITY ASSURANCE AND QUALITY CONTROL

The terms "quality assurance" and "quality control" are often used interchangeably to refer to ways of ensuring the quality of a service or product. The terms, however, have different meanings.

- **Assurance.** The act of giving confidence, the state of being certain or the act of making certain.

  Quality Assurance. The planned and systematic activities implemented in a quality system so that quality requirements for a product or service will be fulfilled.
- **Control.** An evaluation to indicate needed corrective responses; the act of guiding a process in which variability is attributable to a constant system of chance causes.

  Quality Control. The observation techniques and activities used to fulfill requirements for quality.

1.15 COMPARISON CHART

	Quality Assurance	Quality Control
Focus on:	QA aims to prevent defects with a focus on the process used to make the product. It is a proactivequality process.	QC aims to identify defects in the finished product. Quality control, therefore, is a reactive process.
Goal:	The goal of QA is to improve development and test processes so that defects do not arise when the product is being developed.	The goal of QC is to identify defects after a product is developed and before it's released.
Statistical Techniques:	Statistical Tools& Techniques can be applied in both QA & QC. When they are applied to processes (process inputs & operational parameters), they are called Statistical Process Control (SPC); & it becomes the part of QA.	When statistical tools & techniques are applied to finished products (process outputs), they are called as Statistical Quality Control (SQC) & comes under QC.
What:	Prevention of quality problems through planned and systematic activities including documentation.	The activities or techniques used to achieve and maintain the product quality, process and service.
How:	Establish a good quality management system and the assessment of its adequacy & conformance audit of the operation system & the review of the system itself.	Finding & eliminating sources of quality problems through tools & equipment so that customer's requirements are continually met.

1.16 EVOLUTION OF QUALITY CONTROL

Systems for improving and managing quality have evolved rapidly in recent years. During the last two decades or so simple inspection activities have been replaced or supplemented by quality control, quality assurance has been developed and refined, and now many companies, using a process of continuous and company-wide improvement, are working towards TQM. In this progression, four fairly discrete stages can be identified: inspection, quality control, quality assurance and total quality management; it should be noted that the terms are used here to indicate levels in a hierarchical progression of quality management **(figure**).

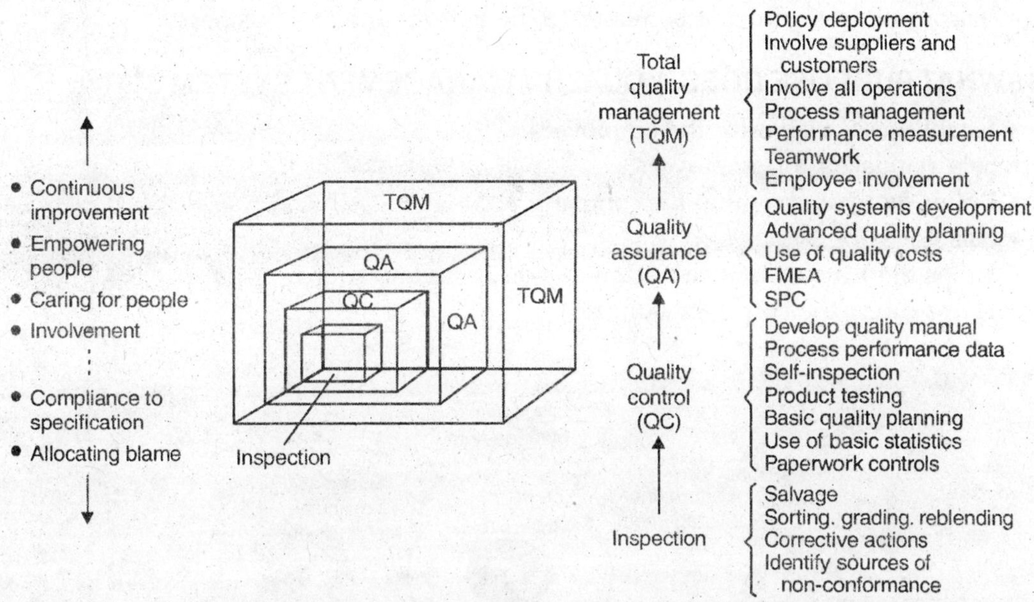

Quality management is a very important part of overall business success. It affects everything from employee performance to customer satisfaction. Quality control is also another important part of this process. Once problems or potential problems are diagnosed, plans are put into place in order to correct them. The idea is to avoid any interruption in the day to day happenings of company or a drop in sales. Teams work hard in various parts of an organization to make sure all business processes continue as normal and to ensure any problems will be resolved. Here the quality is controlled and dealt with in a way that keeps everything running as smoothly as possible.

1.17 QUALITY MANAGEMENT

A quality management system is a management technique used to communicate to employees what is required to produce the desired quality of products and services and to influence employee actions to complete tasks according to the quality specifications.

For more than two decades "quality" and "quality management systems" have been leading buzzwords in the business world. Numerous consultants have built their careers around these topics, and quality issues in business have been responsible for the development of new organizations and even industries, for instance, the American Society for Quality and Six Sigma consulting.

The notion of quality in business focuses on the savings and additional revenue that organizations can realize if they eliminate errors throughout their operations and produce products and services at the optimal level of quality desired by their customers. Errors can take almost any form—for example, producing the wrong number of parts, sending bank statements to customers who have already closed their accounts or sending an incorrect bill to a client. All of these errors are very common, and the costs incurred seem minimal. But over time when mistakes are repeated the costs add up to a significant amount, so eliminating errors can result in significant increases to the bottom line of a business.

1.18 WHAT PURPOSE DOES A QUALITY MANAGEMENT SYSTEM SERVE

- Establishes a vision for the employees.
- Sets standards for employees.
- Builds motivation within the company.
- Sets goals for employees.
- Helps fight the resistance to change within organizations.
- Helps direct the corporate culture.

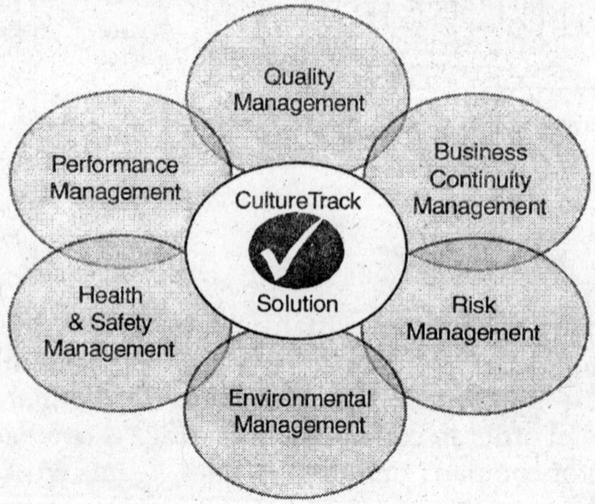

1.19 TOTAL QUALITY MANAGEMENT SYSTEM

TQM is the way of managing for the future, and is far wider in its application than just assuring product or service quality – it is a way of managing people and business processes to ensure complete customer satisfaction at every stage, internally and externally. TQM, combined with effective leadership, results in an organisation doing the right things right, first time.

A core definition of total quality management (TQM) describes a management approach to long-term success through customer satisfaction. In a TQM effort, all members of an organization participate in improving processes, products, services, and the culture in which they work.

A TOTAL QUALITY SYSTEM

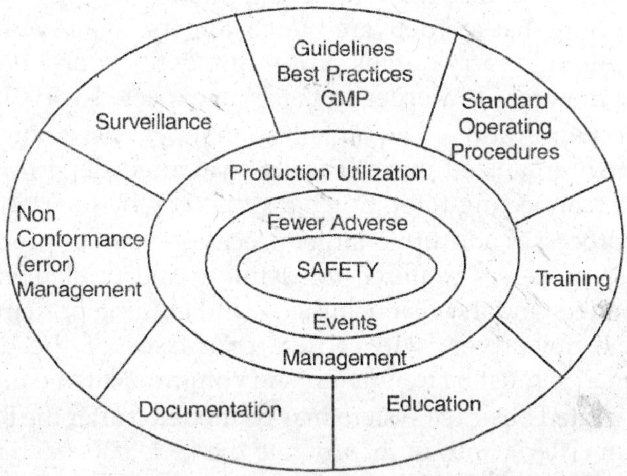

Though the different organization has the different total quality management criterion, in general guideline of total quality management should contain the following items.

- TQM is a customer focused approach
- It is company wide strategy and involves everyone in the organization
- Aims at satisfying the customer or delighting them
- Provides best quality product and satisfy them in a cost effective manner
- Fundamental changes in basic beliefs and practices
- Prevention of defects is the way and the target is zero defects
- Total quality management is methodical
- Provides meaningful measures of performance that guide the self-improvement efforts of everyone involved

1.20 THE PRIMARY ELEMENTS OF TQM

Total quality management can be summarized as a management system for a customer-focused organization that involves all employees in continual improvement. It uses strategy, data, and effective communications to integrate the quality discipline into the culture and activities of the organization.

- **Customer-focused**. The customer ultimately determines the level of quality. No matter what an organization does to foster quality improvement—training employees, integrating quality into the design process, upgrading computers or software, or buying new measuring tools—the customer determines whether the efforts were worthwhile.
- **Total employee involvement**. All employees participate in working toward common goals. Total employee commitment can only be obtained after fear has been driven from the workplace, when empowerment has occurred, and management has provided the proper environment. High-performance work systems integrate continuous improvement efforts with normal business operations. Self-managed work teams are one form of empowerment.

- **Process-centered**. A fundamental part of TQM is a focus on process thinking. A process is a series of steps that take inputs from suppliers (internal or external) and transforms them into outputs that are delivered to customers (again, either internal or external). The steps required to carry out the process are defined, and performance measures are continuously monitored in order to detect unexpected variation.
- **Integrated system**. Although an organization may consist of many different functional specialties often organized into vertically structured departments, it is the horizontal processes interconnecting these functions that are the focus of TQM.
  - Micro-processes add up to larger processes, and all processes aggregate into the business processes required for defining and implementing strategy. Everyone must understand the vision, mission, and guiding principles as well as the quality policies, objectives, and critical processes of the organization. Business performance must be monitored and communicated continuously.
  - An integrated business system may be modeled after the Baldrige National Quality Program criteria and/or incorporate the ISO 9000 standards. Every organization has a unique work culture, and it is virtually impossible to achieve excellence in its products and services unless a good quality culture has been fostered. Thus, an integrated system connects business improvement elements in an attempt to continually improve and exceed the expectations of customers, employees, and other stakeholders.
- **Strategic and systematic approach**. A critical part of the management of quality is the strategic and systematic approach to achieving an organization's vision, mission, and goals. This process, called strategic planning or strategic management, includes the formulation of a strategic plan that integrates quality as a core component.
- **Continual improvement**. A major thrust of TQM is continual process improvement. Continual improvement drives an organization to be both analytical and creative in finding ways to become more competitive and more effective at meeting stakeholder expectations.
- **Fact-based decision making**. In order to know how well an organization is performing, data on performance measures are necessary. TQM requires that an organization continually collect and analyze data in order to improve decision making accuracy, achieve consensus, and allow prediction based on past history.
- **Communications**. During times of organizational change, as well as part of day-to-day operation, effective communications plays a large part in maintaining morale and in motivating employees at all levels. Communications involve strategies, method, and timeliness.

These elements are considered so essential to TQM that many organizations define them, in some format, as a set of core values and principles on which the organization is to operate.

1.21 THE ESSENTIAL COMPONENTS OF TQM – COMMITMENT & LEADERSHIP

TQM is an approach to improving the competitiveness, effectiveness and flexibility of an organisation for the benefit of all stakeholders. It is a way of planning, organising and understanding each activity, and of removing all the wasted effort and energy that is routinely spent in organisations. It ensures the leaders adopt a strategic overview of quality and focus on prevention not detection of problems.

Whilst it must involve everyone, to be successful, it must start at the top with the leaders of the organisation.

All senior managers must demonstrate their seriousness and commitment to quality, and middle managers must, as well as demonstrating their commitment, ensure they communicate the principles, strategies and benefits to the people for whom they have responsibility. Only then will the right attitudes spread throughout the organisation.

A fundamental requirement is a sound quality policy, supported by plans and facilities to implement it. Leaders must take responsibility for preparing, reviewing and monitoring the policy, plus take part in regular improvements of it and ensure it is understood at all levels of the organisation.

Effective leadership starts with the development of a mission statement, followed by a strategy, which is translated into action plans down through the organisation. These, combined with a TQM approach, should result in a quality organisation, with satisfied customers and good business results. The 5 requirements for effective leadership are:

- Developing and publishing corporate beliefs, values and objectives, often as a mission statement
- Personal involvement and acting as role models for a culture of total quality
- Developing clear and effective strategies and supporting plans for achieving the mission and objectives
- Reviewing and improving the management system
- Communicating, motivating and supporting people and encouraging effective employee participation

The task of implementing TQM can be daunting. The following is a list of points that leaders should consider; they are a distillation of the various beliefs of some of the quality gurus:

- The organisation needs a long-term **commitment** to continuous improvement.
- Adopt the philosophy of zero errors/defects to change the **culture** to right first time
- Train people to understand the **customer/supplier** relationships
- Do not buy products or services on price alone – look at the **total cost**
- Recognise that improvement of the **systems** must be managed
- Adopt modern methods of **supervising and training** – eliminate fear
- Eliminate barriers between departments by managing the **process** – improve **communications** and **teamwork**
- Eliminate goals without methods, standards based only on numbers, barriers to pride of workmanship and fiction – get **facts** by studying **processes**
- Constantly educate and retrain – develop **experts** in the organisation
- Develop a **systematic** approach to manage the implementation of TQM

The building blocks of TQM: processes, people, management systems and performance measurement

Everything we do is a Process, which is the transformation of a set of inputs, which can include action, methods and operations, into the desired outputs, which satisfy the customers' needs and expectations.

In each area or function within an organisation there will be many processes taking place, and each can be analysed by an examination of the inputs and outputs to determine the action necessary to improve quality.

In every organisation there are some very large processes, which are groups of smaller processes, called key or core business processes. These must be carried out well if an organisation is to achieve its mission and objectives. The section on Processes discusses processes and how to improve them, and implementation covers how to prioritise and select the right process for improvement.

The only point at which true responsibility for performance and quality can lie is with the **People** who actually do the job or carry out the process, each of which has one or several suppliers and customers.

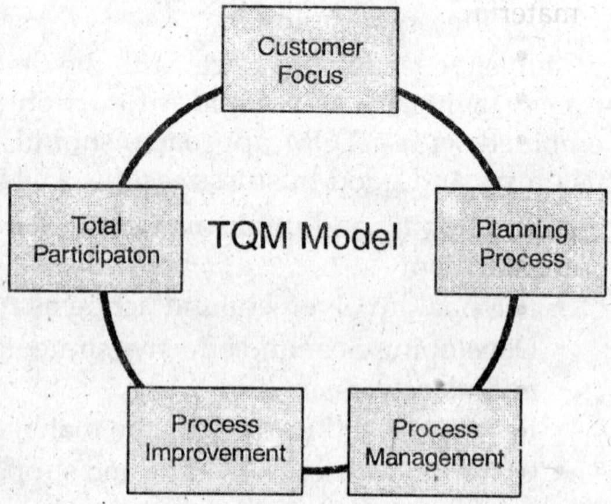

An efficient and effective way to tackle process or quality improvement is through teamwork. However, people will not engage in improvement activities without commitment and recognition from the organisation's leaders, a climate for improvement and a strategy that is implemented thoughtfully and effectively. The section on People expands on these issues, covering roles within teams, team selection and development and models for successful teamwork.

An appropriate documented **Quality Management System** will help an organisation not only achieve the objectives set out in its policy and strategy, but also, and equally importantly, sustain and build upon them. It is imperative that the leaders take responsibility for the adoption and documentation of an appropriate management system in their organisation if they are serious about the quality journey. The Systems section discusses the benefits of having such a system, how to set one up and successfully implement it.

Once the strategic direction for the organisation's quality journey has been set, it needs **Performance Measures** to monitor and control the journey, and to ensure the desired level of performance is being achieved and sustained. They can, and should be, established at all levels in the organisation, ideally being cascaded down and most effectively undertaken as team activities and this is discussed in the section on Performance.

1.22 THE COST OF TQM

Many companies believe that the costs of the introduction of TQM are far greater than the benefits it will produce. However research across a number of industries has costs involved in doing nothing, i.e. the direct and indirect costs of quality problems, are far greater than the costs of implementing TQM.

The American quality expert, Phil Crosby, wrote that many companies chose to pay for the poor quality in what he referred to as the "Price of Nonconformance". The costs are identified in the Prevention, Appraisal, Failure (PAF) Model.

Prevention costs are associated with the design, implementation and maintenance of the TQM system. They are planned and incurred before actual operation, and can include:

- Product Requirements – The setting specifications for incoming materials, processes, finished products/services.
- Quality Planning – Creation of plans for quality, reliability, operational, production and inspections.
- Quality Assurance – The creation and maintenance of the quality system.
- Training – The development, preparation and maintenance of processes.

Appraisal costs are associated with the vendors and customers evaluation of purchased materials and services to ensure they are within specification. They can include:

- Verification – Inspection of incoming material against agreed upon specifications.
- Quality Audits – Check that the quality system is functioning correctly.
- Vendor Evaluation – Assessment and approval of vendors.

Failure costs can be split into those resulting from internal and external failure. Internal failure costs occur when results fail to reach quality standards and are detected before they are shipped to the customer. These can include:

- Waste – Unnecessary work or holding stocks as a result of errors, poor organization or communication.
- Scrap – Defective product or material that cannot be repaired, used or sold.
- Rework – Correction of defective material or errors.
- Failure Analysis – This is required to establish the causes of internal product failure.

External failure costs occur when the products or services fail to reach quality standards, but are not detected until after the customer receives the item. These can include:

- Repairs – Servicing of returned products or at the customer site.
- Warranty Claims – Items are replaced or services re-performed under warranty.
- Complaints – All work and costs associated with dealing with customer's complaints.
- Returns – Transportation, investigation and handling of returned items.

1.23 QUALITY CONCEPTS IN SYSTEM DESIGN

A quality system is composed of the standards and procedures that are developed to ensure that the level of quality desired is repeated in every unit of a product or service. This portion of the quality system is very concrete and can be measured and managed. Before you start, your organization should establish a core team to carry the performance system design process forward.

The eight steps of the design process are:

1. Understand and map all business structures and processes. This forces employees involved in designing a performance measurement system to think through and understand the entire organization, its competitive position, the environment in which

it operates, and its business processes. This will also allow for complete understanding of customer touch points and how the different operations in the organization affect the customer's perception of quality. See Figure for an example of a process map.

2. Develop business performance priorities. The performance measurement system should support the stakeholders' requirements from the organization's strategy through to its business processes. This order of priorities must be in place well before the process enters the actual design phase.
3. Understand the current performance measurement system. Every organization has some kind of measurement system in place. For this reason, there are basically two ways to approach the design and implementation of a new performance measurement system. Either you can scrap the old system and introduce a new one as a replacement, or you can redevelop the existing system. Both approaches can work, but the former approach is more likely to lead to trouble. People will cling to the old measurement system and either use both systems simultaneously or use the old one and simply go through the motions of the new one. You can eliminate this outcome by taking the second approach.
4. Develop performance indicators. The most important element of a performance measurement system is the set of performance indicators you will use to measure your organization's perfor- process where the top-down approach meets the bottom-up design approach and where the broad masses of the organization become involved. The purpose of this step is to develop the performance measurement system with an appropriate number of relevant and accurate performance indicators.
5. Decide how to collect the required data. Developing perfect performance indicators that will tell you everything you ever wanted to know about what goes on in your organization is one thing, but being able to collect the data required to calculate these performance indicators is a completely different matter. This issue must initially be addressed during the development of the performance indicators so that you avoid selecting those that can never actually be measured. There will be trade-offs of cost and time versus the benefits of collecting data, but a likely middle ground between perfect data/high cost and no data/no cost will be found.
6. Design reporting and performance data representation formats. In this step, you decide how the performance data will be presented to the users; how the users should apply the performance data for management, monitoring, and improvement; and who will have access to performance data. After you finish, you should have a performance measurement system that has a solid place in your organization's overall measurement based management system.
7. Test and adjust the performance measurement system. Your first attempt at the performance measurement system will probably not be perfect—there are bound to be performance indicators that do not work as intended, conflicting indicators, undesirable behavior, and problems with data availability. This is to be expected. In this step you should extensively test the system and adjust the elements that do not work as planned.
8. Implement the performance measurement system. Now it's time to put your system to use. This is when the system is officially in place and everyone can start using it. This step involves issues such as managing user access, training, and demonstrating the system.

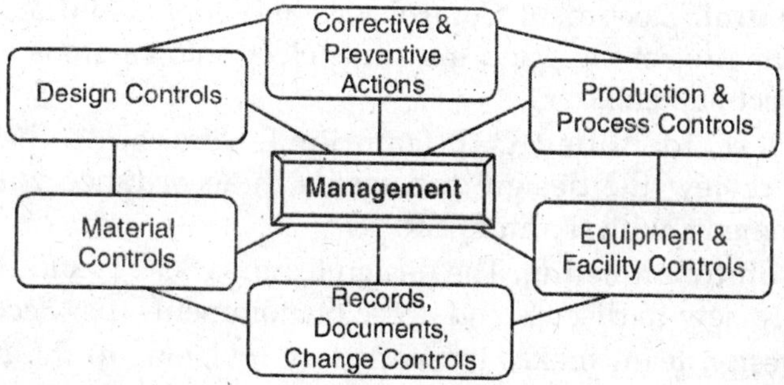

1.24 EVOLUTION OF DESIGN

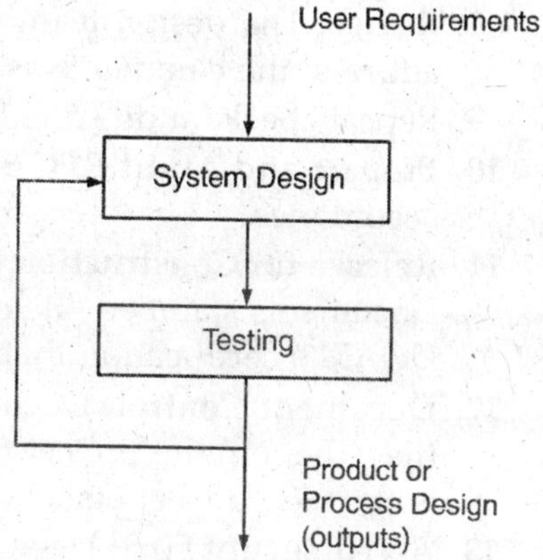

Traditional approach to design process as a feedback system with cycle operation:

The **engineering design process** is the formulation of a plan to help an engineer build a product with a specified performance goal. This process involves a number of steps, and parts of the process may need to be repeated many times before production of a final product can begin.

1.25 OVERVIEW OF DESIGN QUALITY PROGRAM

The DQPs are dynamic documents, and additions/revisions are issued, as needed, when the processes require modifications, refinements, or clarifications.

The design quality program consists of several steps, involving:

- Planning the work.
- Preparing design documents.
- Making revisions.
- Auditing and Certifying.
- Checking and reviewing the documents.
- Releasing documents for construction.

There are iterations to each of the steps, depending on the specific type of document, but the basic design quality process is as shown in Exhibit QMP-5. Specifics regarding the steps are:

1. **Prepare Design Documents.** The design team prepares the design documents, using the established design criteria for the project and appropriate inter-discipline and Task Force coordination (via regular scheduled meetings, written communications, etc.). Task Forces (which include representatives from the Contractor, Designer, and WSDOT) meet weekly or bi-weekly during the design phase and periodically thereafter. Some task forces may be added, combined, or eliminated as design progresses. The Task Forces will generally be discipline specific such as Quality, Roadway/Traffic, and Structures/Geotechnical.
2. **Check.** All design documents are subjected to in-discipline design checking process
3. **Revise.** Checker corrections and comments and review comments are evaluated and incorporated into the documents by the Originator, as appropriate.
4. **Audit.** The DQAM audits the design documents in accordance with Section 4.5 and certifies them as meeting the requirements of the QMP, using Form DQA.

5. **Document Control.** Document Control logs and copies audited design documents, files them in the project files, and transmits electronic versions to WSDOT and other approved project stakeholders.
6. **Review.** WSDOT, identified D/B team Reviewers, and other approved project stakeholders review the design documents in accordance with Section 4.6.1 and document comments with Form RCSR.
7. **Comment Resolution Meeting.** The design team, WSDOT, and other Reviewers meet following the review to discuss and agree on comments, per Section 4.6.1.2.
8. **Revise.** The design team makes the necessary revisions to the design documents to address the comments as agreed upon and advance the design to the next level.
9. Repeat check/audit/review/revise cycle through each required submittal described.
10. **Prepare and Audit RFC Submittal.** The design team prepares the RFC documents in accordance.
11. **Release for Construction (RFC).** The DM transmits the signed and sealed RFC Design Documents stamped "Released for Construction" to Document Control along with the DQAM's certification that the design package may be released for construction.
12. **Document Control.** Document Control logs and copies the audited RFC documents, files them in the project files, and transmits electronic versions to WSDOT and other approved project stakeholders.
13. **Acceptance of Final Design.** WSDOT acceptance of the final design occurs after WSDOT acceptance of construction.

SUMMARY

The quality movement and quality systems have had many different names or terms of reference in the past few decades, and might look like a short-lived business management trend at first glance. With everincreasing competition and consumer expectations, professionals and business managers cannot ignore quality issues and expect to maintain or improve their competitive position. Quality systems, time and again, have been responsible for substantial increases in the bottom line of businesses in every industry and have given organizations the boost they need to meet overall goals and objectives. Organizations that do not accept that quality improvement is going to be ingrained into every part of their business are not going to be around to see what the future brings.

Exercise Questions

1. The chapter discussed four quality gurus. Who are the other major contributors to quality improvement?
2. What is the Malcolm Baldridge National Quality Award? What are the criteria for this award? Which organizations are the past recipients?
3. What is the underlying philosophy of Six Sigma? Which companies spearheaded this movement?
4. Who proposed the "zero defects" concept? Why did this philosophy lose its appeal?
5. How does improvement in quality benefit a manufacturing company?
6. Why do quality and reliability go hand in hand? ❑

Quality Control in Purchasing

2

INTRODUCTION

Quality is an important part of the supply chain, whether it is quality inspections during the manufacturing process, quality checks before goods arrive at the customer, or checking quality as raw materials and parts enter the factory. Before any part or raw material is used in a manufacturer of a finished good that will be delivered to a customer, it is the responsibility of the purchasing department to ensure that the materials that arrive are of the correct quality specification.

2.1 QUALITY IN THE PURCHASING PROCESS

When the purchasing department are looking at the procurement of materials from suppliers they will have been given some guidance by the manufacturing department, research and development, or the quality department. This should include a variety of information about the item to be sourced, such as physical description, dimensional measurements, chemical composition, performance specifications, standards to conform to, or even the brand name of the product.

- **Physical Description.** The purchasing department must know the physical attributes of the part they are required to source. For example, if the required material must be made of a certain shade of a blue, then the purchasing department must be able to communicate that requirement to the potential suppliers to ensure that the specification can be met.
- **Chemical Composition.** This is very important for sourced materials that are used in the **chemical** process. The quality department should give the purchasing team a detailed list of chemical specifications of the required material. This should include a list of characteristics and specifications that the materials should conform to, as well as the ranges that the materials must lie within. For example, a sourced chemical may be required to have a pH of between 5.6 and 5.9; otherwise the material would not be suitable for the manufacturing processes.
- **Dimensional Measurements.** For a part to be used in the manufacturer of a machine the part must conform to certain dimensional specifications. For example, if the manufacture of a finished item required the use of a Pentalobe TS1 screw with a length of 4 mm, then the supplier must be able to produce the item in that correct size.

- **Performance Specifications.** If a part is required to withstand certain forces or perform in a particular manner, the purchasing department must find a supplier that can achieve those specifications. For example, on a household item such as washing machine, the rubber belt that is used must be bale to withstand certain forces and not fail within a certain number of revolutions. This quality measurement is key for a business if they are to produce finished goods that are reliable in the eyes of their customers. Therefore it is important for the purchasing department to find suppliers who can provide parts that meet quality specifications.
- **Industrial Standards.** Some parts required in the production of finished goods must conform to certain industry standards. These standards are set by a number of trade or industry groups who try to maintain a certain level of quality. By having an item that conforms to a particular industry standard, the customer will have a level of confidence in the product. There are a number of industry standards that are used, such as Society of Automotive Engineers (SAE), which is a global association of more than 128,000 engineers and related technical experts in the aerospace, automotive and commercial-vehicle industries. The society has hundreds of standards that relate to different technical aspects of manufacturing.
- **Brand Name.** Sometimes the quality department or development team will inform the purchasing department to only source a particular brand name. This may be due to the specific nature of the part made by one company or the level of quality it has over competitors.

2.1.1 Measuring Purchasing Performance

Measuring purchasing performance is important as the purchasing department plays an ever increasingly important role in the supply chain in an economic downturn. A reduction in the cost of raw material and services can allow companies to competitively market the price of their finished goods in order to win business. An obvious performance measure of the success of any purchasing department is the amount of money saved by the company. However there are a number of performance measurements that businesses can use when they measure purchasing performance.

Administrative costs are the basis for measuring purchasing efficiency. This performance measurement does not relate to the amount of purchased items that the department has procured. The measurement relates to how well the purchasing department is performing in the activities they are expected to perform against the budget that is in place for the department. If the purchasing costs are within the budget then the efficiency of the purchasing department will exceed expectations. If the department is using funds over and above the budget then the purchasing function is not efficient.

2.1.2 Purchasing Effectiveness

The price that the purchasing department paid for an item is not necessarily a good measurement for purchasing performance. The price of an item may fluctuate due to market conditions, its availability, and other demand pressures; therefore the purchasing department may not be able to control the price. A popular method of assessing purchasing effectiveness is to review the inventory turnover ratios. The ratio measures the number of times, on average; the inventory is used, or turned, during the period. The ratio used to measure the liquidity of the inventory. However, this is not always a great measure of purchasing effectiveness as seasonal requirements for having items in stock can make this measurement inaccurate.

2.1.3 Purchasing Functionality

Purchasing performance can be measured against the functional requirements of the purchasing function. The primary function of the department is to provide the correct item at the required time at the lowest possible cost. The performance measurement can take into account these elements, but it does not take into account factors that may relate to the supplier stability, material quality issues and supplier discounts.

2.1.4 Performance Measurements

The performance of the purchasing function can be measured using a variety of measurements. A company can decide which of these measurements of effectiveness are relevant to the performance of their purchasing department. The measurements can include,

- **Cost Savings.** If the purchasing department procure an item at a lower price than they did previously, then it is a cost saving. This can occur when a new supplier is found, a less costly substitute item is used, a new contract has been signed with the vendor, a cheaper transportation method has been found or the purchasing department has negotiated a lower price with the existing supplier.
- **Increased Quality.** When an item has improved quality either by using a different supplier or by negotiating with the existing supplier, the improvement will be reflected in a reduction of waste or production resources.
- **Purchasing Improvements.** Efficiencies in the method used in the purchasing department will increase effectiveness. These can include the introduction of EDI, e-procurement systems, vendor managed inventory and pay on receipt processes.
- **Transportation Improvements.** When a purchasing department negotiates with a carrier or number of carriers to reduce the cost of transporting items from the vendor to the production facilities, the unit cost of the item will be reduced. This cost saving can be used as a measurement of effectiveness.

2.1.5 Purchasing Performance

A number of studies have been carried out on purchasing performance and the results have noted that there is no one method that will cover every purchasing department. However, there are a number of key measures that are found to be common in evaluating performance, namely; cost saving, vendor quality, delivery metrics, price effectiveness and inventory flow. Although these key measures are common, the weight placed on these measures is by no means uniform and will vary between industry to industry and business to business. In addition the importance of these measures to the overall effectiveness of a purchasing department will change over time and therefore need to be assessed and modified on a periodic basis.

2.2 PRODUCT OF VARIOUS PRODUCTS

The product life cycle can be divided into several stages characterized by the revenue generated by the product or range of products, such as a brand. The life cycle can be very short, as pertains to a product that is for an event, such as a Christmas toy, or very long such as a watch or a car. For most products the beginning of the life cycle is the product development stage. Companies develop new products all the time and a small percentage of those reach the market.

2.2.1 Introduction Stage

The introduction of a product into the market will not generate sales until the public is aware of the product. The consumer is introduced to the product by the advertising that a company uses to publicize the product. There are thousands of ways a company can advertise their product and advertising costs usually are high during this stage in order to quickly make consumers aware of the product. There may be additional costs associated with product introduction such as packaging and distribution. The introduction stage of a product generates few sales and the costs of introduction far outweigh the profits from the small sales volume. During this introduction stage, a company is focused on making the consumer aware of the product in the market and seeding a demand for future demand for the product.

2.2.2 Growth Stage

The growth stage in the product life cycle is a period of rapid revenue growth. As the product awareness increases, customers are more likely to purchase the item and sales increase. The success of a product in one area can lead to the product being introduced into other market segments. Continuing increase in sales can lead to additional demand and further sales. During the growth stage, competing products may be introduced by other companies. This can lead to price competition and additional costs in advertising to maintain the demand for the product at the expense of the competition.

2.2.3 Maturity Stage

A product becomes most profitable during the maturity stage. The sales for the product are slower than in the growth stage but continues as the product becomes a market leader. Continued advertising reinforces the product with the consumer, but generally advertising costs are lower than for a new product. For example, companies such as Coca Cola and Clorox advertise their mature products to reinforce the brand with the public. However, competition from other companies or store brands may result in a decreased market share and lower profits. A company may spend more with retailers to obtain more shelf space for their products over competing products, which may differ only very slightly. During the maturity stage, a company's focus is to maintain market share and extend the product life cycle as much as possible. Many companies have been very successful in extending the life cycle of their product when new cheaper alternatives are introduced into the market such as Clorox, Coca Cola, General Mills, Kraft and Pepsi.

2.2.4 Decline Stage

In the decline stage the sales of a product declines, either due to a product becoming obsolete, for example, a slide rule, or where the market becomes saturated. A company does have a number of options when a product has reached the end of its life cycle. It can remove the product from the market completely, reduce advertising and marketing to maximize profits from the small sales volume or reduce costs in manufacturing the product allowing the product more time for competing products to be withdrawn from the market.

2.3 EVALUATION OF SUPPLIES

As a consumer, when you want to purchase an item, whether it is a new car or a flat screen television, you will most likely do some research on the prices of your local stores or from vendors on the internet. When you have narrowed your search you then look at other criteria that may be important to you, like warranty or availability. Lastly you will look at other less tangible criteria such as your previous experiences with the vendor and how their customer service was. This behavior is exactly the same for companies when they want to evaluate the vendors in their supply chain.

Unless your company only uses one vendor for each item they purchase, there will enviably be occasion when a decision has to be made as to which vendor gets your business. There are a number of different scenarios when this will occur, for example when the item is purchased for the first time and when an item is no longer single sourced.

2.3.1 Purchasing an Item for the First Time

When a decision has to be made between vendors, the purchasing department will use some vendor evaluation method to be their tool in the decision. If the item is to be bought for the first time, the purchasing department may have contacted a number of vendors and sent them a Request for Quotation (RFQ). Each vendor would then complete the RDQ with the information that was required, normally price and terms. The purchasing department would then use these completed quotations, in conjunction with other information they have collected on the vendors, to make short list for further evaluation or make a final selection. The purchasing department would evaluate the vendors based on a number of criteria they had decided upon which may include objective criteria such as price and warranty and subjective data which would include past experience with the vendor. Based on the weighting given to these criteria the purchasing department would be able to fairly evaluate each vendor.

2.3.2 Choosing Between Vendors

If the sourcing of an item has been from a single vendor but another vendor has been approved to supply the same item, a decision would need to be made on vendor selection when a requisition has been received by the purchasing department. Many companies use a vendor evaluation tool that allows transaction data to be analyzed to give a comparison between vendors. The vendor evaluation uses criteria that have been determined by the purchasing department to compare vendors such as price, delivery reliability, delivery date adherence and quality of the item. There are any numbers of criteria that can be used in a comparison and these are usually weighted so that important criteria are given more credence. For example, a company may decide that quality of the items it receives from vendors is more important than price, which in turn is more important that delivery reliability. The company would then weight these criteria so that the overall score reflects that requirement.

Supply evaluation is important as it can reduce supply chain costs and improve the quality and timeliness of the delivery of items to your company. The skill in evaluating vendors is to determine which criteria are important and the weighting that these criteria are given. It is important to remember that these criteria may be different for each item you are sourcing and possibly different between regions or countries. Objective data is useful to compare the information that you can obtain from each purchase order and goods receipt, but sometimes the subjective data that your purchasing agents can provide such as customer service and the willingness of the vendor to accommodate your requirements, is as or more important in a vendor evaluation.

2.4 CAPACITY OFVARIFICATION

The term **Varification** refers to moving product from a manufacturing plant and delivers it directly to the customer with little or no material handling in between. Cross docking not only reduces material handling, but also reduces the need to store the products in the warehouse. In most cases the products sent from the manufacturing area to the loading dock has been allocated for outbound deliveries. In some instances the products will not arrive at the loading dock from the manufacturing area, but may arrive as a purchased product that is being re-sold or being delivered from another of the companies manufacturing plants for shipment from the warehouse.

2.4.1 Benefits

Many companies have benefitted from using **Varification.** Some of the benefits include:

- Reduction in labor costs, as the products no longer requires picking and putaway in the warehouse.
- Reduction in the time from production to the customer, which helps improve customer satisfaction.
- Reduction in the need for warehouse space, as there is no requirement to storage the products.

2.4.2 Types of Varification

There are a number of cross docking scenarios that are available to the warehouse management. Companies will use the type of cross docking that is applicable to the type of products that they are shipping.

- **Manufacturing Cross Docking.** This procedure involves the receiving of purchased and inbound products that are required by manufacturing. The warehouse may receive the products and prepare sub-assemblies for the production orders.
- **Distributor Cross Docking.** This process consolidates inbound products from different vendors into a mixed product pallet, which is delivered to the customer when the final item is received. For example, computer parts distributors can source their components from various vendors and combine them into one shipment for the customer.

- **Transportation Cross Docking.** This operation combines shipments from a number of different carriers in the less-than-truckload (LTL) and small package industries to gain economies of scale.
- **Retail Cross Docking.** This process involves the receipt of products from multiple vendors and sorting onto outbound trucks for a number of retail stores. This method was used by Wal-Mart in the 1980's. They would procure two types of products, items they sell each day of the year, called staple stock, and large quantities products which is purchased once and sold by the stores and not usually stocked again. This second type of procurement is called direct freight and Wal-Mart minimize any warehouse costs with direct freight by using cross docking and keeping it in the warehouse for as little time as possible.
- **Opportunistic Cross Docking.** This can be used in any warehouse, transferring a product directly from the goods receiving dock to the outbound shipping dock to meet a known demand, i.e. a customer sales order.

2.4.3 Products Suitable for Varification

There are materials that are better suited to cross docking than others. The list below shows a number of types of material that are more suited to cross docking.

- Perishable items that require immediate shipment
- High quality items that do not require quality inspections during goods receipt
- Products that are pre-tagged (bar coded, RFID), pre-ticketed, and ready for sale at the customer
- Promotional items and items that are being launched
- Staple retail products with a constant demand or low demand variance
- Pre-picked, pre-packaged customer orders from another production plant or warehouse

2.5 DEVELOPMENT OF SOURCE

The Development Source is experienced in a wide range of visual communications.There are various eaxmples that shows the development of soures like-

2.5.1 Digital Publishing

- Editorial and Composition
- ebook design and production
- Rich-media design and creation
- XML workflow
- Conversion Copy-editing, proofreading, and quality guarantee

2.5.2 Mobile Technology

- Mobile / Tablet Development
- Mobile Learning
- Interactive Text Books
- App Design and Development
- Mobile Messaging

2.5.3 eAdvertising

- Integrated Campaign Strategy
- Media Planning and Buying
- Search Engine Optimization
- (SEO / PPC / Mobile)
- Rich Media and Mobile Advertising
- Print, Television, and Radio Advertising
- Digital Advertising
- Email Marketing
- Contests and Viral Campaigns

2.5.4 Design Build

- Scope and Functionality
- User Experience Requirements
- Architecture Design
- Prototyping
- Flowcharts / Wireframes / Sitemaps
- CMS
- E-Commerce
- Custom Component Builds
- Database Development
- Rich Media, Animation, and Interactivity
- Application Development
- Website Development

2.5.5 HD Web Video and Internet Television

- Web Video Production
- Viewer Targeted Video Overview of Company Services
- Deployment on Client's Websites
- Deployment on Client's Social Media Pages / Outlets
- Viral Video Deployment by "Share" features to Targeted user Groups

2.5.6 Social Media

- Consumer Engagement
- Consumer Conversation
- Social Community Development
- Social Network Management and Analysis
- Online Reputation Development
- Press and Blog Relations

2.6 FACTORS THAT INFLUENCE PRODUCT DEVELOPMENT

Product Analysis is the process of identifying, looking at or disassembling a product and identifying its main features. The aim is to understand more about a product and improve it in the future. Many factors influence the development of a product, some are listed below.

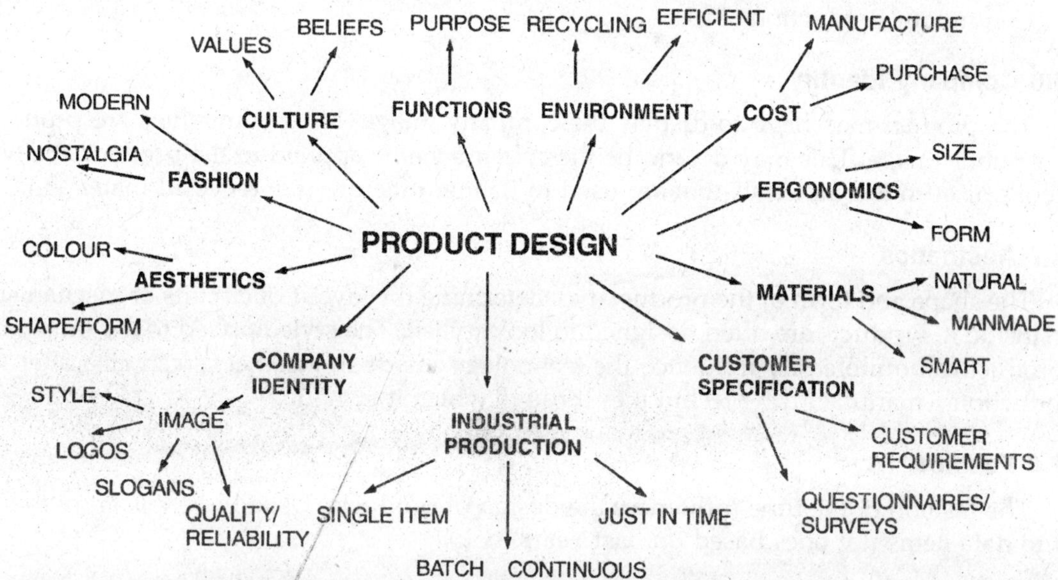

The rich picture above gives an outline to some of the many factors that affect the development of a product. Below is more detail regarding each of the points mentioned above.

2.6.1 Cost

The cost of the materials and labour required to manufacture the product. The price potential customers are prepared to pay for the product.

2.6.2 Ergonomics

The product may be designed for human use. As a result ergonomics (sizes etc...) will pay a major role.

2.6.3 Materials

The availability of materials and the development of new, hi-technology materials will have an influence on the final design of a product.

2.6.4 Customer Requirements

The customer will have great influence over the way a product is designed and develops. As a product is designed it is normal for potential customers to be questioned about the type of product or design that they prefer. For example, when designing a mobile phone a design team will show potential customers several designs and make changes according to their likes and dislikes.

2.6.5 Industrial Production

All products are manufactured through one of the following manufacturing techniques:
Single Item / Prototype / One Off
Batch Production
Continuous Production

2.6.6 Company Identity

The product may have to display the company image. Most companies are proud of their public image. This may determine the colour scheme applied to the product, the way it looks or even the materials that are used in its manufacture (i.e. recycled materials).

2.6.7 Aesthetics

The shape and form of the product may determine the layout of circuits or mechanisms etc..inside it. Products are often designed to look stylish. The style applied to the outside of a product can quite easily influence the technology inside it. Aesthetics can also alter the production / manufacturing techniques through which it is made.

2.6.8 Fashion

The fashion of the time influences the design of products. Usually people want to buy up to date items not ones based on 'last years look'.

2.6.9 Culture

Some products are aimed at different cultures and countries. A product acceptable in one culture may be looked up one as offensive or less desirable in another. The use of colours and colour schemes are a good example of this

2.6.10 Functions

The number of functions a product has to perform will inevitably affect its design. Exactly what is the product going to do?

2.6.11 Environment

Many people (potential customers) are concerned about their environment and the damage to it caused by industrial production. When designing a product it may be wise to ensure that the materials can be recycled or the product itself can be manufactured from a large proportion of recycled material.

2.7 SEVEN STEPS OF PRODUCT DEVELOPMENT

The creation of products with new or different characteristics that offer new or additional benefits to the customer.Product development may involve modification of an existing product or its presentation, or formulation of an entirely new product that satisfies a newly defined customer want or market niche.

2.7.1 Product Idea Brainstorming

The first step is to generate an idea for the product. Ask employees, especially those who deal with customers regularly, for product ideas. Survey customers for feedback on existing products. Examine your industry to see whether there are areas where useful products do not exist. Create an online survey for your customers or social media fans to take. List all ideas for a new product.

2.7.2 Evaluate the Ideas

Make a list of product ideas and share it with the appropriate decision-makers in the company, such as the management team. Discuss the pros and cons of each idea and narrow the list to just a handful of the best ideas, based on their potential to generate revenue, as well as the time and resources you have to actually create the products.

2.7.3 Market Evaluation

Seek feedback from customers, employees and partners on which idea is most appealing. Ask customers for feedback via email or phone calls. Send an email to partners and employees and ask which of the products seems most useful or valuable. Whittle the list to just one or two product ideas.

2.7.4 Analysis

Analyze the remaining product idea from a business perspective. Determine how much, if any, competition exists for similar products. Determine the demand for the product, and estimate all costs affiliated with the product, such as development costs and operational costs, to help determine the profit margin.

2.7.5 Prototype and Marketing

Develop a prototype of the product, then share it with a handful of good customers and key partners. Ask them to try it out and provide feedback. The marketing team should use that feedback to craft marketing messages and developing marketing campaign ideas, such as email campaigns, websites, billboards or posters. Base the marketing messages on the most common positive comments or reactions from customers and partners during the prototype evaluation.

2.7.6 Market Testing

Make adjustments to the prototype or develop a new version, if necessary. Develop additional prototypes for market testing. Do a small product release in select areas. See whether the product sells well, and evaluate why sales are high or low. Evaluate the price and the effectiveness of the marketing messages. A small launch helps determine what needs to be done before an official launch.

2.7.7 Prepare for Launch

Begin production for the first round of the product launch. Evaluate how many products to produce based on your market testing and demand for the product. Advertise and speak to product distributors about ordering the product, if the product will be sold in stores.

2.7.8 Quality Assurance in Purcahsing

A process is described for quality assurance in pharmaceutical purchasing and inventory control. A quality assurance program should ensure that quality drugs are purchased at the lowest price, drug products are available when needed, the system is managed efficiently, internal controls are provided, drug products are stored under appropriate conditions, and laws, regulations, accreditation standards, and procedures are followed. To meet these objectives, product quality, vendor performance, the department's system of internal controls, purchasing data, and storage conditions should be monitored. A checklist for evaluating purchasing and inventory practices and a sample audit form listing quality assurance criteria, standards, procedures, and recommended actions are provided. A quality assurance program for pharmaceutical purchasing and inventory control should define institution-specific criteria and standards and use these standards for continual evaluation of all aspects of the purchasing and inventory control system. Documentation of quality assurance activities should be provided for use by the purchasing department, hospital administration, and regulatory bodies procurement procedures and processes.

Procurement is the acquisition of goods, services or works from an external source. It is favorable that the goods, services or works are appropriate and that they are procured at the best possible cost to meet the needs of the purchaser in terms of quality and quantity, time, and location. Corporations and public bodies often define processes intended to promote fair and open competition for their business while minimizing exposure to fraud and collusion.

Almost all purchasing decisions include factors such as delivery and handling, marginal benefit, and price fluctuations. Procurement generally involves making buying decisions under conditions of scarcity. If good data is available, it is good practice to make use of economic analysis methods such as cost-benefit analysis or cost-utility analysis.

An important distinction made between analyses without risk and those with risk. Where risk is involved, either in the costs or the benefits, the concept of expected value may be employed.

Direct procurement and indirect procurement				
		TYPES		
		Direct procurement	**Indirect procurement**	
		Raw material and production goods	**Maintenance, repair, and operating supplies**	**Capital goods and services**
FEATURES	**Quantity**	Large	Low	Low
	Frequency	High	Relatively high	Low
	Value	Industry specific	Low	High
	Nature	Operational	Tactical	Strategic
	Examples	Crude oil in petroleum industry	Lubricants, spare parts	Crude oil storage facilities

Based on the consumption purposes of the acquired goods and services, procurement activities are often split into two distinct categories. The first category being direct, production-related procurement and the second being indirect, non-production-related procurement.

Direct procurement occurs in manufacturing settings only. It encompasses all items that are part of finished products, such as raw material, components and parts. Direct procurement, which is the focus in supply chain management, directly affects the production process of manufacturing firms. In contrast, Indirect procurement activities concern "operating resources" that a company purchases to enable its operations. It comprises a wide variety of goods and services, from standardized low value items like office supplies and machine lubricants to complex and costly products and services;[2][3] like heavy equipment and consulting services.

2.8 TEN TOP TIPS FOR A SUCCESSFUL PROCUREMENT PROCESS

2.8.1 Spend plenty of time planning

- Consider at the outset the full extent of what needs to be done, by whom, and by when. Who needs to be involved? Are they being consulted?
- Seek advice from others (departments, local authorities etc.). It's always harder if you start with a blank piece of paper.
- Establish a complete procedure timetable with consultation periods, approval dates, invitation, receipt and evaluation of tenders, interviews, contract award etc.
- Ensure adequate time is allowed for the whole process.
- If you think that the project might be right for a partnering or framework agreement, build this in at the start.

2.8.2 Establish roles and responsibilities

- Establish the roles and responsibilities of all involved. For example, who is to decide/ approve the short list? Who will be responsible for the quality and price evaluations?
- Get everyone to contribute to the planning process, including internal Lawyers and Auditors. Be clear what approvals are required from elected Members and their role in the whole process.

2.8.3 Ensure transparency of proceedings

- Be seen to be fair to all potential tenderers and that the process is conducted without favouritism.
- Engage widely with stakeholders and existing contractors in advance of formal proceedings.
- Get all internal players to contribute to the critical success factors and key evaluation criteria, and record these!
- Allow sufficient time for tenderers to 'put their case' during evaluation, at interviews, presentations etc.

2.8.4 Observe legalities

- Ensure compliance with EC Procurement Directives, domestic legislation, Contract Standing Orders etc., particularly in respect of advertisements, invitations, and receipt/ opening of tenders, evaluation procedure and approvals.

- Seek legal advice and involvement in the process at the outset. You are initiating events that will result in a contract with an outside firm! You want it to be right.

2.8.5 Accommodate innovation and secure Best Value

- Do not 'handcuff' tenderers. Do not be too prescriptive in how you want the work to be delivered. Describe the 'outcomes' you require.
- Try to find ways in which specialist suppliers and contractors can contribute their expertise; allow tenderers to innovate and offer you their best solutions.
- Make sure you secure Best Value by considering quality, design, and Whole Life costs, and not just lowest tender price.

2.8.6 Prepare sound and complete tender documents

- Specify clearly what you want and describe in detail how tenderers are to price their submissions.
- Give sufficient thought to various pricing mechanisms such as lump-sum or schedules of rates, and how good these will be at accommodating changes.
- Remember, the more information you provide, particularly on the desired outcomes, the greater your chances of success.

2.8.7 Consider monitoring and payment arrangements at the outset

- Be clear as to how payments to the successful tender are to be calculated once they have been awarded the contract, and make payments on time.
- Establish the monitoring procedures that are required to satisfy the Council that the service is being delivered in accordance with that specified.
- Consider 'default' procedures, performance incentives and profit sharing.
- Incorporate these processes within the tender documents, as they will provide the basis of the subsequent contract document.

2.8.8 Ensure procedures provide for probity and accountability

- Ensure that the whole process is adequately documented and recorded to demonstrate the decision-making processes to others.
- Ensure all key documents are signed, dated etc. and retained to ensure that those responsible for making decisions can be held accountable.
- Communicate all decisions to the whole team.

2.8.9 Think before you act

- Review your plans before commencing. Do not 'rush' things – unless it is a real emergency. Inadequate time in the planning stage will lead to problems.
- Think what can go wrong? What if delays occur? What contingencies do you have? (e.g. slack in the timetable)? What if a key person leaves or goes off sick?
- Is the price/quality model practical robust and will it deliver Best Value?
  Ensure you test it thoroughly.

2.8.10 Learn from the Process

- Learn, experiment, and don't fear mistakes. Ask yourself and the rest of the team, how would you do it better next time? How can we repeat what went well, and not what went badly?

SUMMARY

The quality of the parts and raw materials that are used by a company makes a difference to the finished products that are sold to their customers. By ensuring that the purchased parts are of a specific quality as defined by the development, manufacturing, or quality departments, the purchasing department are ensuring that the quality of the finished goods are maintained.

Exercise Questions

1. Define the term quality.
2. Define TQM.
3. Name dimensions of quality?
4. Name any four prominent TQM pioneers.
5. What are the necessary characteristics of a good quality product?
6. What is serviceability?
7. What is durability?
8. What is quality planning?
9. What are the objectives of quality planning?
10. What is meant by quality costs?
11. Give examples of internal failure costs?
12. Give examples of external failure costs?
13. What do you mean by total cost of quality?
14. List the techniques used for analyzing the quality costs.
15. Define strategic planning.
16. Name any four role of senior management.
17. What is a quality council?
18. What is a quality policy statement?
19. List any four characteristics of a quality policy statement.
20. Mention any four duties and responsibilities of the quality council.
21. What is mission statement?
22. Define leadership?
23. What is management by wandering?
24. Name any four tangible benefits of TQM.
25. Name any two popular awards for quality.

❑

Manufacturing Quality— Origins and Principles of Lean Manufacturing

3

Manufacturing is basically the production of goods for use or sale using labor and resources. Manufacturing is the basis of industrial development and is key indicator on how a nation's economy performing. Companies of all sizes manufacture products using a number of different processes and methodologies.

When a manufacturing company has a production line, it will usually have some operations that are performed on the line. These process control systems could be testing equipment, scanners, print machines, or any number of items that can perform operations to the work in progress materials as they pass along the production line. The process control systems can be connected to the company's enterprise resource planning (ERP) application by means of software called Manufacturing Execution Systems (MES). The systems can be seamlessly placed along the production line so that the ERP system can control operations on the plant floor.

3.1 USING MES WITH ERP

The use of manufacturing execution systems with ERP allows companies to have a visibility of the production line from the ERP system. Before the two applications were integrated, the MES operations would operate independently and at some point the data would be uploaded or remain locally. The ERP system would have access to the data, but not real-time and therefore issues that would occur were not dealt with at the time. This led to quality issues creeping into the manufacturing process, which could cause materials to be scraped or reworked. This could be costly with a long production run and also lead to issues with delivery times to customers, as well as possible customer satisfaction problems.

The integration of the MES and ERP systems have allowed the data from the MES equipment to be recorded real-time in the ERP and it is possible for the production department to immediately be informed of issues with production, whether they are equipment related or quality issues. The response times for work-in-progress issues is dramatically reduced as monitoring in the ERP system can trigger personnel to be informed and decisions can be made rapidly.

3.1.1 Benefits of MES

The MES applications can give a company significant benefits in their manufacturing process. By having an application that takes data from a process control machine and passes that to the ERP system, there is no longer any need for a human interface between the two. This removes the manual data collection and data entry process that used to occur, which led to data issues, such as validation rules being ignored, incorrect calculations, value limits exceeded, or simple data entry errors.

One benefit of MES that is of increased important is that of data security. An automatic link between the process control and ERP means that the security of the data is maintained, unlike manual entry sheet which could be lost of incorrectly discarded.

An important benefit of MES is that the data recorded and transmitted can be retrieved at a later date. This could be important for future modeling exercises or testing of upgrades to any component in the production process. Having data available means that there is increased traceability, which is so vital in regulated industries, such as the food industry and the pharmaceutical sector. Audit trail availability is important for investigation of issues when they occur.

The use of MES also allows companies to introduce best practices into their manufacturing process. Production improvement models such as Lean Manufacturing would benefit from the advantages offered by MES. Other best practices such as Process Analytical Technology (PAT) can be implemented the PAT process requires in-line and on-line analytical instruments used to measure critical process parameters (CPP) of the production equipment used to manufacturing the finished goods. PAT is a useful tool to reduce production cycle times, as well as faster batch release times, fewer batch failures, and improving energy and raw material usage.

MES applications can also assist a company with achieving compliance with 21 CFR Part 11, which refers to the guidelines on electronic records and electronic signatures. This FDA regulation requires companies in the regulated industries to implement controls, which can include audits, system validations, electronic signatures, and documentation for software and systems involved in processing electronic data.

3.2 PHARMACEUTICAL MANUFACTURING

Pharmaceutical products save lives every day. Manufacturers of these important drugs spend many millions of dollars over many years to bring a product to the market. A report from Tuffs University estimates that the full cost of developing a new prescription medication is around $1.3 billion. Pharmaceutical companies have to follow strict rules on the way the products are developed and manufactured. The Federal Drug Administration (FDA) regulates and monitors the way the products are manufactured and sold to patients. There are a number of functions in a pharmaceutical company that follow the product from its original discovery to the sale of the product to the public.

3.2.1 Discovery of the Product

At the beginning of the process that ends with a new pharmaceutical product is the research into a specific ailment. The researchers investigate the specific disorder to understand all aspects and perform experiments to investigate possible methods of controlling it. Depending on the results of laboratory experiments, some of these will be taken into the development stage. A study from Tuffs University estimates that there is only one successful drug out of 5,000 to 10,000 compounds developed in the laboratory.

3.2.2 Differences Between Manufacturing and Service Organizations

Defining quality in manufacturing organizations is often different from that of services. Manufacturing organizations produce a tangible product that can be seen, touched, and directly measured. Examples include cars, CD players, clothes, computers, and food items. Therefore, quality definitions in manufacturing usually focus ontangible product features.

The most common quality definition in manufacturing is conformance, which is the degree to which a product characteristic meets preset standards. Other commondefinitions of quality in manufacturing include performance— such as acceleration of a vehicle; reliability— that the product will function as expected without failure; features— the extras that are included beyond the basic characteristics; durability— expected operational life of the product; and serviceability— how readily a product can be repaired. The relative importance of these definitions is based on the preferences of each individual customer. It is easy to see how different customers can have different definitions in mind when they speak of high product quality.

In contrast to manufacturing, service organizations produce a product that is intangible. Usually, the complete product cannot be seen or touched. Rather, it is experienced. Examples include delivery of health care, experience of staying at a vacation resort, and learning at a university. The intangible nature of the product makes defining quality difficult. Also, since a service is experienced, perceptions can be highly subjective. In addition to tangible factors, quality of services is often defined by perceptual factors. These include responsiveness to customer needs, courtesy and friendliness of staff, promptness in resolving complaints, and atmosphere. Other definitions of quality in services include time— the amount of time a customer has to wait for the service; and consistency— the degree to which the service is the same each time. Today's customers demand and expect high quality. Companies that do not make quality a priority risk long-run survival.

World-class organizations such as General Electric and Motorola attribute their success to having one of the best quality management programs in the world. These companies were some of the first to implement a quality program called, SixSigma, where the level of defects is reduced to approximately 3.4 parts per million. To achieve this, everyone in the company is trained in quality. For example, individuals highly trained in quality improvement principles and techniques receive a designation called "Black Belt." The full-time job of Black Belts is to identify and solve quality problems. In fact, Motorola was one of the first companies to win the prestigious Malcolm Baldrige National Quality Award in 1988, due to its high focus on quality.

Both GE and Motorola have had a primary goal to achieve total customer satisfaction.

To this end, the efforts of these organizations have included eliminating almost all defects from products, processes, and transactions. Both companies consider quality to be the critical factor that has resulted in significant increases in sales and market share, as well as cost savings in the range of millions of dollars.

3.2.3 Development of the Product

After the laboratory experiments produced favorable results, the product is then moved to the development stage. The product will undergo a four phase clinic trial, where each stage of the trial is designed to answer a separate research question.

- **Phase 1.** Company researchers test a new product in a small group of people for the first time to evaluate its safety, determine a safe dosage range, and identify the side effects.
- **Phase 2.** The product is given to a larger group of people to see if it is effective and to further evaluate its safety.
- **Phase 3.** The product is given to large groups of people to confirm its effectiveness, monitor the side effects, compare it to commonly used treatments, and collect information that will allow the product to be used safely.
- **Phase 4.** Studies are complete after the product has been marketed to assemble information on the drug's effect in various populations and any side effects associated with long-term use.

To get approval to manufacture and sell a new pharmaceutical product to the public, a company must provide the FDA with proof of the quality, efficacy, and safety of the product. In the European Union, each member country has its own regulatory agency, but these are coordinated by the European Medicines Evaluation Agency (EMEA).

Manufacturing of the Product

To ensure that the product is manufactured to the highest quality standards as determined by current good manufacturing processes (cGMP), there are a number of steps to be followed. These include,

- **Quality Assurance** – monitors quality and regulatory requirements across the enterprise. This includes developing and monitoring standard operating procedures (SOP), implementing corrective and preventive actions, and conducting internal audits for regulatory complicance.
- **Quality Control** – monitors and controls the manufacturing operations, inspects and approves material in the production process.
- **Maintenance** – preventative and emergency maintenance to ensure that the manufacturing operation is as efficient as possible.

3.2.4 Marketing

The marketing of a new product is very important to a company as it introduces the product into the market. Some companies can expend a third of the overall sales revenue on the marketing of a new product, which can be far in excess of what a company spends on research and development.

3.3 SALES EFFORT

A pharmaceutical company will employ an experienced sales force that will publicize the new product to the medical community. The financial success of a new drug depends on a large part in the ability of the pharmaceutical sales organization to establish and grow the products once they have been approved by the FDA.

3.3.1 Methods and Techniques for manufacture

Organisations will adopt a variety of techniques to produce their goods or services. The technique adopted will depend on a number of factors including;

- The product or service
- Quality of the product or service
- Quantity of the product or service
- Size of the organisation
- The type of organisation
- The organisation's resources

3.3.2 Legislation applicable to the organisation

The most common methods of production include Line Production, Continuous flow production, Batch Production and Just in Time Production. The aim of all is to add value. Adding value is the process of converting the input to an output so that it's desirability to the customer increases. The input is the product or service at the start of the production process. The output is the product or service at the end of the production process.

3.3.3 Line Production

Just as the name suggests line production is producing goods along a line of production. The goods will be passed along a line containing different stages. At each stage in the line the goods will be altered. Often a person/group of people will be responsible for just one stage in the process. Car assembly or fast food "drive thrus", often adopt Line production as identical products are produced each day. Nowadays some organisations will employ robots rather than people to undertake the stages in line production. Robots are believed to be more efficient and unlike humans will not get bored and cause errors.

3.3.4 Continuous Flow Production (CFP)

This is simply adopting line production 24 hours day/seven days a week, using automatic equipment. The automatic equipment will operate in the same manner day in day out. The ability to work in this manner is another advantage robots/machinery have over humans. CFP does not involve humans so it is not used in the service industry unlike line production.

3.3.5 Batch Production

This is the method employed when the organisation needs to produce a fixed amount of each of the type of goods it produces. In this instance production technique and resources will be adapted, to produce the product required and to produce just the amount required. A good example is a pizza factory. Let's imagine the factory produces 150 pepperoni pizzas, 265 ham and pineapple pizzas and 75 cheese and tomato pizzas each day. Each batch (or variety) of pizza have its own ingredients, cooking times and production method. When the factory switches from the production of one type of pizza to another, it will need to change its production methods. Some of the tasks for one type of bread can be completed at the same time as producing the other types of bread such as making dough for the cheese and tomato pizza, whilst waiting for the pepperoni pizzas to cook. However the factory will have to be careful to ensure that they do not confuse the production of one type of pizza with the production of another.

3.3.6 Just In Time Production (JIT)

This method of production generates goods/services "just in time" for them to be sold rather than preparing them months or weeks in advance. To save storage costs, the parts needed to make the end product will arrive just before they are used to manufacture the product. This means that the production process is carefully planned and organised. Production must be efficient and speedy otherwise the goods will not be manufactured "in time" for the customer.Conversely if there are no/few orders then production will slow down or stop altogether.

3.4 INSPECTION AND CONTROL OF CONTROL

3.4.1 Inspection

Inspection is the most common method of attaining standardisation, uniformity and quality of workmanship. It is the cost art of controlling the product quality after comparison with the established standards and specifications. It is the function of quality control. If the said item does not fall within the zone of acceptability it will be rejected and corrective measure will be applied to see that the items in future conform to specified standards.

Inspection is an indispensable tool of modern manufacturing process. It helps to control quality, reduces manufacturing costs, eliminate scrap losses and assignable causes of defective work.

3.4.2 Objectives of Inspection

(1) To collect information regarding the performance of the product with established standards for the use of engineering production, purchasing and quality control etc.

(2) To sort out poor quality of manufactured product and thus to maintain standards.

(3) To establish and increase the reputation by protecting customers from receiving poor quality products.

(4) Detect source of weakness and failure in the finished products and thus check the work of designer.

3.4.3 Purpose of Inspection

(1) To distinguish good lots from bad lots

(2) To distinguish good pieces from bad pieces.

(3) To determine if the process is changing.

(4) To determine if the process is approaching the specification limits.

(5) To rate quality of product.

(6) To rate accuracy of inspectors.

(7) To measure the precision of the measuring instrument.

(8) To secure products – design information.

(9) To measure process capability.

3.4.4 Stages of Inspection

(1) Inspection of incoming material

(2) Inspection of production process
(3) Inspection of finished goods.

(1) **Inspection of incoming materials.** It is also called receiving inspection. It consists of inspecting and checking of all the purchased raw materials and parts that are supplied before they are taken on to stock or used in actual manufacturing. Inspection may take place either at supplier's end or at manufacturer's gate. If the incoming materials are large in quantity and involve huge transportation cost it is economical to inspect them at the place of vendor or supplier.

(2) **Inspection of production process.** The work of inspection is done while the production process is simultaneously going on. Inspection is done at various work centres of men and machines and at the critical production points. This had the advantage of preventing wastage of time and money on defective units and preventing delays in assembly.

(3) **Inspection of finished goods.** This is the last stage when finished goods are inspected and carried out before marketing to see that poor quality product may be either rejected or sold at reduced price.

3.4.5 Inspection Procedures

There are three ways of doing inspection. They are Floor inspection, Centralised inspection and Combined inspection.

3.4.6 Floor Inspection

It suggests the checking of materials in process at the machine or in the production time by patrolling inspectors. These inspectors moves from machine to machine and from one to the other work centres. Inspectors have to be highly skilled. This method of inspection minimise the material handling, does not disrupt the line layout of machinery and quickly locate the defect and readily offers field and correction.

3.4.7 Advantages

(1) Encourage co-operation of inspector and foreman.
(2) Random checking may be more successful than batch checking.
(3) Does not delay in production.
(4) Saves time and expense of having to more batches of work for inspection.
(5) Inspectors may see and be able to report on reason of faculty work.

3.4.8 Disadvantages

(1) Difficult in inspection due to vibration.
(2) Possibility of biased inspection because of worker.
(3) Pressure on inspector.
(4) High cost of inspection because of numerous sets of inspections and skilled inspectors.

3.4.9 Suitability

(1) Heavy products are produced.
(2) Different work centres are integrated in continuous line layout.

3.4.10 Centralised Inspection

Materials in process may be inspected and checked at centralised inspection centre which are located at one or more places in the manufacturing industry.

3.4.11 Advantages

(1) Better quality checkup.
(2) Closed supervision.
(3) Absence of workers pressure.
(4) Orderly production flow and low inspection cost.

3.4.12 Disadvantages

(1) More material handling.
(2) Delays of inspection room causes wastage of time.
(3) Work of production control increases.
(4) Due to non-detection of machining errors in time, there may be more spoilage of work.

3.4.13 Suitability

(1) Incoming materials inspection.
(2) Finished product inspection.
(3) Departmental inspection.
(4) High precision products of delicate products.
(5) Small and less expensive products.

3.4.14 Combined Inspection

Combination of two methods what ever may be the method of inspection, whether floor or central. The main objective is to locate and prevent defect which may not repeat itself in subsequent operation to see whether any corrective measure is required and finally to maintained quality economically.

3.4.15 Methods of Inspection

There are two methods of inspection. They are 100% inspection and Sampling inspection.

3.4.16 100% Inspection

This type will involve careful inspection in detail of quality at each strategic point or stage of manufacture where the test involved is non-destructive and every piece is separately inspected. It requires more number of inspectors and hence it is a costly method.

There is no sampling error. This is subjected to inspection error arising out of fatigue, negligence, difficulty of supervision etc. Hence complete accuracy of influence is seldomly attained.

It is suitable only when a small number of pieces are there or a very high degree of quality is required. Example : Jet engines, Aircraft, Medical and Scientific equipment.

3.4.17 Sampling Inspection

In this method randomly selected samples are inspected. Samples taken from different batches of products are representatives. If the sample prove defective. The entire concerned is to be rejected or recovered. Sampling inspection is cheaper and quicker. It requires less number of Inspectors. Its subjected to sampling errors but the magnitude of sampling error can be estimated. In the case of destructive test, random or sampling inspection is desirable. This type of inspection governs wide currency due to the introduction of automatic machines or equipments which are less susceptible to chance variable and hence require less inspection, suitable for inspection of products which have less precision importance and are less costly.

Example :Electrical bulbs, radio bulbs, washing machine etc.

Destructive tests conducted for the products whose endurance or ultimate strength properties are required.

Example :Flexible strength, resistance capacity, compressibility etc.

3.4.18 Drawbacks of Inspection

(1) Inspection adds to the cost of the product but not for its value.

(2) It is partially subjective, often the inspector has to judge whether a product passes or not.

Example :Inspector discovering a slight burnish on a surface must decide whether it is bad enough to justify rejection even with micrometers a tight or loose fit change measurement by say 0.0006 inches. The inspectors design is important as he enforces quality standards.

(3) Fatigue and Monotony may affect any inspection judgement.

(4) Inspection merely separates good and bad items. It is no way to prevent the production of bad items.

3.5 QUALITY

Different meaning could be attached to the word Quality under different circumstances. The word Quality does not mean the Quality of manufactured product only. It may refer to the Quality of the process (i.e., men, material, machines) and even that of management. Where the quality of manufactured product referred as or defined as "Quality of product as the degree in which it fulfills the requirement of the customer. It is not absolute but it judged or realised by comparing it with some standards".

It is usually determined by some characteristics namely design, size, material, chemical composition, mechanical functioning workmanship, finish and other properties. In the final analysis the Quality standards for the products are established by the customer.

Example :Gear used in sugarcane extracting machine through not of the same material and without possessing good finish, tolerance and accuracy as that of gear used in the hand stock of a teeth may be considered of good quality if it work satisfactory in the juice extracting machine.

Quality begins with the design of a product in accordance with the customer specification further it involves the established measurement standards, the use of proper material, selection of suitable manufacturing process and the necessary tooling to manufacture the product, the performance of the necessary manufacturing operations and the inspection of the product to check the manufacturing operations and the inspection of the product to check on performance with the specifications. Quality characteristics can be classified as follows :

(1) Quality of design
(2) Quality of conformance with specifications
(3) Quality of performance.

3.5.1 Control

The process through which the standards are established and met with standards is called control. This process consists of observing our activity performance, comparing the performance with some standard and then taking action if the observed performance is significantly to different from the standards.

The control process involves a universal sequence of steps as follows :

(1) Choose the control subject.
(2) Choose a unit of measure.
(3) Set a standard value i.e., specify the quality characteristics
(4) Choose a sensing device which can measure.
(5) Measure actual performance.
(6) Interpret the difference between actual and standard.
(7) Taking action, if any, on the difference.

3.5.2 Quality Control

Quality control can be defined as that Industrial Management technique by means of which product of uniform acceptable quality is manufactured.

3.5.3 Factors Affecting Quality

(1) Men, Materials and Machines
(2) Manufacturing conditions
(3) Market research in demand of purchases
(4) Money in capability to invest
(5) Management policy for quality level
(6) Production methods and product design
(7) Packing and transportation
(8) After sales service

3.5.4 Objectives of Quality Control

(1) To decide about the standard of Quality of a product that is easily acceptable to the customer.
(2) To check the variation during manufacturing.
(3) To prevent the poor quality products reaching to customer.

3.6 STATISTICAL QUALITY CONTROL (SQC)

A Quality control system performs inspection, testing and analysis to conclude whether the quality of each product is as per laid quality standard or not. It's called "Statistical Quality Control" when statistical techniques are employed to control quality or to solve quality control problem. SQC makes inspection more reliable and at the same time less costly. It controls the quality levels of the outgoing products.

SQC should be viewed as a kit of tools which may influence related to the function of specification, production or inspection.

A successful SQC programme is expected to yield the following results :

(1) Improvement of quality.
(2) Reduction of scrap and rework.
(3) Efficient use of men and machines.
(4) Economy in use of materials.
(5) Removing production bottle-necks.
(6) Decreased inspection costs.
(7) Reduction in cost/unit.
(8) Scientific evaluation of tolerance.
(9) Scientific evaluation of quality and production.
(10) Quality consciousness at all levels.
(11) Reduction in customer complaints.

3.6.1 Tools of SQC

The principle tools of SQC are as follows :

(1) Frequency distribution.
(2) Control charts for measurement and attribute data.
(3) Acceptance sampling techniques.
(4) Regression and correlation analysis.
(5) Tests of significance.
(6) Design of experiments.

3.6.1.1 Quality Characteristics

3.6.1.2 Quality of Design

Quality design is a technical term. It can be regarded as a composite of 3 separate terms or steps in a common progression of activities.

(i) Identification of what constitutes fitness for use to the user (Quality of market research).
(ii) Choice of concept of product or service to be responsible to the identified needs of the user (Quality of concept).
(iii) Translation of the chosen product concept into a detailed set of specifications which is faithfully executed, will then meet the user's need (Quality of specification).

The total progression composed of these three activities is called "Quality of Design" and it may be said to consist of Quality of market research: Quality of concept and Quality of specification.

Example : All automobiles provide the user with the service of transportation. The various models differ as to size, comfort, appearance, performance, economy, status conferred etc. These differences are in turn the results of intended or designed differences in the size, styling, materials, tolerances, test programs etc. Higher quality of design can be attained only at an increase in costs.

3.6.1.3 Quality of Comformance

The design must reflect the needs of fitness for use, and the products must also confirm to the design. The extent to which the product does confirm to the design is called "Quality of conformance". This extent of conformance is determined by variables as :

(i) Choice of process i.e., whether they are able to hold the tolerances.

(ii) Training of the supervision and the work force.

(iii) Degree of adherence to the program of inspect, test, audit etc. motivation for quality.

Higher quality of conformance can be attained with an accompanying reduction in cost.

Example : Two scooters both are produced at the same level of time but one may be 100% according to the drawing and specification of the same design; the second scooter may be 90% according to the drawing and specification and probably a few dimensions may be different from those of drawing. Therefore quality of conformance of 1st scooter is better than the 2nd scooter even though both are of same design.

3.6.1.4 Quality Costs

Quality costs are the incurring in introducting quality and benefits. This is done by identifying and defining the following categories of costs which are associated with making, finding, repairing or avoiding (preventing) defects.

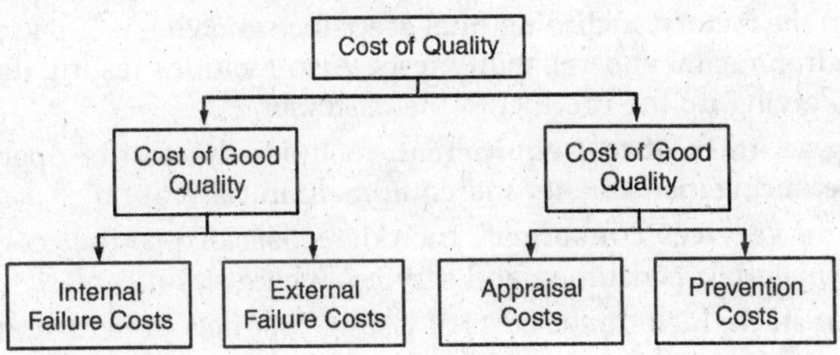

Fig. 1.1 Hierarcy of quality cost or Brakdown of quality cost.

3.6.1.4.1 Failure costs

Internal failure costs. These are costs which would disappear if no defects exit in the product prior to shipment to the customer. They include.

Scrap. The net loss in labour and material resulting from defectives which cannot economically be repaired or used.

Rework. The cost of correcting defectives to make them fit for use.

Retest. The cost of inspection and retest of products that have undergone rework or other revision.

Down time. The cost of idle facilities resulting from defects. (**Example :**Aircraft idle due to unreliability, printing press down due to paper break).

Yield losses. The cost of process yield lower that might be attainable by improved controls. Includes "overfill" of containers (going to customers) due to variability in filling and measuring equipment.

External failure costs. These costs would also disappear if there were no defects.

They are disguished from the internal failure costs by the fact that the defects are found at the shipment to the customer. They include :

Complaint adjustment. All costs of investigation and adjustment of justified complaints attributable to defective product or installation.

Returned material. All costs associated with receipts and returned from the field.

Warranty charges. All costs involved in service to customers under warranty contracts.

Allowances. Costs of concessions made to customers due to substandard products being accepted by the customer as is include loss in income due to down grading products for sale as seconds.

3.6.1.4.2 Appraisal Costs

These are costs incurred to discover the conditions of the products, mainly during the "first come through" costs include.

Incoming material inspection. The cost of determining the quality of vendor made products, whether by inspection on receipt or at source or by surveillance method.

Inspection and test. The cost of checking the conformance of the product throughout its progression, in the factory, including final aceptance and check of packing and shipping includes life, environmental and reliability tests. Also includes testing done at customer's premises prior to giving up the product to the customer.

Maintaining accuracy of test equipment. Includes the cost of operating the system that keeps the measuring instruments and equipment in calibration.

Materials and services consumed. Includes costs of product consumed through destructive tests, materials consumed and services where significant.

Evaluation of stock. Include the costs of testing products in field storage or in stock to evaluate degradation.

3.6.1.4.3 Prevention Costs

These costs are incurred to keep future and appraisal costs at a minimum. It includes :

Quality Planning. This includes the broad array of activities which collectively create quality plan, the inspection plan, reliability plan, data system and numerac specialized plans. It includes also preparation of the manuals and procedures needed to communicate these plans to all concerned.

New Product review. Includes preparation of bid proposals evaluation of new design, preparation of test and experiment programs and other quality activities associated with the launching of new designs.

Training. The costs of preparing training programs for attaining and improving quality performance includes the cost of conducting formal training programs as well.

Process control. Includes that part of process control which is conducted to achieve fitness for use as distinguished from achieving productivity, safety etc.

Quality data acquisition and analysis. This is the work of running the quality of data systems to acquire continuing data on quality performance. It includes analysis of these data to identify the quality troubles, to sound alarms etc.

Quality reporting. Includes the work of summaring and publishing quality information to the middle and upper management.

Improvement Projects. Includes the work of structuring and carrying out programs for break through to new levels of performance i.e., defective prevention programs, motivation programs etc.

3.7 TOTAL QUALITY CONTROL

Total Quality Control defined as an effective system for intergrating the quality development, quality maintainance and quality improvement efforts of the various groups in an organisation so as to enable production and service at the most economical level which allow for full customer satisfaction.

It may be classified as a "Management Tool" for many industries outstanding improvement in product quality design and reduction in operating costs and losses.

Product quality is defined as "The composite product of engineering and manufacture that determine the degree to which the product in use will meet the expectations of the customer".

"Control" represents a tool with four steps :

- Setting up of quality standards.
- Appraising conformance to these standards
- Acting when these standards are exceeded.
- Planning for improvements in these standards.

Quality control emerges as a based function based on the collection analysis and interpretations of data on all aspects of the enterprise.

Total quality control is an aid for good engineering designs, good manufacturing methods and conscious inspection activity that have always been required for the production of high quality articles.

Quality of any product is effected at many stages of the industrial cycle :

Marketing. Evaluates the level of Quality which customers want for which they are willing,to pay.

Engineering. Reduces this marketing evaluations to exact specification.

Purchasing. Chooses, contracts with and retains vendors for parts and materials.

Manufacturing Engineering. Select the jigs, tools and processes for production.

Manufacturing Supervision and shop operators. Exert a major quality influence during parts making, sub assembly and final assembly.

Mechanical Inspection and function Test. Check conformance to specifications.

Shipping. Influences the calibre of packaging and transportation.

Installation. Helps ensure proper operations by installing the product according to proper instructions and maintaining it through product service.

In other words, the determination of both quality and quality costs actually takes place throughout the entire industrial cycle.

Quality control is responsible for quality assurance at optimum quality costs. The benefits resulting from Total Quality Control programmes are :

- Improvements in product quality and design
- Reduction in operating costs and losses
- Reduction in production line bottle necks
- Improvement in employee morale
- Improved inspection methods
- Setting time standards for labour
- Definite schedule for preventive maintainance
- Availability of purposeful data for use in co-advertising
- Furnishing of actual basis for cost accounting for standard and for scrap, rework and inspection.

3.8 QUALITY IN SALES AND SERVICE

The quality for sale described by following points as-

3.8.1 Customers' knowledge

A sales representative is first and foremost characterized by its knowledge of its customers. A good sales representative has good customer base and maintains good relationships with all of individual clients. Good sales agents visit their customers or call them regularly. They know their needs and they know how to answer them.

Knowing its customers also means that your sales representative must know the purchasing pattern of their customers. What is the purchasing cycle, who makes decisions along the way? These are a few questions that a good sales representative will know the answers to.

3.8.2 Knowledge of the industry

A good sales representative not only understand each and every individual customer, but it also understands the market as a whole. What is the customer's demand for such and such product, what are the market trends, who are the competitors.

3.8.3 Product knowledge

Your sales representative must also know the product it represents. It can seem obvious but it has numerous consequences. It means for example that in order to sell technical products a sales representative must have a good technical education, good enough to understand its customers' questions and give clear answers.

It also means that a sales representative can be good at selling one product but not good at another product. Some products require technical sales, some others require negotiation capabilities, others require to understand the emotions behind the purchase, and others require a constant presence on the field.

Training a sales representative is crucial. Most companies do not give enough training to their sales representatives. This is a serious mistake because representatives can only be efficient if they answer their customers' needs. A good sales representative must be able to demonstrate a product or give a detailed presentation; it must be able to answer the main questions from the customers; and it must understand its own limits in order to come back to the company it represents and ask for details or answers to questions it has been asked. This capacity at dialoguing with the company it represents is an excellent indication of a good sales representative.

3.9 COMMUNICATION CAPACITIES

Communication capacities of a sales representative are crucial. A sales representative is the link between two parties, one selling products and the other one purchasing them. A good sales representative must have the capability to communicate with both parties quickly and efficiently. The representative must bring answers to its customers, but it must also bring answers to the company it represents.

3.9.1 Follow-up

Finding prospects is a good start. But a sales representative must have tenacity. It must follow up with its customers, understand their sales cycles and know when to push. This follow up will make the difference between a sales representative that brings prospects and one that brings purchase orders. And there can be a huge gap between the two.

3.9.2 Reporting

It is very important for a sales representative to keep the company it represents up to date on its progress. All companies require regular reporting from their inside sales force. This includes new contracts, new offers, follow up of existing prospects, probability to win existing opportunities, and revenue forecasts.

It is normal to require the same level of reporting from independant sales representatives. Unfortunately most companies do not have enough contacts with their sales representatives and do not get detailed reports.

A good representative must define with its principal the level of reporting to provide. Then he must conform to this requirement and send its report by itself, without being asked. It is very frustrating for a company to be forced to ask regularly its sales representatives for reports. Very few give reports by themselves.

Most sales representatives have a very bad reporting. Therefore, a representative that gives regular and complete reports without being asked is very much appreciated.

Reporting can be a determining factor in the long run in the relationship between a company and its sales representative. Any company will prefer a representative that gives regular reports. A sales representative that reports brings less revenue but that gives better reporting can in certain cases be preferred to a representative that does not report on its activities. Managing representatives is crucial for a company.

3.9.3 Feedback

Customer contact is very important for any company, in order to get feedback on its products, to know about new trends and new customers requests, and to know about new products that customers would like to see. Selling through sales representatives cuts the direct link between a company and its customers. A good sales representative must relay customers concerns and requests to the company it represents. Sales representatives must be opened to discussion and must listen to their clients.

A good sales representative must also report negative comments from the customers. Any company is interested in constructive criticism, which can make products evolve to better serve the customer. Sales representatives must understand customers' criticisms and must provide constructive feedback to the principals.

3.9.4 Reactivity

It is almost obvious that a good sales representative must be reactive. It must answer requests both from its principal and from its customers.

3.9.5 Results

In the end, a sales representative is judged upon its results. A good sales representative is one that adapts to its customers and knows how to get the order. Certain sales representatives practices can be surprising, especially in foreign countries. But the sale representative must be the one who decides how to interact with its customers to sell the products it represents.

3.10 QUALITY OF SERVICE

Quality of Service (QoS) is a set of technologies for managing network traffic in a cost-effective manner to enhance user experiences for home and enterprise environments. QoS technologies allow you to measure bandwidth, detect changing network conditions (such as congestion or availability of bandwidth), and prioritize or throttle traffic. For example, QoS technologies can be applied to prioritize traffic for latency-sensitive applications (such as voice or video) and to control the impact of latency-insensitive traffic (such as bulk data transfers).When you want service in Quality You face a special challenge: Meet customer needs while remaining economically competitive. Automated processes can make an impact, but services are still labor-intensive. There can be no substitute for high-quality personal interaction between service employees and customers. Use quality practices to:

- Understand and improve operational processes.
- Identify problems quickly and systematically.
- Establish valid and reliable service performance measures.
- Measure customer satisfaction and other performance outcomes.

3.10.1 Product Guarantee and Recall Insurance

Over recent years, the number of cases where faulty products have led to personal injury and property damage has increased dramatically. In today's litigious climate, manufacturers are increasingly aware of their responsibilities to monitor products and as a result the number ofproduct recalls are on the rise.

3.10.2 Protection for the Worst Case Scenarios

How much would it cost you to recall and replace some or all of your products Or to compensate customers for a serious flaw in your service? Either would probably be enough to seriously weaken, if not destroy, your business.

Your Public and Product Liability insurance almost certainly falls short of protecting you from these eventualities. In most cases, these policies specifically exclude Product Guarantee and Recall Claims.

3.10.3 The Product Guarantee and Recall Minefield

In the current environment, even the most conscientious organisation can be caught out. The slightest error or misjudgement - one that may not even be your fault - and your company's reputation and finances could be seriously affected. An error of judgement, an oversight, a simple mistake, or incorrect information from a third party could threaten your very livelihood.

When you sell a product or service to a customer, you enter into a contractual relationship and you can be liable not only for correcting your own failings, but also for compensating your client for the effect upon their company and possibly on their customers. Product integrity and brand name protection, by the efficient removal or rectification of defective products, should be recognised by any manufacturer or supplier as a priority.

Companies are advised to take a path that is designed to give further peace of mind and, should the unthinkable happen, makes it possible for you to help maintain customer relations. It may even be the means that enables your organisation to survive and live another day.

Research repeatedly shows that those companies that retain the greatest customer loyalty are the ones that react quickly and positively to a crisis. Taking responsibility and concentrating on putting things right wins understanding and earns respect and that is a good foundation for rebuilding relationships. Contrary to popular opinion, customers do understand that mistakes can happen, the issue is how readily will you put things right.

Insurance companies are likely to push non-participating (without profit) products, as compared to participating (with profit) ones after implementation of the new product guidelines from October. With a guaranteed surrender value of 90 per cent and maturity corpus' assured returns of four per cent and eight per cent, insurers said there were few design options under the new structure for participating products.

3.11 ANALYSIS OF CLAIM

Claims analysis is a technique for examining the positive and negative consequences of design features that are described in current or future scenarios of use. A "claim" is a statement of the consequences of a specific design feature or artifact on users and other stakeholders.

The criteria for determining whether claims are positive or negative for a particular scenario include:

- Attributes of the target user groups
- Theories from cognitive psychology
- Human-computer interaction (HCI) research, principles and guidelines
- Domain knowledge
- Environmental factors

The claims are the most important part of a patent. The goal of the claims is to particularly point out and distinctly claim the subject matter which the applicant regards as his or her invention. There must be at least one claim in a patent, and the reasoning is that possible infringers must be able to understand what is and is not protected based on the claims.

3.11.1 Parts of a Claim

A claim is generally presented in three parts, the **preamble**, a **transitional phrase** (or word), and the **body**.

3.11.1.1 Preamble

The preamble is an introductory statement that names the invention that is to be claimed. For example, "A method for making a genetically modified plant."

3.11.1.2 Transitional Phrase

The transitional phrase (or word) specifies whether the claim is limited to only the elements listed, or whether the claim may cover items or processes that have additional elements. Commonly used transitional phrases include "comprising"and "consisting of". See also Transitional Language in Patent Claims for a more in-depth description of transitional phrases.

3.11.1.3 Body

The body of a claim lists the elements (also referred to as "limitations") or steps of the named invention.

3.11.2 Claims may be Independent or Dependent

3.11.2.1 Independent Claims

An independent claim defines an operative, complete invention by itself, without referring to, or including limitations of other claims. The intention of independent claims is to broadly cover all embodiments of the invention without reading on prior art.

3.11.2.2 Dependent Claims

Dependent claims refer back to and further defines an invention recited in another claim. In doing so, a dependent claim includes all of the limitations of the claim to which it refers. Dependent claims are often used to define the scope of the elements in an independent claim, and are written to protect specific embodiments of an invention. Should a court find that the main independent claim was wrongly granted, a dependent claim may still be valid, and is used as a "fallback position". Dependent claims also make it easier for a jury to determine whether infringement as occurred, if the infringing activity is clearly spelled out in a claim rather than just inferred.

3.11.3 Types of Claims

There are a number of different types of claims that are designed for claiming different types of inventions, including:

3.11.3.1 Composition of Matter Claims

Composition of matter claims list the constituents of a new material, as well as the amount of each constituent, if applicable. Nucleic acids and amino acid sequences are often claimed as compositions of matter.

3.11.3.1 Apparatus or Device Claims

Apparatus, or device claims are claims to an apparatus or device.

3.11.3.1 Method (or Process) Claims

Method or process claims describe a novel method or process used to achieve a particular goal.

3.11.3.1 Product-By-Process Claims

In a product-by-process claims, a product is defined by the method used to manufacture it.

3.11.3.1 Markush-Type Claims

Markush-type claims have a list of functionally-equivalent elements. Components not on the list are excluded from the claim.

SUMMARY

A manufacturing network is a group of individual SMEs that cooperate in ways that increase their quality, productivity, and resultant competitiveness to levels beyond what the individual member companies could achieve by themselves.What makes a network succeed are two concepts: interdependence of member companies and mutual need. The member companies depend on each other in developing mutual solutions to common problems. Manufacturing networks are characterized by relationships of collaboration or interdependence among firms. The interactions between participants are neither dominated by any one firm nor are they simple economic exchanges motivated by calculations of price and quantity. Firms in these networks are partners: they must rely on each other in order to accomplish their objectives.

Exercise Question

1. What are quality statements? Discuss with examples.
2. . Explain the Deming Philosophy for improving quality, productivity and competitiveness.
3. Define quality cost. Explain the different types of quality costs.
4. What are the barriers for implementing TQM in industries? Explain.
5. Explain the roles of senior management in successful implementation of TQM.
6. Describe the process of strategic planning and state its importance.

❑

Quality Management—Organization Structure and Design

4

An **organizational structure** consists of activities such as task allocation, coordination and supervision, which are directed towards the achievement of organizational aims. It can also be considered as the viewing glass or perspective through which individuals see their organization and its environment. Organizational structure is the way in which the members of an organization and their job responsibilities are arranged. The key components of an organizational structure include roles and responsibilities (task allocation), coordination processes and relationships between members and groups of members, hierarchical structure of power and authority (supervision), monitoring and control mechanisms, and channels for communications and information flows.

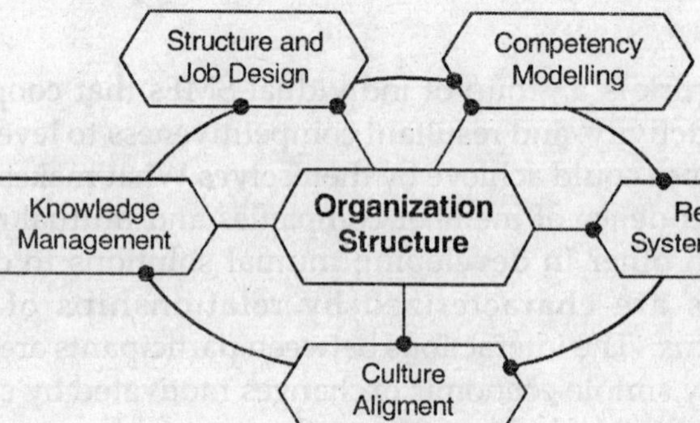

An organization can be structured in many different ways, depending on their objectives. The structure of an organization will determine the modes in which it operates and performs.

Organizational structure allows the expressed allocation of responsibilities for different functions and processes to different entities such as the branch, department, workgroup and individual.

Organizational structure affects organizational action in two big ways. First, it provides the foundation on which standard operating procedures and routines rest. Second, it determines which individuals get to participate in which decision-making processes, and thus to what extent their views shape the organization's actions.

Principles of Organizational Structure

Organizational structure

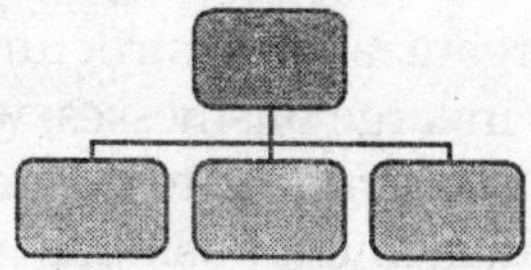

- The sum of ways an organization divides its labor into distinct, coordinated tasks
- Control, coordination, and motivation issues

Organizational design

- Assessing the organization's strategy and environmental demands and determining the appropriate organizational structure

The concept of organization structure is at the heart of organizational studies, historically and contemporaneously . . . understanding organizational structure is central and the thrust of the discipline of organization theory is to understand effective and efficient organizing, through structural design.

4.1 TYPES OF ORGANIZATIONAL STRUCTURE

Organizational structure can be divided into two categories: flat and high structures. Flat or horizontal organizational structures minimize the amount of levels in the organizational hierarchy. Flat organizations allow for feedback, free-thinking and the involvement of team members in decision-making processes. High or horizontal structures have many levels in the hierarchy and do not promote employee feedback or involvement. Leadership expects subordinates to follow directives without question.

4.2 TYPES OF ORGANIZATIONAL DESIGN

Organizational design can use one of three, or a combination of, different styles: authoritative, democratic or delegative. Authoritative organizational design places all authority and responsibility in the hands of the leadership. Democratic design uses members on every level to accomplish goals and tasks. In this way, lower management is given free rein to govern its teams or department as it sees fit. Delegative design creates smaller teams that are self-governed and do not have to report to leadership.

4.3 DIFFERENCE BETWEEN ORGANIZATIONAL STRUCTURE & DESIGN

Two important factors in organizational development are organizational structure and design. These two components help define the corporate culture, expectations and management style. When the structure and design of an organizational work together, they create a productive and efficient working environment where employees are motivated and customers are satisfied. People and tasks don't get lost in the company as the structure and design ensure that everyone is taken care of and tasks are completed on time with accuracy.

Organizational structure and design are two closely related concepts in business. The former represents the structure of positions, power, and responsibilities in a company. The structure flows from the top executive to the lowest frontline employee. Organizational design is a strategy that defines how a company unifies its departments and individuals in order to achieve goals. Essentially, this latter activity is about planning rather than organizing, and while they are different, changes to one often results in changes to the other.

Creating an organizational structure is not often an easy process. It takes some time to organize positions in large businesses, which are often the users of organizational structure. The biggest issue is often how to create a formal link for supervisory purposes. Each link between upper management positions needs to oversee employees that have relatable skills and attributes. This creates a strong sense of management–employee relationships in each line of the organizational structure.

A company's organizational structure and design are distinctly different due to the differences between creation and planning. For example, after a company creates its organizational structure, it needs to design the work flow for the business operations. These may be designed based on product lines, functions, or a hybrid between these two designs or others. In many cases, the design process must begin after the creation of an organizational structure. Changes may be more frequent in organizational design but not structure.

4.4 COMMON BUSINESS ORGANIZATIONAL STRUCTURES

4.4.1 Matrix Organizational Structure

A matrix structure provides for reporting levels both horizontally as well as vertically. Employees may be part of a functional group (i.e. engineer) but may serve on a team that supports new product development (i.e. new album). This kind of structure may have members of different groups working together to develop a new product line.

For example, a recording engineer who works for a music publisher, may have engineers who report to him but may also use his expertise and work with teams to develop new music albums. The advantage of a matrix organizational structure is that employees have responsibility not only for their department but for organizational projects. A challenge with this type of structure presents itself when employees are given direction from two different managers and they need to prioritize their work responsibilities.

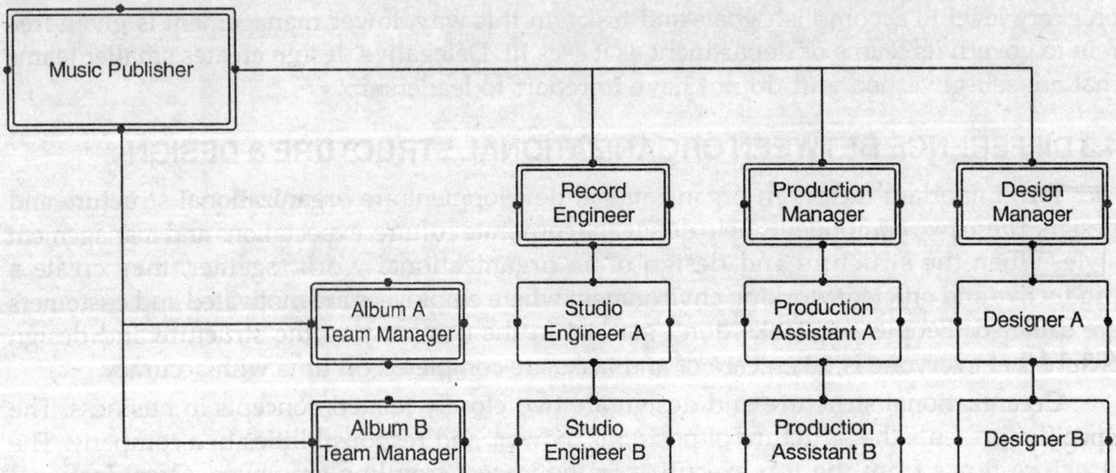

4.4.2 Functional Organizational Structure

Functional organizational structures are the most common. A structure of this type groups individuals by specific functions performed. Common departments such as human resources, accounting and purchasing are organized by separating each of these areas and managing them independently of the others.

For example, managers of different functional areas all report up to one director or vice president who has responsibility for all of the operational areas. The advantage of this type of structure is that functions are separated by expertise but the challenges comes in when different functional areas turn into silos that focus only on their area of responsibility and don't support the function of other departments.

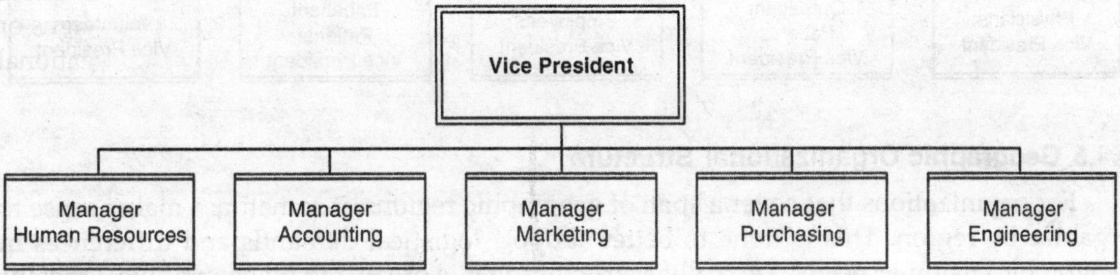

4.4.3 Product Organizational Structure

Another common structure is to be organized by a specific product type. Each product group falls within the reporting structure of an executive and that person oversees everything related to that particular product line.

For example an executive over Kraft products would be responsible for every product under that label – dressings, meats, sauces, etc. The advantage of this type of structure is that it organizes products by category but can create completely separate processes from other product lines within the organization.

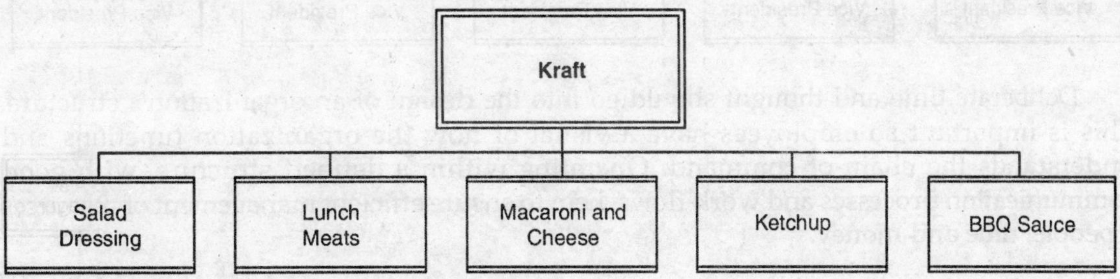

4.4.4 Customer Organizational Structure

Certain industries will organize by customer type. This is done in an effort to ensure specificcustomer expectations are met by a customized service approach.

An example of this would be in healthcare. A patient seen as an outpatient has very different needs than those of patients who spend time in the hospital as inpatients. A customer centered structure creates customized care for those patients. The advantage of this type of structure is that it specializes in the needs of each customer group but can ignore the needs of different customer types.

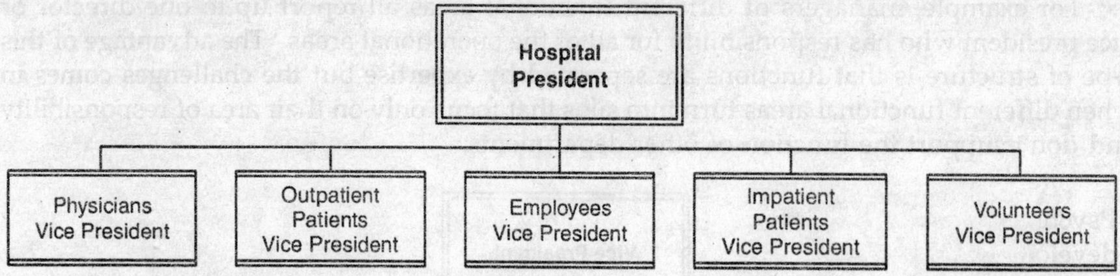

4.4.5 Geographic Organizational Structure

For organizations that cover a span of geographic regions, it sometimes makes sense to organize by region. This is done to better support logistical demands and differences in geographic customer needs. Typically a structure that is organized by geographical regions reports up to a central oversight person. You see this type of structure in companies that go beyond a city or state limit and may have customers all across the country or in multiple states.

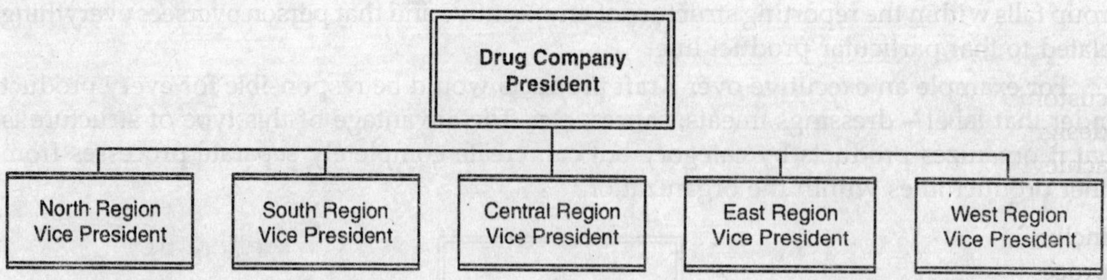

Deliberate time and thought should go into the design of an organization's structure. This is important so employees have a visual of how the organization functions and understands the chain-of-command. Operating within a defined structure, with good communication processes and work-flows, help to ensure efficient management of resources – people, time and money.

4.5 QUALITY FUNCTION DEPLOYMENT

Quality function deployment (QFD) is a "method to transform user demands into design quality, to deploy the functions forming quality, and to deploy methods for achieving the design quality into subsystems and component parts, and ultimately to specific elements of the manufacturing process."

Quality Function Deployment (QFD) was developed to bring this personal interface to modern manufacturing and business. In today's industrial society, where the growing distance between producers and users is a concern, QFD links the needs of the customer (end user) with design, development, engineering, manufacturing, and service functions.

QFD is:

1. Understanding Customer Requirements
2. Quality Systems Thinking + Psychology + Knowledge/Epistemology
3. Maximizing Positive Quality That Adds Value
4. Comprehensive Quality System for Customer Satisfaction
5. Strategy to Stay Ahead of The Game

As a quality system that implements elements of Systems Thinking with elements of Psychology and Epistemology (knowledge), QFD provides a system of comprehensive development process for:

- Understanding 'true' customer needs from the customer's perspective
- What 'value' means to the customer, from the customer's perspective
- Understanding how customers or end users become interested, choose, and are satisfied
- Analyzing how do we know the needs of the customer
- Deciding what features to include
- Determining what level of performance to deliver
- Intelligently linking the needs of the customer with design, development, engineering, manufacturing, and service functions
- Intelligently linking Design for Six Sigma (DFSS) with the front end Voice of Customer analysis and the entire design system

QFD is a comprehensive quality system that systematically links the needs of the customer with various business functions and organizational processes, such as marketing, design, quality, production, manufacturing, sales, etc., aligning the entire company toward achieving a common goal.

The QFD methodology can be used for both tangible products and non-tangible services, including manufactured goods, service industry, software products, IT projects, business process development, government, healthcare, environmental initiatives, and many other applications.

4.5.1 History of QFD

QFD was invented in Japan by Yoji Akao in 1966, but was first implemented in the Mitsubishi's Kobe shipyard in 1972, possibly out of the teaching of Deming. Then later it was adopted and developed by other Japanese companies, notably Toyota and its suppliers.

In the USA the first serious exponents of QFD were the 'big three' automotive manufacturers in the 1980's, and a few leading companies in other sectors such as electronics. However, the uptake of QFD in the Western world appears to have been fairly slow. There is also some reluctance among users of QFD to publish and share information - much more so than with other quality-related methodologies.

4.5.2 Processes of QFD

According to Lockamy and Khurana (1995) [6], the idea of QFD is timing, performance evaluation, and resource commitment. And the four phases of QFD are:

1. Product concept planning. It starts with customers and market research with leads to product plans, ideas, sketches, concept models, and marketing plans.
2. Product development and specification. It would lead to the development to prototypes and tests.
3. Manufacturing processes and production tools. They are designed based on the product and component specifications.
4. Production of product. It starts after the pilot have been resolved

After the products have been marketed, the customer's voice is taken again.

4.5.3 Benefits of QFD

According to Don Clausing, the author of Total Quality Development book, pointed out that the QFD has been evolved by product development people in response to the major problems in the traditional processes, which were:

1. Disregard the voice of customer
2. Disregard the competition
3. Concentration on each specification in isolation
4. Low expectations
5. Little input from design and production people into product planning
6. Divergent interpretation of the specifications
7. Lack of structure
8. Lost information
9. Weak commitment to previous decisions

4.5.4 Tools of QFD

Matrix diagrams, which are very useful to organize the data collected, help to facilitate the improvement process. They can be used to display information about the degree to which employee expectations are being met and the resources that exist to meet those expectations. The structure in which QFD uses to organize information is known as the House of Quality.

In its broadest sense, the QFD House of Quality displays the relationship between dependent (WHATS) and independent (HOWS) variables (Woods, 1994) [8]. Figure 1 shows the typical House of Quality.

This House of Quality should be created by a team of people with first-hand knowledge of both company capabilities and the expectations of the employee. Effective use of QFD requires team participation and discipline inherent in the practice of QFD, which has proven to be an excellent team-building experience.

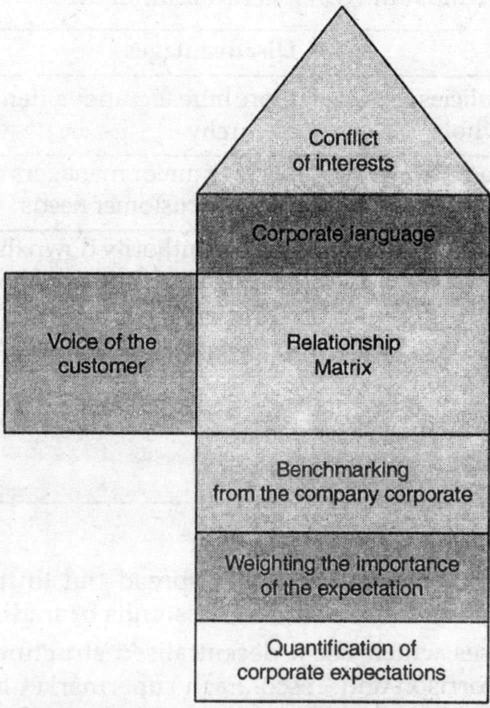

Fig. 1 The Typical House of Quality Decentralization.

4.6 ORGANISATIONAL STRUCTURE—CENTRALISATION Vs DECENTRALISATION

One of the issues that a business needs to address is where decision-making power resides in the organisational structure.

Decision-making is about **authority**. A key question is whether authority should rest with senior management at the centre of a business **(centralised)**, or whether it should be delegated further down the hierarchy, away from the centre **(decentralised)**

The choice between centralised or decentralised is not an either/or choice. Most large businesses necessarily involve a degree of decentralisation when it starts to operate from several locations or it adds new business units and markets.

The issue is really how much **independence** do business units or groups within a business have when it comes to the key decisions?

4.6.1 Centralised Structures

Businesses that have a centralised structure keep decision-making firmly at the top of the hierarchy (amongst the most senior management).

Fast-food businesses like Burger King, Pizza Hut and McDonalds use a predominantly centralised structure to ensure that control is maintained over their many thousands of outlets. The need to ensure consistency of customer experience and quality at every location is the main reason.

The main advantages and disadvantages of centralisation are:

Advantages	Disadvantages
Easier to implement common policies and practices for the business as a whole	More bureaucratic – often extra layers in the hierarchy
Prevents other parts of the business from becoming too independent	Local or junior managers are likely to much closer to customer needs
Easier to co-ordinate and control from the centre – e.g. with budgets	Lack of authority down the hierarchy may reduce manager motivation
Economies of scale and overhead savings easier to achieve	Customer service does not benefit from flexibility and speed in local decision-making
Greater use of specialisation	
Quicker decision-making (usually) – easier to show strong leadership	

4.6.2 Decentralisation

In a decentralised structure, decision-making is spread out to include more junior managers in the hierarchy, as well as individual business units or trading locations.

Good examples of businesses which use a decentralised structure include the major supermarket chains like WM Morrison and Tesco. Each supermarket has a store manager who can make certain decisions concerning areas like staffing, sales promotions. The store manager is responsible to a regional or area manager. Hotel chains are particularly keen on using decentralised structures so that local hotel managers are empowered to make on-the-spot decisions to handle customer problems or complaints.

The main advantages and disadvantages of this approach are:

Advantages	Disadvantages
Decisions are made closer to the customer	Decision-making is not necessarily "strategic"
Better able to respond to local circumstances	More difficult to ensure consistent practices and policies (customers might prefer consistency from location to location)
Improved level of customer service	May be some diseconomies of scale – e.g. duplication of roles
Consistent with aiming for a flatter hierarchy	Who provides strong leadership when needed (e.g. in a crisis)?
Good way of training and developing junior management	Harder to achieve tight financial control – risk of cost-overruns
Should improve staff motivation	

4.7 THE ADVANTAGES OF A DECENTRALIZED ORGANIZATIONAL STRUCTURE

Decentralization is a type of organizational structure in which daily operations and decision-making responsibilities are delegated by top management to middle and lower-level mangers within the organization, allowing top management to focus more on major decisions. For a small business, growth may create the need to decentralize to continue efficient operations. Decentralization offers several advantages, though relinquishing control may be difficult for a business owner accustomed to making all the decisions.

4.7.1 Empowering Employees

Employees can be empowered by having more autonomy to make their own decisions, giving them a sense of importance and making them feel as if they have more input in the direction of the organization. It also allows them to make better use of the knowledge and experience they have gained and implement some of their own ideas.

4.7.2 Relieving the Burden

Decentralizing takes some of the burden of daily business operations off the business owner. When the owner allows others to perform such tasks as hiring new employees or ordering supplies, this frees her up to spend more time on big-picture items, such as pplanning for expansion or meeting with important clients.

4.7.3 Preparing for Emergencies

A situation may arise where the business owner must be away from the business for an extended period time because of illness or another type of emergency. A decentralized structure provides a better chance that the organization will maintain self-sufficiency because managers and employees are accustomed to working autonomously.

4.7.4 More Efficient Decision-Making

A decentralized organization is able to make decisions more quickly than one with a centralized structure. A manager often can make a decision without having to wait for it to go up a chain of command, allowing the organization to react quickly to situations where fast action can mean the difference between gaining and losing a customer.

4.7.5 Ease of Expansion

For a growing business, decentralization can facilitate the process of expansion. For example, if expansion results in opening a new business unit in a different geographic area, decentralization allows the new unit to operate as an independent entity, meaning it can react more easily to the specific needs of the area, such as deciding to sell products that appeal to the local market.

4.7.6 Implications of Decentralization

1. There is less burden on the Chief Executive as in the case of centralization.
2. In decentralization, the subordinates get a chance to decide and act independently which develops skills and capabilities. This way the organization is able to process reserve of talents in it.

3. In decentralization, diversification and horizontal can be easily implanted.
4. In decentralization, concern diversification of activities can place effectively since there is more scope for creating new departments. Therefore, diversification growth is of a degree.
5. In decentralization structure, operations can be coordinated at divisional level which is not possible in the centralization set up.
6. In the case of decentralization structure, there is greater motivation and morale of the employees since they get more independence to act and decide.
7. In a decentralization structure, co-ordination to some extent is difficult to maintain as there are lot many department divisions and authority is delegated to maximum possible extent, i.e., to the bottom most level delegation reaches. Centralization and decentralization are the categories by which the pattern of authority relationships became clear. The degree of centralization and de-centralization can be affected by many factors like nature of operation, volume of profits, number of departments, size of a concern, etc. The larger the size of a concern, a decentralization set up is suitable in it.

4.8 DESIGNING AND FITTING OF ORGANIZATION

Many people equate organization design with an organization's structure: The words "lean" and "flat" are used to describe organization design as well as it's structure. In fact, organizational design encompasses much more than simply the structure: Organization design is the process of aligning an organization's structure with its mission. This means looking at the complex relationship between tasks, workflow, responsibility and authority, and making sure these all support the objectives of the business.

Good organizational design helps communications, productivity, and innovation. It creates an environment where people can work effectively.

Many productivity and performance issues can be traced back to poor organization design. A company can have a great mission, great people, great leadership, etc. and still not perform well because of poor organizational design.

Take the example of a company whose sales department and production department both work well as separate units. Yet they need to communicate about customer needs and have not been organized to do so: Company performance suffers as a result. Then take the example of a company that wants to grow by acquiring new customers. Yet its sales team is rewarded for customer retention instead: Again, company performance is compromised as a result.

How work is done, business processes, information sharing and how people are incentivized; all of these directly affects how well the organization performs. All of these factors are facets of the organization's design and each facet is important to organization's success.

Given the importance of organizational design, why is it so often to blame for inefficiency and ineffectiveness? The reason is because organizations often evolve rather than get designed. With little or no planning and intervention, the organization design that emerges is likely to be flawed with misaligned incentives, processing gaps and barriers to good communications.

Without due planning, an organization's design often takes on a hierarchical structure. This structure is common because business executives and managers are often reluctant to relinquish control. However, such structures can lack flexibility, soak up resources and under-use key people and skills. When it comes to good organization design, it's a question of getting the right balance – getting the right controls, the right flexibility, the right incentives; and getting the most from people and other key resources.

In this article, we first look at types of organization design and their uses. We then look in more detail at the key facets of organization design and offer some tips on how to ensure your organization is aligned with your business objectives.

4.9 TYPES OF ORGANIZATION STRUCTURE

Most organizations are designed, or evolve, to have elements of both hierarchy and more flexible, organic structures within. (Organic structures are more informal, less complex and more "ad-hoc" than hierarchical structures. They rely on people within the organization using their initiative to change the way they work as circumstances change.)

Before looking at some of the common types of organization structure, its worth looking at what characterizes a hierarchical structure and how it contrasts with an organic structure. It's worth saying that one type of structure is not intrinsically better than another. Rather, it's important to make sure that the organization design is fit for organization's purpose and for the people within it. And the section on **Making Organization Design Decisions** below discusses this in more detail.

Characteristic	Hierarchical structure	Organic structure
Complexity	High – with lots of horizontal separation into functions, departments and divisions	Usually lower – less differentiation or functional separation
Formality	High – lots of well defined lines of control and responsibility	Lower – no real hierarchy and less formal division of responsibilities
Participation	Low – employees lower down the organization have little involvement with decision making	Higher participation – lower level employees have more influence on decision makers.
Communication	Downward – information starts at the top and trickles down to employees	Lateral, upward, and downward communication – information flows through the organization with fewer barriers

Functional structures and divisional structure are both examples of hierarchical organization structures.

In a **functional structure**, functions (accounting, marketing, HR etc) are quite separate; each led by a senior executive who reports to the CEO. The advantage can be efficiency and economies of scale where functional skills are paramount. The main disadvantage is that functional goals can end up overshadowing the overall goals of the organization.

In a **divisional structure**, the company is organized by office or customer location. Each division is autonomous and has a divisional manager who reports to the company CEO. Each business unit is typically structured along functional lines. The advantage here relates to local results, as each division is free to concentrate on its own performance. The disadvantage is that functions and effort may be duplicated. For example, each division may have a separate marketing function, and so risk being inefficient in its marketing efforts.

More organic structures include: simple, flat structures, matrix organizations and network structures:

Simple Structure. Often found in small businesses, the simple organization is structure is flat. It may have only two or three levels; employees tend to work as a large team with everyone reporting to one person. The advantages are efficiency and flexibility, and responsibilities are usually clear. The main disadvantage is that this structure can hold back growth when the company gets to a size where the founder or CEO cannot continue to make all the decisions.

Matrix Structure. In a matrix structure, people typically have two or more lines of report. For example, a matrix organization may combine both functional and divisional lines of responsibility. For example, in this structure, a marketing manager may report both to the functional marketing director and the country director of the division he or she works in. The advantage is that the organization focuses on divisional performance whilst also sharing functional specialist skills and resources. The (often serious) downfall is its complexity – effectively with two hierarchies, and with the added complexity of tensions between the two.

Network Structure. Often known as a lean structure, this type of organization has central, core functions that operate the strategic business. It outsources or subcontracts non-core functions which, depending on the type of business, could include manufacturing, distribution, information technology marketing and other functions. This structure is very flexible and often can adapt to the market almost immediately. The disadvantage is inevitable loss of control, dependence on third parties and the complexity of managing outsource and sub-contract suppliers.

4.10 MAKING ORGANIZATION DESIGN DECISIONS

Given the many choices of structure, how do you go about making organization design decision for your business? Different organization structures have different benefits in different situations. What matters is the overall organization design is aligned with the business strategy and the market environment in which the business operates. It must then have the right business controls, the right flexibility, the right incentives, the right people and the right resources.

Here are just some of the many things that you can consider when thinking about the structure of your organization.

Strategy. The organization design must support your strategy. If your organization intends to be innovative then a hierarchical structure will not work. If however, your strategy is based on low cost, high volume delivery then a rigid structure with tight controls may be the best design.

Size. The design must take into account the size of your organization. A small organization could be paralyzed by too much specialization. In larger organizations, on the other hand, there may be economies of scale that can be gained by maintaining functionally specialist departments and teams. A large organization has more complex decision making needs and some decision making responsibilities are likely to be devolved or decentralized.

Environment. If the market environment you work in (customers, suppliers, regulators, etc.) is unpredictable or volatile, then the organization needs to be flexible enough to react to this.

Controls. What level of control is right in your business? Some activities need special controls (such as patient services in hospitals, money handling in banks and maintenance in air transport) whilst others are more efficient when there is a high degree of flexibility.

Incentives. Incentives and rewards must be aligned with the business's strategy and purpose. When these are misaligned, there is a danger that units within the organization become self-serving. Using the earlier example of a company that wants to grow by acquiring new customers, the sale team is incentivized on customer retention, and therefore is self-serving rather than aligned with the business purpose.

There is much more to organization design than deciding on its structure. This list shows just some of the facets organization design that can be taken into accounting thinking about this. With each stage of growth or each change, the organization design needs to be reassessed and realigned as necessary. The list can also help you identify issues that might be causing team problems or holding back you business.

4.11 ORGANIZATION FOR DIFFERENT TYPES OF PRODUCTS AND SERVICES

A product can be defined as a collection of physical, service and symbolic attributes which yield satisfaction or benefits to a user or buyer. A product is a combination of physical attributes say, size and shape; and subjective attributes say image or "quality". A customer purchases on both dimensions. As cited earlier, an avocado pear is similar the world over in terms of physical characteristics, but once the label CARMEL, for example, is put on it, the product's physical properties are enhanced by the image CARMEL creates. In "postmodernisation" it is increasingly important that the product fulfills the image which the producer is wishing to project. This may involve organisations producing symbolic offerings represented by meaning laden products that chase stimulation-loving consumers who seek experience - producing situations. So, for example, selling mineral water may not be enough. It may have to be "Antarctic" in source, and flavoured. This opens up a wealth of new marketing opportunities for producers.

A product's physical properties are characterised the same the world over. They can be convenience or shopping goods or durables and nondurables; however, one can classify products according to their degree of potential for global marketing:

(i) local products - seen as only suitable in one single market.
(ii) international products - seen as having extension potential into other markets.
(iii) multinational products - products adapted to the perceived unique characteristics of national markets.
(iv) global products - products designed to meet global segments.

Quality, method of operation or use and maintenance (if necessary) are catchwords in international marketing. A failure to maintain these will lead to consumer dissatisfaction. This is typified by agricultural machinery where the lack of spares and/or foreign exchange can lead to lengthy downtimes. It is becoming increasingly important to maintain quality products based on the ISO 9000 standard, as a prerequisite to export marketing.

Consumer beliefs or perceptions also affect the "world brand" concept. World brands are based on the same strategic principles, same positioning and same marketing mix but there may be changes in message or other image. World brands in agriculture are legion. In fertilizers, brands like Norsk Hydro are universal; in tractors, Massey Ferguson; in soups, Heinz; in tobacco, BAT; in chemicals, Bayer. These world brand names have been built up over the years with great investments in marketing and production. Few world brands, however, have originated from developing countries. This is hardly surprising given the lack of resources. In some markets product saturation has been reached, yet surprisingly the same product may not have reached saturation in other similar markets.

In industry, **product lifecycle management (PLM)** is the process of managing the entire lifecycle of a product from its conception, through design and manufacture, to service and disposal.[1] PLM integrates people, data, processes and business systems and provides a product information backbone for companies and their extended enterprise.

PLM integrates a multitude of critical cross-functional activities, such as:

- product strategy
- product management
- product design
- product validation and compliance
- product quality
- manufacturing
- portfolio management
- idea and requirements gathering
- product engineering
- product costing
- direct material sourcing
- after-market services product retirement

4.12 FOUR WAYS TO IMPROVE PLM

True enterprise PLM requires building an end-to-end framework that spans multiple solutions and accom¬modates business processes and data from marketing, design, product portfolio management and more. A one-size-fits-all answer does not exist, but Accenture has identified four best practices to get the most out PLM:

Step 1. Create an enterprise-wide framework to define PLM capabilities. Define what is and is not PLM, then formally break down and re-evaluate current PLM capabilities. Review all processes, applications, metrics, organization and data that underpin product development process flow from initial concept to product retirement. Then examine the performance and maturity of each as objectively as possible. High-performance businesses structure PLM as a hierarchy of capabilities that span the process, represent various organizations and competencies, and connect all corners of the PLM landscape with each another. Most companies that go through this exercise are surprised by how disjointed and fragmented their overall PLM approaches are and by how many gaps and redundancies they uncover. And they are often alarmed to find how few metrics and how little docu¬mentation supports their PLM activities.

Step 2. Link the PLM framework's capabilities to key corporate and product priorities. Settle on five-to-ten business metrics that track the effectiveness and efficiency of innovation and product development outputs, transcending any one department or function. They might relate to pipeline throughput, cost of engineering, reuse of platforms or components or resource use. For instance, if plans call for more new products to be developed in lower-cost countries, the PLM framework would link that objective to the corresponding capabilities and metrics.

Step 3. Use the prioritized PLM framework As An investment planning tool. It is relatively straightforward to turn the results of these exercises into a powerful tool for ongoing planning activities. The organization's varied constituents can more easily analyze trade-offs, guide investments in product development improvement projects, and measure the impact of those projects over time. For example, one high-technology company used this framework to concentrate its future PLM focus and investment to improve software product development processes rather than mechanical design. Basically, the firm chose to improve the productivity of its thousands of software designers instead of its hundreds of mechanical designers.

Step 4. Establish a group to own and update the PLM framework and corporate roadmap. As with CRM, ERP and supply chain management, there has to be a single, formal organization to advance and support PLM. That organization should have visible, unambiguous sponsorship from a senior executive. This helps ensure PLM becomes part of the company's innovation fabric rather than a one-time project.

4.13 ECONOMICS OF QUALITY VALUE AND CONTRIBUTION

The economics of quality include the fact that there are costs to prevention, appraisal, as well as costs of failure. Ultimately the goal is to be able to track the costs and benefits of each to determine the most cost effective solution. The cost of quality (COQ) relates to the costs of Prevention, Appraisal, and Failure (PAF). The COQ can be further broken down into the cost of good quality (conformance) and poor quality (non?conformance) as shown below (Cokins, 2006).

Cost of Conformance (good quality) = Prevention Costs +Appraisal Costs

Cost of Non? Conformance (poor quality) = Internal Failure Costs + External

Failure Costs .In other words, the cost to achieve high quality consists of the cost to prevent errors plus the cost to monitor or appraise performance to detect errors. The cost of poor quality (non?conformance), on the other hand, is equal to the cost of correcting failures before delivery to the customer (Internal Failure) and the cost of failures after delivery to the customer(External Failures).

The cost of poor quality or chronic waste can be reduced by focusing on the three fundamentals of quality, planning, control and improvement.

Cost of quality measures the costs connected with either attaining the desired level of quality in a service or product, or missing the desired level of quality. These are the costs of preventing quality issues, appraising quality level, controlling quality level, or failing to make the desired quality level.

Quality of product, quality of service, and quality of process are all included.

Setting up a formal measure of these costs allows many benefits, largely unobtainable with other approaches.

1. To avoid using trial and error methods and quality safety nets while integrating improvement approaches into functional areas, cost of quality is a significant part of managing. Only cost of quality provides a means to reduce inspection while retaining control of risks.
2. Some forms of improvement will shift costs around. When quality costs are applied correctly, these cost reductions are directly added to profits, and trade-offs are avoided.
3. Looking at the range of business measures from the top to the bottom of an organization, top managers use money in the measures, and lower level areas use pieces or transactions to measure work. Cost of quality creates an improvement measure from senior management's perspective.
4. The salient points of the economic case for improvement are:
    - Businesses are highly competitive
    - Improvement is a strategic tool
    - Quality is the 'right thing to do`' besides being a market imperative
    - To apply improvement methods in varying functional areas, there needs to be a translation of process improvement measures into the common language of business: money.

4.14 QUALITY COST

Over the last several decades, quality costs have been divided into several categories. These are: (1) prevention, (2) appraisal, and (3) failure costs.

Prevention costs. Costs of all activities specifically designed to prevent poor quality in products or services. All improvement approaches (six sigma, ISO, Baldrige, for example) will invest in some prevention activity.

Appraisal costs. Costs associated with measuring, evaluating or auditing products or services to assure conformance to quality standards and performance requirements. Most improvement programs enable reduction of these classic "quality" area expenses as work processes are better controlled and prevention investments bear fruit.

Failure costs: costs resulting from products or services not conforming to requirements or customer/user needs. Failure costs are divided into internal and external failure cost categories.

Internal failure costs: failure costs occurring prior to delivery or shipment of the product, or the furnishing of a service, to the customer. In the service environment, effort that does not support service delivery may be considered internal failure.

External failure costs: failure costs occurring after delivery or shipment of the product, and during or after furnishing of a service, to the customer. Service businesses often count second and third customer contacts as external failures.

4.14.1 What are the core values of cost of quality?

4.14.1.1 Flexibility

Cost of quality can be applied at any organization. Service organizations can apply cost of quality; there are costs of poor processes in service industries as well as costs of measuring quality levels (appraisal) and investments to prevent poor outcomes. Most importantly, the elements of cost of quality are meant to be applied in the context of each organization. Because of this, these techniques can be applied to many types of organizations, and all improvement approaches.

4.14.1.2 Cost reduction via prevention

You can manage your improvement programs with a balance of prevention activity cost, measurement activity cost, and connected costs. Increased and refocused prevention activities are used to first attack failure costs, then reduce appraisal costs.

4.14.1.3 Reducing the overall costs is the goal

Improvement programs will show bottom-line savings while avoiding the pitfalls that accompany simplistic cost cutting. These pitfalls may include decreases of product or service quality, increased customer dissatisfaction, added rework costs, or simple shifts of costs from one area to another.

4.14.1.4 The later a problem is found, the more it costs to fix

The central theme behind cost of quality is that the largest costs occur after product has shipped or a service has been performed; that is, in the category of external failure costs. By showing costs in the order of flow, managers will focus improvement efforts on issues at the earliest possible point in the flow.

4.14.1.5 Showing the qualitypayoff

A cost of quality system shows the payoff of improvement activities. Has the organization reached the point where added improvement activity consumes more resources than it returns in benefits An ongoing cost of quality program will answer that by showing the pace of improvement.

4.14.1.6 A global look

Cost of quality allows a monetary measure of overall organizational progress. No longer will departments waste time arguing that their improvement trumps the contribution of another department's. All improvement will be measured in terms of their contribution to the bottom line.

4.15 THE WHOLE ORGANIZATION

With a comprehensive cost of quality program, the costs from each organizational area can be totaled. By comparing the pace of change of each area to its own track record, senior managers can allocate resources according to measured need and strategic plans.

Improvement methodologies such as lean, six sigma, ISO, and Baldrige-type programs all reference the need to measure an organization's performance. Cost of quality provides the way to measure improvement so that measure can be integrated into an organization's strategic plan.

The core values of the Baldrige approach drive a holistic approach to improvement. 'Management by Fact,' 'Focus on Results and Creating Value,' and 'Systems Perspective' in particular support the use of cost of quality.

Linkage is the key. From improvement approaches to dollars and cents, from early flow to late flow of product, from supply chain beginnings to final customer and the end of the waste stream; linkage of key costs allows strategic improvement.

4.16 THE FINAL ANALYSIS

The name of the game is dollars and cents. Cost of quality will demonstrate the value of improvement approaches. Cost of quality makes an ongoing "economic case" for the value of improvement, excellence, and quality, no matter what improvement approach is used.

4.17 Optimizing Quality Cost

Quality costs are used to identify costs related to product nonconformance and to measure their relative importance. This understanding of how and why resources nave been wasted can provide direction for improvement. Quality costs exist in terms of four common categories: external failure costs include the costs of responding to customer complaints, customer returns, warranty claims, and product recalls; internal failure costs occur before product delivery, and include the costs of scrap, reinspection, retesting, and downgrading; appraisal costs are associated with measuring, evaluating, and auditing of products; and prevention costs include quality planning, quality improvement, and quality training. Products which deviate significantly from customer specifications can cause large external costs. Accordingly, it is more profitable to rework materials and processes to absorb smaller internal costs; external costs should be transformed into internal costs. Reworking is not the only approach. Avoiding expensive product deviations in the first place can be more economical. Choosing the best approach requires a balance of failure, appraisal, and prevention costs.

4.18 SEDUCTION PROGRAM

Many manufacturing organizations we work with are still reeling from the impact of organizational change programs:

- **Wasted Time:** Several supervisors at an auto parts manufacturer complained, "We finally documented our processes for ISO certification then management went on an industry best-practices tour. They found out our processes weren't the best in the first place. All we did was waste our time certifying poor processes."
- **Increased Politics:** A power systems manufacturer's quality program failed as interdepartmental feedback data wasn't used to improve processes, but seen as an attack from being "written up." The ensuing write-up wars brought the organization to its knees.
- **Functional Distractions:** A hi-tech manufacturer development team was frustrated as they tried to figure out how to make their R&D meet the mandatory quality policies. How would they know which "idea" had enough quality?
- **Strategic Misdirection:** One plant manager complained about the overhead of six-sigma process. "Our bottle caps work great at 3-sigma. We"e achieved no more market share or profit from the extra quality. I think management forgot to look at how the program would support our strategy."

But why do some manufacturing changes implement well while others flounder using the same methods? Seeking an answer led our research to a unique laboratory — the death zone; that altitude above 26,000 feet which makes survival for a long period of time impossible because of the lack of available oxygen. In this environment climbers reveal insights previously unnoticed by mainstream management experts.

Climbers bear a resemblance to manufacturing executives.They live passionately while confronting impossible odds. Some are deeply humble; others are psychotic narcissists. They come with all levels of competence; from naive wannabes to elite athletes. And when put to the test, they react like all of us: sometimes like heroes, other times like self-destructive villains.

In our study we expected to find new leadership principals, but we found something else. Executives who produce peak performance in the face of extreme challenges — what we call high altitude leaders — walk a different path. Instead of being seduced by the latest leadership platitudes, cliches or feel-good organizational change theories, they succeed by recognizing and surviving specific dangers; dangers that always emerge on the journey to higher performance. Eight dangers seem to threaten peak performance:Fear, Selfishness, Tool Seduction, Arrogance, Lone Heroism, Cowardice, Comfort, and Gravity. If we had to choose one for manufacturing, we'd choose Tool Seduction.

SUMMARY

An **organizational structure** consists of activities such as task allocation, coordination and supervision, which are directed towards the achievement of organizational aims. It can also be considered as the viewing glass or perspective through which individuals see their organization and its environment. Organizational structure is the way in which the members of an organization and their job responsibilities are arranged.

Exercise Question

1. What is customer satisfaction?
2. Name the five important principle of TQM.
3. What do you mean by customer perceived quality?
4. What is service quality?
5. What are the components of service quality?
6. What do you mean by customer defection?
7. Define customer retention.
8. What is employee motivation?
9. What do you mean by safety needs?
10. Define empowerment.
11. Give any two benefits of empowerment.
12. Define a team and teamwork.
13. List the stages of team building.
14. List out the characteristics of a successful team. ❑

5 Human Factor in Quality

Our employees make a decisive contribution to product quality. Their qualifications, motivation and commitment are important factors in success, the responsibilities assumed in the individual working area presupposing a high degree of self-sufficiency and conscientiousness. Customer-oriented thinking and action are much in demand and not only the purchaser is to be seen as a client. Instead, the aim must be to live up to the expectations of all those, who rely on the performance shown during the development and production process, or during component supply.

The ongoing optimization of internal procedures is also the result of employee involvement. The workforce is able to introduce its ideas and suggestions regarding the workplace, processes and plants within the framework of a continuous improvement process (CIP). This has a positive effect upon quality, productivity, safety and environmental protection within company plants.

The term human factors has grown increasingly popular as the commercial aviation industry realize that human error, rather than mechanical failure, underlies most aviation accidents and incidents. Human factors science or technologies are multidisciplinary fields incorporating contributions from psychology, engineering, industrial design, statistics, operations research, and anthropometry. It is a term that covers the science of understanding the properties of human capability, the application of this understanding to the design, development, and deployment of systems and services, and the art of ensuring successful application of human factor principles into the maintenance working environment.

The list of human factors that can affect aviation maintenance and work performance is broad. They encompass a wide range of challenges that influence people very differently as humans do not all have the same capabilities, strengths, weaknesses, or limitations. Unfortunately, aviation maintenance tasks that do not account for the vast amount of human limitations can result in technical error and injuries.

Cost of Ignoring Human Factors Is

Poor Quality!

Increased probability of accidents and errors

Less spare capacity to deal with emergencies

Increased labor turnover

Lower productive output

Increases in lost time
Higher medical costs
Higher material costs
Increased absenteeism
Low quality work
Injuries, strains

5.1 ELEMENTS OF HUMAN FACTORS

Human factors are comprised of many disciplines. This section discusses ten of those disciplines: Clinical Psychology, Experimental Psychology, Anthropometrics, Computer Science, Cognitive Science, Safety Engineering, Medical Science, Organizational Psychology, Educational Psychology, and Industrial Engineering.The study and application of human factors is complex because there is not just one simple answer to fix or change how people are affected by certain conditions or situations. Aviation maintenance human factors research has the overall goal to identify and optimize the factors that affect human performance in maintenance and inspection.

The focus initiates on the technician but extends to the entire engineering and technical organization. Research is optimized by incorporating the many disciplines that affect human factors and help to understand how people can work more efficiently and maintain work performance.

By understanding each of the disciplines and applying them to different situations or human behaviors, we can correctly recognize potential human factors and address them before they develop into a problem or create a chain of problems that result in an accident or incident.

5.2 CLINICAL PSYCHOLOGY

Clinical psychology includes the study and application of psychology for the purpose of understanding, preventing, and relieving psychologically-based distress or dysfunction and to promote subjective well-being and personal development. It focuses on the mental well-being of the individual. Clinical psychology can help individuals deal with stress, coping mechanisms for adverse situations, poor self image, and accepting criticism from coworkers.

5.3 EXPERIMENTAL PSYCHOLOGY

Experimental psychology includes the study of a variety of basic behavioral processes, often in a laboratory environment. These processes may include learning, sensation, perception, human performance, motivation, memory, language, thinking, and communication, as well as the physiological processes underlying behaviors, such as eating, reading, and problem solving. In an effort to test the efficiency of work policies and procedures, experimental studies help measure performance, productivity, and deficiencies.

5.4 ANTHROPOMETRICS

Anthropometry is the study of the dimensions and abilities of the human body. This is essential to aviation maintenance due to the environment and spaces that AMTs have to work with. For example, a man who is 6 feet 3 inches and weighs 230 pounds may be required to fit into a small crawl space of an aircraft to conduct a repair. Another example is the size and weight of equipment and tools. Men and women are generally on two different spectrums of height and weight. Although both are equally capable of completing the same task with a high level of proficiency, someone who is smaller may be able to perform more efficiently with tools and equipment that is tailored to their size. In other words, one size does not fit all and the term "average person" does not apply when employing such a diverse group of people.

5.5 COMPUTER SCIENCE

The technical definition for computer science is the study of the theoretical foundations of information and computation and of practical techniques for their implementation and application in computer systems. How this relates to aviation maintenance is a lot simpler. As mentioned earlier, AMTs spend as much time documenting repairs as they do performing them. It is important that they have computer work stations that are comfortable and reliable. Software programs and computer-based test equipment should be easy to learn and use, and not intended only for those with a vast level of computer literacy.

5.6 COGNITIVE SCIENCE

Cognitive science is the interdisciplinary scientific study of minds as information processors. It includes research on how information is processed (in faculties such as perception, language, reasoning, and emotion), represented, and transformed in a nervous system or machine (e.g., computer). It spans many levels of analysis from low-level learning and decision mechanisms to high-level logic and planning. AMTs must possess a great ability to problem solve quickly and efficiently. They constantly have to troubleshoot a situation and quickly react to it. This can be a viscous cycle creating an enormous amount of stress. The discipline of cognitive science helps us understand how to better assist AMTs during situations that create high levels of stress so that their mental process does not get interrupted and effect their ability to work.

5.7 SAFETY ENGINEERING

Safety engineering assures that a life-critical system behaves as needed even when the component fails. Ideally, safety engineers take an early design of a system, analyze it to find what faults can occur, and then propose safety requirements in design specifications up front and changes to existing systems to make the system safer. Safety cannot be stressed enough when it comes to aviation maintenance, and everyone deserves to work in a safe environment. Safety engineering plays a big role in the design of aviation maintenance facilities, storage containers for toxic materials, equipment used for heavy lifting, and floor designs to ensure no one slips, trips, or falls. In industrial work environments, the guidelines of the Occupational Safety and Health Administration (OSHA) are important.

5.8 MEDICAL SCIENCE

Medicine is the science and art of healing. It encompasses a variety of health care practices evolved to maintain and restore health by the prevention and treatment of illness. Disposition and physical well-being are very important and directly correlated to human factors. Just like people come in many shapes and sizes, they also have very different reactions to situations due to body physiology, physical structures, and biomechanics.

5.9 ORGANIZATIONAL PSYCHOLOGY

Organizational psychologists are concerned with relations between people and work. Their interests include organizational structure and organizational change, workers' productivity and job satisfaction, consumer behavior, and the selection, placement, training, and development of personnel. Understanding organizational psychology helps aviation maintenance supervisors learn about the points listed below that, if exercised, can enhance the work environment and productivity.

- Rewards and compensations for workers with good safety records.
- Motivated workers that want to do well and work safely. Unified work teams and groups that get along and work together to get the job done right.
- Treat all workers equally.

5.10 EDUCATIONAL PSYCHOLOGY

Educational psychologists study how people learn and design the methods and materials used to educate people of all ages. Everyone learns differently and at a different pace. Supervisors should design blocks of instruction that relate to a wide variety of learning styles.

5.11 INDUSTRIAL ENGINEERING

Industrial engineering is the organized approach to the study of work. It is important for supervisors to set reasonable work standards that can be met and exceeded. Unrealistic work standards create unnecessary stressors that cause mistakes. It is also beneficial to have an efficient facility layout so that there is room to work. Clean and uncluttered environments enhance work performance. Another aspect of industrial engineering that helps in the understanding of human factors is the statistical analysis of work performance. Concrete data of work performance, whether good or bad, can show the contributing factors that may have been present when the work was done.

5.12 ATTITUDE OF TOP MANAGEMENT

Here are the four most common bad attitudes in the workplace:

- **Negative emotions toward the organization.** It's not uncommon to have those select employees who continuously make snide remarks about company leaders or co-workers. These negative feelings toward the organization clash with organizational goals and hurt the workplace environment.
- **Insubordinate challenges to authority.** Bad attitude employees might refuse to perform a task just in order to prove a point. That is disrespectful, unprofessional and sure isn't helping your organization!
- **Overly argumentative.** Employees who aggravate and pick fights in the workplace create an uncomfortable and distrusting team setting. These employees don't make efforts to compromise or settle disagreements with coworkers.

- **Lazy, unmotivated.** These are the employees who aren't engaged in their work and spend most of their time goofing off and causing distractions. An infographic created from the National Business Research Institute shared that disengaged employees spend their time sleeping, playing games, using social media and socializing.

5.13 COOPERATION OF GROUPS

What is cooperation

- **Cooperation is the common effort of a group for their mutual benefit.**
- **Cooperation is teamwork.**
- **Cooperation is working together peacefully.**

Cooperation (sometimes written **co-operation** or **coöperation**) is the process of working or acting together. In its simplest form it involves things working in harmony, while in its more complicated forms, it can involve something as complex as the inner workings of a human being or even the social patterns of a nation. It is the opposite of working separately in competition. Cooperation can also be accomplished by computers, which can handle shared resources simultaneously, while sharing processor time.

Cooperation is the process by which the components of a system work together to achieve the global properties. In other words, individual components that appear to be "selfish" and independent work together to create a highly complex, greater-than-the-sum-of-its-parts system.Examples:

- The components in a cell work together to keep it living.
- Neurons create thought and consciousness, other cells work together and communicate to produce multicellular organisms.
- Organisms form food chains and ecosystems.
- People form families, tribes, cities and nations.
- Atoms cooperate in a simple way, by combining to make up molecules.

Understanding the mechanisms that create cooperating agents in a system is one of the most important and least well understood phenomena in nature, though there has not been a lack of effort.Individual action on behalf of a larger system may be coerced (forced), voluntary (freely chosen), or even unintentional, and consequently individuals and groups might act in concert even though they have almost nothing in common as regards interests or goals. Examples of that can be found in market trade, military wars, families, workplaces, schools and prisons, and more generally any institution or organization of which individuals are part (out of own choice, by law, or forced)

5.14 OPERATORS ATTITUDES

When discussing data quality and the process from raw data to information, three key occupational groups can be identified data collectors or producers, data analysers and data consumers. In an engineering asset context data collectors are those tasked with the responsibility of collecting, recording or documenting the raw data produced by engineering assets. While those involved in the data collection process are typically onsite maintenance operators or production technicians, the nature of the task does not limit it to these specific roles. For the sake of conciseness the term "operator" is used to denote personnel tasked with the responsibility of manually recording and documenting engineering data. As would be expected this data may come about as part of maintenance activities such as equipment monitoring, condition assessment reports and routine inspections. Despite the vital role played by this group far more attention has been paid in the literature to the skills required by data analysers and data consumers. The need to pay attention to the role of data collection personnel in the data quality process is considered important for two key reasons. One, those tasked to record the data in its raw state represent the first weak link in a vulnerable chain.

Arguably data collected in a consistent and timely manner, that is both complete and accurate reduces the amount of manipulation and cleansing required later in the process. The flowon effects of poor manually acquired data are likely to result in significant difficulties for analysis and to be of reduced utility to consumers. Two, in many instances the potential for human error can be significant, with a high degree of performance variance between individuals for the same task – irrespective of standardised procedures and training equivalence.

Typical approaches to improving the performance of data collectors appear to centre on aspects such as standardising the data collection process and improving the training and competency of those responsible for data quality. However, while best practice protocols may exist to instruct those responsible for data collection, empirical and anecdotal evidence indicates that organisations still have difficulty in convincing operators to comply with data collection procedures and to have an overall appreciation of good data and its consequences. Cases routinely recount stories of gauges being misread, information being omitted, incorrect information being provided or in extreme cases, gauges and thresholds altered to reduce operational inconvenience. Consequently while standardised forms, training and the threat of discipline (e.g. demotion, sacking) may be useful tools to encourage short termcompliance, efforts are likely to be focused on the bareminimum and are unlikely to be sustained in the long term. In response it is suggested that an increased level of attention be paid to the attitudes, motivations and behaviours of those responsible for data collection. An improved understanding of these aspects will allow engineering asset managers the opportunity to implement a number of strategies able to guarantee operator commitment to data quality over a sustained period. The remainder of the paper represents an attempt to further this line of enquiry, using the Theory of Planned Behaviour (TPB) as a theoretical framework to consider the psychological underpinnings of operator behaviour when collecting engineering data.

5.15 RESPONSIBILITYTOWARDS QUALITY

Responsibilities for the core quality functions include:

- **Customer Quality.** Drives identification of the root cause of quality issues and execution of product quality improvements through preventive or corrective actions.
- **External Quality.** Interfaces with final manufacturing subcontractors and foundries for quality-related tasks, audits and incidents. This is the primary quality interface for outsourced products.

- **Failure Analysis Lab.** Performs electrical and physical product analysis to support new product development, customer issue resolution and manufacturing effectiveness improvements. Provides an expert voice in new product development teams.
- **Field Quality.** Interfaces with customers for quality-related tasks, audits and incidents and collects and summarizes customer quality data to drive improvement within Freescale.
- **Manufacturing Quality.** Provides support and the voice of the customer for internal manufacturing sites regarding change management, discrepant material and product qualifications. Overviews and performs quality audit activities, provides expert knowledge with quality tools and methods and helps to ensure quality of manufactured products.
- **NPI Quality.** Drives quality into product development activities and helps to ensure that new product releases meet customer and standards requirements. These activities focus on the quality and reliability of new products, qualifies new materials and new products and performs reliability engineering for all NPI qualification definitions and new product qualifications.
- **Quality Standards and Bodies.** Voices Freescale's position and interests within industry standard bodies such as IEC and JEDEC; Communicates within Freescale industry standard trends and changes (planned or actual).
- **Quality Systems.** Manages Freescale quality rules, process structure and documents. Coordinates internal and certification audits. Leads continuous improvement activities. Helps to ensure that customer-specific requirements are available and understood.
- **Reliability Lab.** Operates life and environmental stress labs used to validate long-term reliability of Freescale products.
- **Software Quality.** Drives quality into software development activities and helps to ensure that new software releases meet customer and standards requirements.
- **Supplier Quality.** Interfaces with suppliers for Quality related tasks, audits and incidents. Drives supplier quality improvements and handle supplier audits, data collection and analysis and quality related items, including issues and changes.

5.16 MANAGEMENT RESPOSIBILITY

5.16.1 Management commitment

Top management shall provide evidence of its commitment to the development and implementation of the quality management system and continually improving its effectiveness by

1. communicating to the organization the importance of meeting customer as well as statutory and regulatory requirements,
2. establishing the quality policy,
3. ensuring that quality objectives are established,
4. conducting management reviews, and
5. ensuring the availability of resources.

5.16.2 Process efficiency

Top management shall review the product realization processes and the support processes to assure their effectiveness and efficiency.

5.16.3 Customer focus

Top management shall ensure that customer requirements are determined and fulfilled with the aim of enhancing customer satisfaction.

5.16.4 Quality policy

Top management shall ensure that the quality policy

1. is appropriate to the purpose of the organization,
2. includes a commitment to comply with requirements and continually improve the effectiveness of the quality management system,
3. provides a framework for establishing and reviewing quality objectives,
4. is communicated and understood within the organization, and
5. is reviewed for continuing suitability.

5.17 PLANNING

5.17.1 Quality objectives

Top management shall ensure that quality objectives, including those needed to meet requirements for product are established at relevant functions and levels within the organization. The quality objectives shall be measurable and consistent with the quality policy.

5.17.2 Quality objectives - Supplemental

Top management shall define quality objectives and measurements that shall be included in the business plan and used to deploy the quality policy.

5.17.3 Quality management system planning

The quality management system is maintained when changes to the quality management system are planned and implemented.

5.18 RESPONSIBILITY, AUTHORITY AND COMMUNICATIONAND AUTHORITY

Top management shall ensure that the responsibilities and authorities are defined and communicated within the organization.

5.18.1 Responsibility for quality

Managers with responsibility and authority for corrective action shall be promptly informed of products or processes which do not conform to requirements. Personnel responsible for product quality shall have the authority to stop production to correct quality problems.

Production operations across all shifts shall be staffed with personnel in charge of, or delegated responsibility for, ensuring product quality.

5.18.2 Management representative

Top management shall appoint a member of management who, irrespective of other responsibilities, shall have responsibility and authority that includes

1. ensuring that processes needed for the quality management system are established, implemented and maintained,
2. reporting to top management on the performance of the quality management system and any need for improvement, and
3. ensuring the promotion of awareness of customer requirements throughout the organization.

NOTE The responsibility of a management representative can include liaison with external parties on matters relating to the quality management system.

5.18.3 Customer representative

Top management shall designate personnel with responsibility and authority to ensure the customer requirements are addressed This includes selection of special characteristics, setting quality objectives and related training, corrective and preventive actions, product design and development.

5.19 INTERNAL COMMUNICATION

Top management shall ensure that appropriate communication processes are established within the organization and that communication takes place regarding the effectiveness of the quality management system.

5.20 MANAGEMENT REVIEW

5.20.1 General

Top management shall review the organization's quality management system, at planned intervals, to ensure its continuing suitability, adequacy and effectiveness. This review shall include assessing opportunities for improvement and the need for changes to the quality management system, including the quality policy and quality objectives.

5.20.2 Quality management system performance

These reviews shall include all requirements of the quality management system and its performance trends as an essential part of the continual improvement process.

Part of the management review shall be the monitoring of quality objectives, and the regular reporting and evaluation of the cost of poor quality .These results shall be recorded to provide, as a minimum, evidence of the achievement of

- the quality objectives specified in the business plan, and
- customer satisfaction with product supplied.

5.20.3 Review input

The input to management review shall include information on

(a) results of audits,
(b) customer feedback,
(c) process performance and product conformity,
(d) status of preventive and corrective actions,
(e) follow-up actions from previous management reviews,
(f) planned changes that could affect the quality management system, and
(g) recommendations for improvement.

5.20.4 Review input - Supplemental

Input to management review shall include an analysis of actual and potential field-failures and their impact on quality, safety, or the environment.

5.20.5 Review output

The output from the management review shall include any decisions and actions related to

(a) improvement of the effectiveness of the quality management system and its processes,
(b) improvement of product related to customer requirements, and
(c) resource needs.

5.21 CAUSES OF APPARATUS ERROR AND CORRECTIVE METHOD

Every organization runs into an issue or nonconformance at one time or another. It's what they do when it happens that separates effective companies from ineffective companies and creates better products, higher customer satisfaction and a competitive advantage.

Inefficient or ineffective problem solving can occur when a company fails to:

- Focus on the meaningful problems
- Use an effective problem solving process
- Get the necessary functions and "opinion leaders" involved
- Utilize sufficient problem solving skills to determine the root cause
- Translate the problem and solution into dollars
- Automate or otherwise link the corrective action system to other activities within the organization, such as the quality management system
- Follow through
- Be sensitive but direct

Corrective action and preventive action (**CAPA**, also called **corrective action / preventive action**) are improvements to an organization's processes taken to eliminate causes of non-conformities or other undesirable situations. CAPA is a concept withingood manufacturing practice (GMP). It focuses on the systematic investigation of the root causes of non-conformities in an attempt to prevent their recurrence (for corrective action) or to prevent occurrence (for preventive action).

Corrective actions are implemented in response to customer complaints, undesired levels of internal nonconformity, nonconformities identified during an internal audit or adverse or unstable trends in product and process monitoring such as would be identified by SPC. Preventive actions are implemented in response to the identification of potential sources of non-conformity.

To ensure that corrective and preventive actions are effective, the systematic investigation of the root causes of failure is pivotal. CAPA is part of the overall quality management system (QMS)

Examples of corrective actions

- Visible or Audible Alarms
- Process Redesign
- Product Redesign
- Training or enhancement/ modification of existing training programmes
- Improvements to maintenance schedules
- Improvements to material handling or storage

SUMMARY

The term human factors has grown increasingly popular as the commercial aviation industry realize that human error, rather than mechanical failure, underlies most aviation accidents and incidents. Human factors science or technologies are multidisciplinary fields incorporating contributions from psychology, engineering, industrial design, statistics, operations research, and anthropometry. It is a term that covers the science of understanding the properties of human capability, the application of this understanding to the design, development, and deployment of systems and services, and the art of ensuring successful application of human factor principles into the maintenance working environment.

Exercise Questions

1. Name types of teams?
2. What is performance appraisal?
3. What is PDSA?
4. What is 5 S?
5. What is sourcing?
6. What are the types of sourcing?
7. What is Muda?
8. What do you mean by continuous process improvement?
9. Define Kaizen.
10. Define partnering.
11. 60. What is MalcolmBalridge National Quality Award?

Control Charts in Quality Management 6

A **control chart** is a graphic tool used by quality technicians to control, analyze and document the processes in production and other quality-relevant areas.

Control charts were developed by Dr. Walter A. Shewhart (1891 - 1967) in 1924 to detect systematic deviations of a quality characteristic from a target value (signals) against the background of inevitable, random fluctuations in individual measured values (noise). Today, the control chart is the central element of **statistical process control** (SPC).

6.1 HOW ARE CONTROL CHARTS USED

In statistical process control, one or more **control variables** of the observed characteristic are selected and determined by taking samples from the process at uniform intervals, if possible. These statistic variables are plotted in the chart in a chronological order. The most important control variables are:

- Mean value □x
- Standard deviation s
- Median
- Range
- Original value of a sample
- Number of nonconforming units
- Number of defects

Two control variables of a characteristic are often maintained simultaneously as two **tracks** in a control chart (for example, as a mean value and standard deviation). In this example, the location and dispersion of the process can be observed at the same time.

Apart from the control variable itself, each track on the control chart also contains **control limits** for the process. You must intervene in the process if these limits are violated. In addition to these action limits, you can also define warning limits or a mean line for individual chart types.

The limits are generally determined from the current process data or the results of preliminary test using statistical methods. The limits are calculated using various algorithms that are based on different mathematical approaches.

6.2 WHY SHOULD TEAMS USE CONTROL CHARTS?

A stable process is one that is consistent over time with respect to the center and the spread of the data. Control Charts help you monitor the behavior of your process to determine whether it is stable. Like Run Charts, they display data in the time sequence in which they occurred. However, Control Charts are more efficient that Run Charts in assessing and achieving process stability.

It will benefit from using a Control Chart when you want to

Differentiate between special cause and common cause variation.

Assess the effectiveness of changes to improve a process.

Communicate how a process performed during a specific period.

6.3 TYPES OF CONTROL CHARTS

There are two main categories of Control Charts, those that display attribute data, and those that display variables data.

Attribute Data: This category of Control Chart displays data that result from counting the number of occurrences or items in a single category of similar items or occurrences. These "count" data may be expressed as pass/fail, yes/no, or presence/absence of a defect.

Variables Data: This category of Control Chart displays values resulting from the measurement of a continuous variable. Examples of variables data are elapsed time, temperature, and radiation dose.

While these two categories encompass a number of different types of Control Charts (Viewgraph 3), there are three types that will work for the majority of the data analysis cases you will encounter. In this module, we will study the construction and application in these three types of Control Charts:

6.4 X-BAR AND R CHART

Individual X and Moving Range Chart for Variables Data

Individual X and Moving Range Chart for Attribute Data

Viewgraph 4 provides a decision tree to help you determine when to use these three types of Control Charts.

In this module, we will study only the Individual X and Moving Range Control Chart for handling attribute data, although there are several others that could be used, such as the np, p, c, and u charts. These other charts require an understanding of probability distribution theory and specific control limit calculation formulas which will not be covered here. To avoid the possibility of generating faulty results by improperly using these charts, we recommend that you stick with the Individual X and Moving Range chart for attribute data.

The following six types of charts will not be covered in this module:

X-Bar and S Chart

Median X and R Chart

c Chart

u Chart

p Chart

np Chart

Chart details

A control chart consists of:

- Points representing a statistic (e.g., a mean, range, proportion) of measurements of a quality characteristic in samples taken from the process at different times [the data]
- The mean of this statistic using all the samples is calculated (e.g., the mean of the means, mean of the ranges, mean of the proportions)
- A centre line is drawn at the value of the mean of the statistic
- The standard error (e.g., standard deviation/sqrt(n) for the mean) of the statistic is also calculated using all the samples
- Upper and lower control limits (sometimes called "natural process limits") that indicate the threshold at which the process output is considered statistically 'unlikely' and are drawn typically at 3 standard errors from the centre line

The chart may have other optional features, including:

- Upper and lower warning limits, drawn as separate lines, typically two standard errors above and below the centre line
- Division into zones, with the addition of rules governing frequencies of observations in each zone
- Annotation with events of interest, as determined by the Quality Engineer in charge of the process's quality

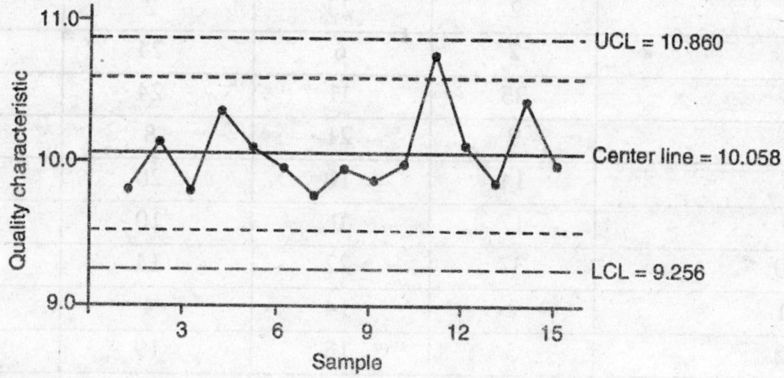

6.5 HOW TO CALCULATE CONTROL CHARTS

In quality improvement, a control chart is used to determine if a process is stable. In a control chart, data points are plotted on a graph and compared to upper and lower control-limits. The control limits are designed to contain 99 percent of all the data points of the process if the process is in control. If your data points routinely fall above or below these control limits, the process is deemed out of control. Causes for variation in process quality should be investigated and remediated before any systematic changes to the process as a whole can be made and evaluated.

6.6 CONSTRUCTION AND ANALYSIS OF C CHART

Control charts are an efficient way of analyzing performance data to evaluate a process. Control charts have many uses; they can be used in manufacturing to test if machinery are producing products within specifications. Also, they have many simple applications such as professors using them to evaluate tests scores. To create a control chart, it is helpful to have Excel; it will simplify your life.

1. Method

- Data should usually be normally distributed revolving around a mean (average).
  - In the example below, a bottle company fills their bottles to 16 oz. (mean); they are evaluating if their process is "in-control". The amount in ounces over 16 oz. is normally distributed around the mean.
- Measurements need to be independent of one another.
  - In the example, the measurements are in subgroups. The data in the subgroups should be independent of the measurement number; each data point will have a subgroup and a measurement number.

Hundredths of an ounce over 16 ounces in bottle filling process

Subgroup Number	a	b	c	d
1	24	17	9	4
2	19	13	9	28
3	5	16	12	13
4	2	23	2	23
5	7	6	24	6
6	25	11	24	18
7	9	21	8	19
8	14	10	20	7
9	17	0	10	25
10	37	22	14	18
11	2	14	4	5
12	3	15	19	18
13	25	8	25	26
14	26	10	23	12
15	1	6	5	17
16	15	28	2	5
17	25	21	4	18
18	10	24	5	19
19	2	12	3	1
20	13	12	15	11

2. Find the mean of each subgroup.

- To find the mean, add all measurements in the subgroup and divide by the number of measurements in the subgroup.
  - In the example, there are 20 subgroups and in each subgroup there are 4 measurements.

Hundredths of an ounce over 16 ounces in bottle filling process

Subgroup Number	a	b	c	d	$\bar{X}$
1	24	17	9	4	13.5
2	19	13	9	28	17.25
3	5	16	12	13	11.5
4	2	23	2	23	12.5
5	7	6	24	6	10.75
6	25	11	24	18	19.5
7	9	21	8	19	14.25
8	14	10	20	7	12.75
9	17	0	10	25	13
10	37	22	14	18	22.75
11	2	14	4	5	6.25
12	3	15	19	18	13.75
13	25	8	25	26	21
14	26	10	23	12	17.75
15	1	6	5	17	7.25
16	15	28	2	5	12.5
17	25	21	4	18	17
18	10	24	5	19	14.5
19	2	12	3	1	4.5
20	13	12	15	11	12.75

3. Find the mean of all of the means from the previous step (X).
This will give you the overall mean of all the data points.

- The overall mean will be the centerline in the graph (CL), which is 13.75 for our example.
  1. **Calculate the standard deviation (S) of the data points**
  2. **Calculate the upper and lower control limits (UCL, LCL) using the following formula:**

     UCL = CL + 3*S

     LCL = CL – 3*S

The formula represents 3 standard deviations above and 3 standard deviations below the mean respectively.

Hundredths of an ounce over 16 ounces in bottle filling process

Subgroup Number	a	b	c	d	$\bar{X}$
1	24	17	9	4	13.5
2	19	13	9	28	17.25
3	5	16	12	13	11.5
4	2	23	2	23	12.5
5	7	6	24	6	10.75
6	25	11	24	18	19.5
7	9	21	8	19	14.25
8	14	10	20	7	12.75
9	17	0	10	25	13
10	37	22	14	18	22.75
11	2	14	4	5	6.25
12	3	15	19	18	13.75
13	25	8	25	26	21
14	26	10	23	12	17.75
15	1	6	5	17	7.25
16	15	28	2	5	12.5
17	25	21	4	18	17
18	10	24	5	19	14.5
19	2	12	3	1	4.5
20	13	12	15	11	12.75
					275

Standard Dev.	8.400609	
$\bar{X}$	13.75	
UCLx	38.97883	
LCLx	– 11.4788	

6. Refer to the below chart with steps 7 through 10.

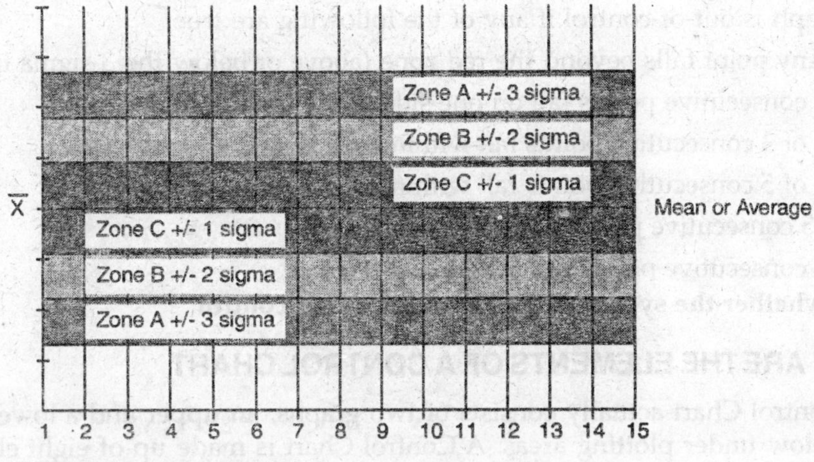

7. Draw a line at each deviation.

1. In the above example, there is a line drawn at one, two, and three standard deviations (sigma's) away from the mean.
   1. Zone C is 1 sigma away from the mean (green).
   2. Zone B is 2 sigma away from the mean (yellow).
   3. Zone A is 3 sigma away from the mean (red).

8. Graph the X-bar Control Chart, by graphing the subgroup means (x-axis) verses measurements (y-axis).

Your graph should look like something like this:

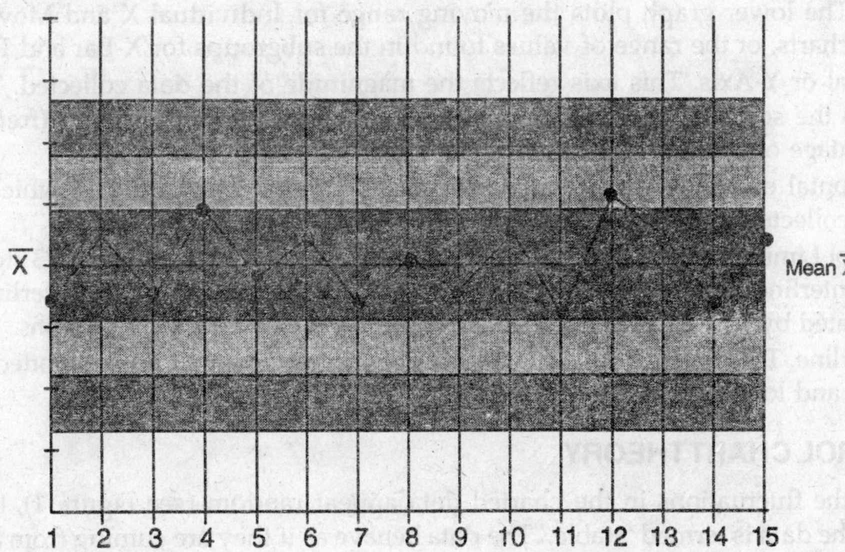

9. **Evaluate the graph to see if the process is out-of-control**

   The graph is out-of-control if any of the following are true:

   1. Any point falls beyond the red zone (above or below the 3-sigma line).
   2. 8 consecutive points fall on one side of the centerline.
   3. 2 of 3 consecutive points fall within zone A.
   4. 4 of 5 consecutive points fall within zone A and/or zone B.
   5. 15 consecutive points are within Zone C.
   6. 8 consecutive points not in zone C.

10. **State whether the system is in-control or out-of-control.**

6.7 WHAT ARE THE ELEMENTS OF A CONTROL CHART

Each Control Chart actually consists of two graphs, an upper and a lower, which are described below under plotting areas. A Control Chart is made up of eight elements. The first three are identified in Viewgraphs 5; the other five in Viewgraph6.

1. Title. The title briefly describes the information which is displayed.
2. Legend. This is information on how and when the data were collected.
3. Data Collection Section. The counts or measurements are recorded in the data collection section of the Control Chart prior to being graphed.
4. Plotting Areas. A Control Chart has two areas—an upper graph and a lower graph—where the data is plotted.
   (a) The upper graph plots either the individual values, in the case of an Individual X and Moving Range chart, or the average (mean value) of the sample or subgroup in the case of an X-Bar and R chart.
   (b) The lower graph plots the moving range for Individual X and Moving Range charts, or the range of values found in the subgroups for X-Bar and R charts.
5. Vertical or Y-Axis. This axis reflects the magnitude of the data collected. The Y-axis shows the scale of the measurement for variables data, or the count (frequency) or percentage of occurrence of an event for attribute data.
6. Horizontal or X-Axis. This axis displays the chronological order in which the data were collected.
7. Control Limits. Control limits are set at a distance of 3 sigma above and 3 sigma below the centerline [Ref. 6, pp. 60-61]. They indicate variation from the centerline and are calculated by using the actual values plotted on the Control Chart graphs.
8. Centerline. This line is drawn at the average or mean value of all the plotted data. The upper and lower graphs each have a separate centerline.

6.8 CONTROL CHART THEORY

When the fluctuations in the charted data appear random (see Figure 1), the system producing the data is termed 'stable.' The data behave as if they are coming from a binomial random process with parameter P. The points are predictable in terms of the random process, and all fall within three-sigma control limits.

All points are in 'statistical control.' The PSU whose data are charted in Figure 1 is moderate in terms of an average monthly sample size of 134, but its P of 0.072 is small, hence the narrow control limits. In addition, the fluctuations seen from month to month in the control limits are small, indicating low variability in the monthly sample sizes.

The use of two base years to estimate the centerline and control limits is based on Deming's notion that a system in statistical control is predictable, at least in the short run. If the system producing the data is in statistical control, then the data in the extension year should continue to fall between the control limits determined from the base years.

For percent of unrestrained passenger vehicle occupants from FARS, the data are not instatistical control. In January of the third year charted, the point goes "out-of-control" beyond the lower control limit. Each successive point is also out-of-control. It appears that the process producing the data stabilizes around March at a much lower value than in the preceding two years. In short, the process

becomes inconsistent with a binomial model with a fixed P for all three years.

Western Electric (1956) recommends four rules to identify patterns (and implicitly, points) in control charts as out-of-control. The first is the three-sigma rule that is, the chart has at least one point falling outside of the three-sigma control limits. The other rules are: rule 2, two out of three consecutive points more than two sigma away from the centerline (with the two points on the same side of the centerline); rule 3, four out of five consecutive points more that one sigma away from the centerline (with all four on the same side of the centerline); and rule 4, eight consecutive points on the same side of the centerline.

6.9 THEORETICAL BASIS FOR A CONTROL CHART

Control charts are used to routinely monitor quality. Depending on the number of process characteristics to be monitored, there are two basic types of control charts. The first, referred to as a univariate control chart, is a graphical display (chart) of one quality characteristic. The second, referred to as a multivariate control chart, is a graphical display of a statistic that summarizes or represents more than one quality characteristic.

6.10 CHARACTERISTICS OF CONTROL CHARTS

If a single quality characteristic has been measured or computed from a sample, the control chart shows the value of the quality characteristic versus the sample number or versus time. In general, the chart contains a center line that represents the mean value for the in-control process. Two other horizontal lines, called the upper control limit (UCL) and the lower control limit (LCL), are also shown on the chart. These control limits are chosen so that almost all of the data points will fall within these limits as long as the process remains in-control. The figure below illustrates this.

6.11 CHART DEMONSTRATING BASIS OF CONTROL CHART

Theoretical Basis for a Control Chart

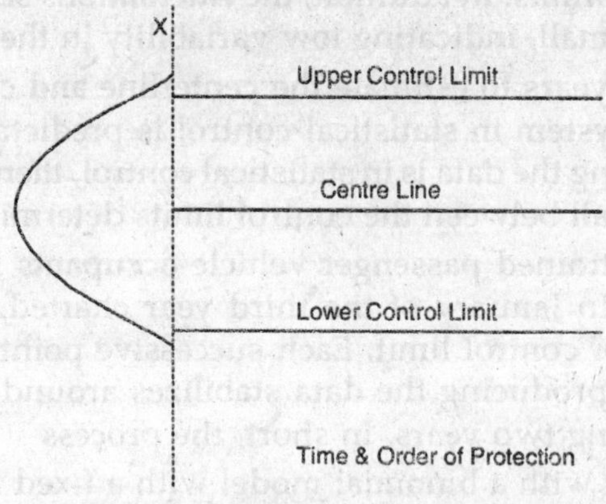

6.12 WHY CONTROL CHARTS "WORK"

The control limits as pictured in the graph might be .001*probability* limits. If so, and if chance causes alone were present, the probability of a point falling above the upper limit would be one out of a thousand, and similarly, a point falling below the lower limit would be one out of a thousand. We would be searching for an assignable cause if a point would fall outside these limits. Where we put these limits will determine the risk of undertaking such a search when in reality there is no assignable cause for variation.

Since two out of a thousand is a very small risk, the 0.001 limits may be said to give practical assurances that, if a point falls outside these limits, the variation was caused be an assignable cause. It must be noted that two out of one thousand is a purely arbitrary number. There is no reason why it could not have been set to one out a hundred or even larger. The decision would depend on the amount of risk the management of the quality control program is willing to take. In general (in the world of quality control) it is customary to use limits that approximate the 0.002 standard.

Letting X denote the value of a process characteristic, if the system of chance causes generates a variation in X that follows the normal distribution, the 0.001 probability limits will be very close to the 3σ limits. From normal tables we glean that the 3σ in one direction is 0.00135, or in both directions 0.0027. For normal distributions, therefore, the 3σ limits are the practical equivalent of 0.001 probability limits.

6.13 PLUS OR MINUS "3 SIGMA" LIMITS ARE TYPICAL

In the U.S., whether X is normally distributed or not, it is an acceptable practice to base the control limits upon a multiple of the standard deviation. Usually this multiple is 3 and thus the limits are called 3-sigma limits. This term is used whether the standard deviation is the universe or population parameter, or some estimate thereof, or simply a "standard value" for control chart purposes. It should be inferred from the context what standard deviation is involved. (Note that in the U.K., statisticians generally prefer to adhere to probability limits.)

If the underlying distribution is skewed, say in the positive direction, the 3-sigma limit will fall short of the upper 0.001 limit, while the lower 3-sigma limit will fall below the 0.001 limit. This situation means that the risk of looking for assignable causes of positive variation when none exists will be greater than one out of a thousand. But the risk of searching for an assignable cause of negative variation, when none exists, will be reduced. The net result, however, will be an increase in the risk of a chance variation beyond the control limits. How much this risk will be increased will depend on the degree of skewness.

If variation in quality follows a Poisson distribution, for example, for which $np = .8$, the risk of exceeding the upper limit by chance would be raised by the use of 3-sigma limits from 0.001 to 0.009 and the lower limit reduces from 0.001 to 0. For a Poisson distribution the mean and variance both equal np. Hence the upper 3-sigma limit is 0.8 + 3 *sqrt*(.8) = 3.48 and the lower limit = 0 (here *sqrt* denotes "square root"). For $np = .8$ the probability of getting more than 3 successes = 0.009.

6.14 STRATEGIES FOR DEALING WITH OUT-OF-CONTROL FINDINGS

If a data point falls outside the control limits, we assume that the process is probably out of control and that an investigation is warranted to find and eliminate the cause or causes.

Does this mean that when all points fall within the limits, the process is in control? Not necessarily. If the plot looks non-random, that is, if the points exhibit some form of systematic behavior, there is still something wrong. For example, if the first 25 of 30 points fall above the center line and the last 5 fall below the center line, we would wish to know why this is so. Statistical methods to detect sequences or nonrandom patterns can be applied to the interpretation of control charts. To be sure, "in control" implies that all points are between the control limits and they form a random pattern.

6.15 WHAT ARE VARIABLES CONTROL CHARTS?

During the 1920's, Dr. Walter A. Shewhart proposed a general model for control charts as follows:

6.16 SHEWHART CONTROL CHARTS FOR VARIABLES

Let w be a sample statistic that measures some continuously varying quality characteristic of interest (e.g., thickness), and suppose that the mean of w is μ_w, with a standard deviation of σ_w. Then the center line, the UCL and the LCL are

$$\text{UCL} = \mu_w + k\sigma_w$$
$$\text{Center Line} = \mu_w$$
$$\text{LCL} = \mu_w - k\sigma_w$$

where k is the distance of the control limits from the center line, expressed in terms of standard deviation units. When k is set to 3, we speak of 3-sigma control charts.

Historically, $k = 3$ has become an accepted standard in industry.

The centerline is the process mean, which in general is unknown. We replace it with a *target* or the average of all the data. The quantity that we plot is the sample average, $\bar{X}$. The chart is called the $\bar{X}$ chart.

We also have to deal with the fact that σ is, in general, unknown. Here we replace σ_w with a given standard value, or we estimate it by a function of the *average standard deviation*. This is obtained by averaging the individual standard deviations that we calculated from each of *m* preliminary (or present) samples, each of size *n*. This function will be discussed shortly.

It is equally important to examine the standard deviations in ascertaining whether the process is in control. There is, unfortunately, a slight problem involved when we work with the usual estimator of σ. The following discussion will illustrate this.

6.17 SAMPLE VARIANCE

If σ^2 is the unknown variance of a probability distribution, then an unbiased estimator of σ^2 is the sample variance

$$s^2 = \frac{\sum_{i=1}^{n}(x_i - \bar{x})^2}{n-1}$$

However, *s*, the sample standard deviation is *not* an unbiased estimator of σ. If the underlying distribution is normal, then *s* actually estimates $c_4\,\sigma$, where c_4 is a constant that depends on the sample size *n*. This constant is tabulated in most text books on statistical quality control and may be calculated using

C_4 *factor*
$$c_4 = \sqrt{\frac{2}{n-1}}\,\frac{\left(\frac{n}{2}-1\right)!}{\left(\frac{n-1}{2}-1\right)!}$$

Note that in some sources the formula is given in terms of $\sigma = c_4 * s$, in which case c_4 will be the reciprocal of the formula given above.

6.18 FRACTIONAL FACTORIALS

To compute this we need a *non-integer factorial*, which is defined for $n/2$ as follows:

$$\left(\frac{n}{2}\right)! = \left(\frac{n}{2}\right)\left(\frac{n}{2}-1\right)\left(\frac{n}{2}-2\right)\ldots\left(\frac{1}{2}\right)\sqrt{\pi}$$

For example, let $n = 7$. Then $n/2 = 7/2 = 3.5$ and

$$\left(\frac{7}{2}\right)! = (3.5)! = (3.5)\,(2.5)\,(1.5)\,(0.5)\,(1.77246) = 11.632$$

With this definition the reader should have no problem verifying that the c_4 factor for $n = 10$ is .9727.

6.19 MEAN AND STANDARD DEVIATION OF THE ESTIMATORS

So the mean or expected value of the sample standard deviation is $c_4\,\sigma$.

The standard deviation of the sample standard deviation is

$$\sigma_5 = \sigma\sqrt{1-c_4^2}$$

What are the differences between control limits and specification limits ?

6.20 CONTROL LIMITS VS. SPECIFICATIONS

Control Limits are used to determine if the process is in a state of statistical control (i.e., is producing consistent output).

Specification Limits are used to determine if the product will function in the intended fashion.

How many data points are needed to set up a control chart?

Shewhart gave the following rule of thumb:

6.21 HOW MANY SAMPLES ARE NEEDED?

"It has also been observed that a person would seldom if ever be justified in concluding that a state of statistical control of a given repetitive operation or production process has been reached until he had obtained, under presumably the same essential conditions, a sequence of not less than twenty five samples of size four that are in control."

It is important to note that control chart properties, such as false alarm probabilities, are generally given under the assumption that the parameters, such as μ and σ, are known. When the control limits are not computed from a large amount of data, the actual properties might be quite different from what is assumed

6.21.1 Constructing Control Charts

Control Charts come in many varieties, but all Control Charts have some common features. The data is plotted in time order from left to right. A centerline is drawn to represent the calculated mean of the data. Each new data point is added as it is collected, and the chart is interpreted each time a data point is added.

Look at the sample Control Chart below:

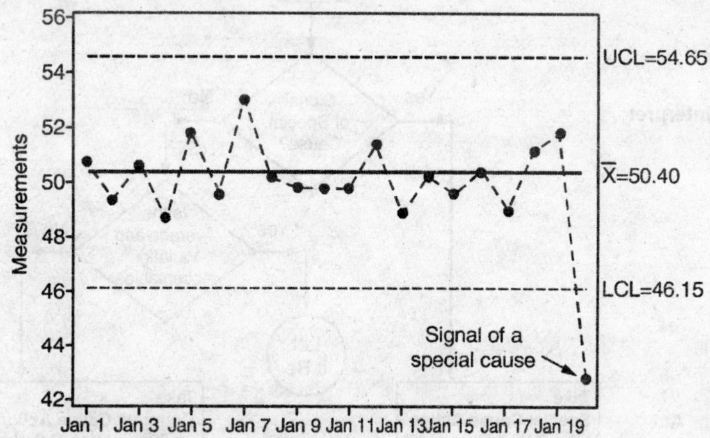

In this chart, you can see that the last data point is just below the LCL which means something is wrong and it has to be looked into.

All Control Charts show control limits that reflect the extremes (limits) for the expected variation, called Common Cause variation. As a rule, the limits are set at three standard deviations from the mean so that almost all the Common Cause variation is captured within the limits. It's highly unlikely that a stable process would have a data point beyond these control limits. When that occurs, we call it a Special Cause.

It's important to know that control limits are calculated on the basis of the variation in the data from the process. The control limits represent the voice of the process, telling us what extent of variation we can expect to see. Specification limits are different. They represent the voice of the customer and, as such, tell you what extent of variation that is desired.

6.21.2 Interpreting a Control Chart

By now, you have a good idea of What a Control Chart is, what it is used for and the types of Control Charts. As a Process Owner, you need to properly interpret the Control Chart because that tells you what actions to take, or not to take. Variation always exists, so your job is to separate variation into its two categories of Common and Special Cause. Then you use your centerlines, control limits, and plots of data to make your interpretation.

A common mistake that inexperienced process owners do is - assigning someone to create lots of Control Charts. While the walls become covered with pretty charts, no one has responsibility to interpret and act on the charts. Acting on just one Control Chart is better than plastering the wall with many charts that go unattended.

6.21.3 Interpreting a Control Chart

Interpreting your control chart is not easy because, your future course of action is going to be based on this interpretation. So, it is imperative that we interpret/understand the control chart in the right way. The following flow chart gives you a decision pathway for taking action on your process.

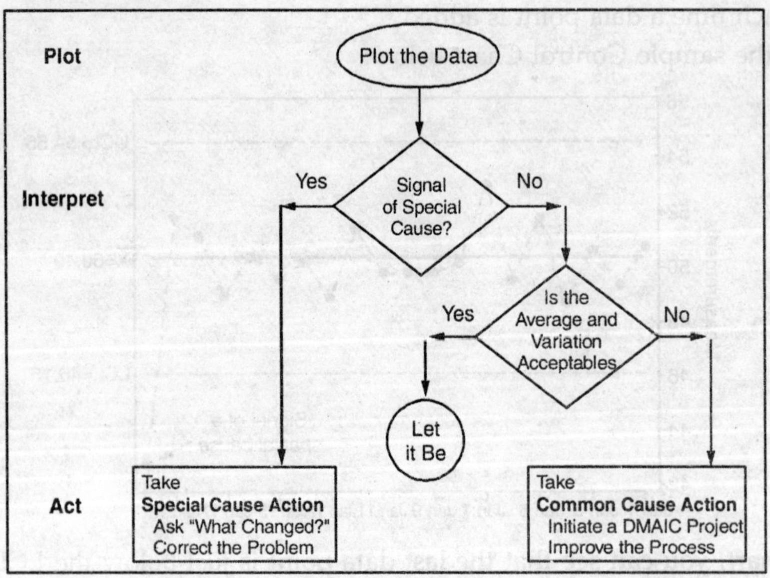

As you can see - Special Causes require special action, while Common Causes require Lean Six Sigma–type improvement.

6.22 SPECIAL CAUSES

Any occurrence or pattern in the data that isn't just random variation is called a Special Cause. Statisticians have created several signals for detecting Special Causes, the most common of which are outliers, shifts, trends, or cycles. Let's look at each one of these in detail.

1. **Outliers.** An outlier is any data point that is above the UCL or below the LCL. Because the control limits are calculated from probability theory, an outlier is highly unlikely in a process with just Common Cause variation.
2. **Shifts.** The likelihood of a stable process generating nine points in a row on the same side of the centerline is like tossing a coin and getting heads nine times in a row. It's possible, but highly unlikely. Therefore, a run of nine consecutive points all on the same side of the centerline indicates a shift in the mean. This is a strong indicator that the process has changed and warrants investigation.
3. **Trends.** A trend is defined as six consecutive points, each higher than the previous point or six consecutive points, each lower than the previous point. This indicates a Special Cause with a gradual effect. Look for a process change that began at approximately the start of the trend.
4. **Cycles.** Repeating patterns, called cycles, are signaled by 14 consecutive points that alternate up and down. This pattern signals cyclical change in the process that is repetitive and certainly warranting investigation. Possible causes include over-adjustment, shift-to-shift variation, and machine-to-machine variation.

The picture below shows you how you can identify the above special causes from your Control Chart.

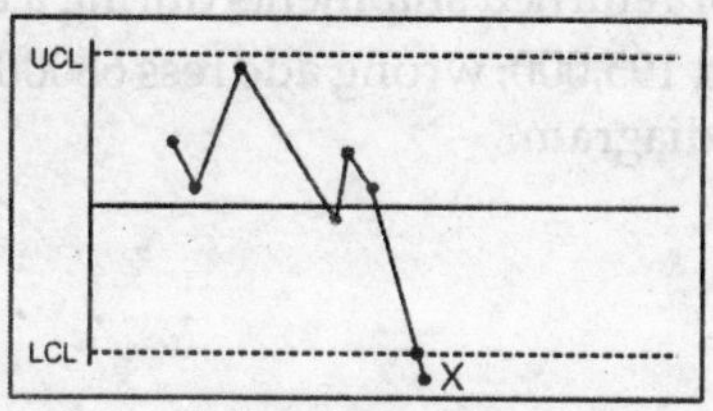

Outliers

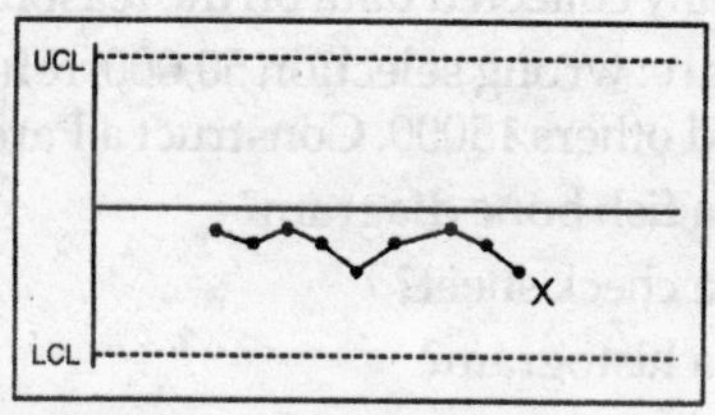

Shifts

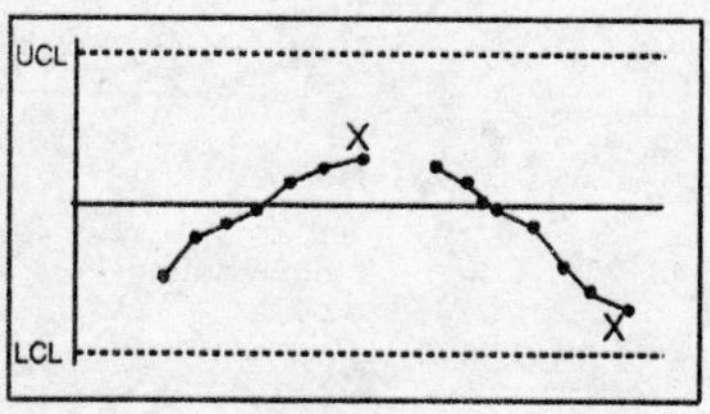

Trends

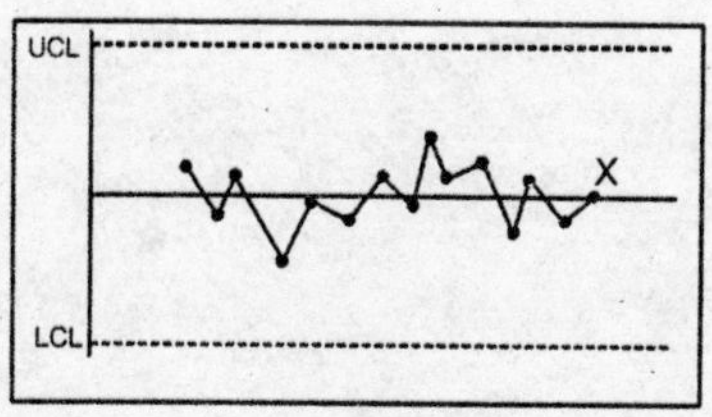

Cycles

These signals (outliers, shifts, trends and cycles) apply to all Control Charts Common Causes

When no Special Cause signals are present, we deem the process to be in control, not out of control. In other words, the process is stable and not changing and only Common Cause variation is affecting its behavior. The example charts we saw in the previous chapters are examples of control charts that have common cause signals.

SUMMARY

A stable process is one that is consistent over time with respect to the center and the spread of the data. Control Charts help you monitor the behavior of your process to determine whether it is stable. Like Run Charts, they display data in the time sequence in which they occurred. However, Control Charts are more efficient that Run Charts in assessing and achieving process stability.

Exercise Questions

1. What do you mean by measure of central tendency?
2. What do you mean by measures of dispersion?
3. Define population.
4. Define data and information.
5. 3, 4, 5, 6, 8, 8 and 10, what are average, median, and mode?
6. List seven quality control tools.
7. Give examples of vital few.
8. Give examples of useful many.
9. What is Pareto diagram?
10. A company collected data on the reasons for returned shipments during a quarter.
11. Results are: wrong selection 50,000; refused 195,000; wrong address 68000; order cancelled 5000; and others 15000. Construct a Pareto diagram.
12. What is a fish bone diagram?
13. What is a check sheet?
14. What is a histogram?

❑

Attributes Control Charts 7

The Shewhart control chart plots quality characteristics that can be measured and expressed numerically. We measure weight, height, position, thickness, etc. If we cannot represent a particular quality characteristic numerically, or if it is impractical to do so, we then often resort to using a quality characteristic to sort or classify an item that is inspected into one of two "buckets".

An example of a common quality characteristic classification would be designating units as "conforming units" or "nonconforming units". Another quality characteristic criteria would be sorting units into "non defective" and "defective" categories. Quality characteristics of that type are called *attributes.*

Note that there is a difference between "nonconforming to an engineering specification" and "defective" — a nonconforming unit may function just fine and be, in fact, not defective at all, while a part can be "in spec" and not function as desired (i.e., be defective).

Examples of quality characteristics that are attributes are the number of failures in a production run, the proportion of malfunctioning wafers in a lot, the number of people eating in the cafeteria on a given day, etc.

7.1 TYPES OF ATTRIBUTE CONTROL CHARTS

Control charts dealing with the number of *defects* or *nonconformities* are called *c* charts (for count).

Control charts dealing with the *proportion* or *fraction* of defective product are called *p* charts (for proportion).

There is another chart which handles *defects per unit,* called the*u* chart (for unit). This applies when we wish to work with the average number of nonconformities per unit of product.

For additional references, see Woodall (1997) which reviews papers showing examples of attribute control charting, including examples from semiconductor manufacturing such as those examining the spatial dependence of defects.

7.2 COUNTS CONTROL CHARTS

7.2.1 Defective items vs individual defects

The literature differentiates between *defect* and *defective*, which is the same as differentiating between *nonconformity* and*nonconforming units*. This may sound like splitting hairs, but in the interest of clarity let's try to unravel this man-made mystery.

Consider a wafer with a number of chips on it. The wafer is referred to as an "item of a product". The chip may be referred to as "a specific point". There exist certain specifications for the wafers. When a particular wafer (e.g., the item of the product) does not meet at least one of the specifications, it is classified as a nonconforming item. Furthermore, each chip, (e.g., the specific point) at which a specification is not met becomes adefect or nonconformity.

So, a nonconforming or defective item contains at least one defect or nonconformity. It should be pointed out that a wafer can contain several defects but still be classified as conforming. For example, the defects may be located at noncritical positions on the wafer. If, on the other hand, the number of the so-called "unimportant" defects becomes alarmingly large, an investigation of the production of these wafers is warranted.

Control charts involving counts can be either for the *total number* of nonconformities (defects) for the sample of inspected units, or for the *average number* of defects per inspection unit.

7.2.2 Poisson approximation for numbers or counts of defects

Let us consider an assembled product such as a microcomputer. The opportunity for the occurrence of any given defect may be quite large. However, the probability of occurrence of a defect in any one arbitrarily chosen spot is likely to be very small. In such a case, the incidence of defects might be modeled by a *Poisson* distribution. Actually, the Poisson distribution is an approximation of the *binomial* distribution and applies well in this capacity according to the following rule of thumb:

The sample size n should be equal to or larger than 20 and the probability of a single success, p, should be smaller than or equal to .05. If $n \geq 100$, the approximation is excellent if np is also ≤ 10.

7.2.3 Illustrate Poisson approximation to binomial

To illustrate the use of the Poisson distribution as an approximation of a binomial distribution, consider the following comparison: Let p, the probability of a single success in $n = 200$ trials, be .025.

Find the probability of exactly 3 successes. If we assume that $p$remains constant then the solution follows the binomial distribution rules, that is:

$$p(x) = \binom{n}{x} p^x (1-p)^{n-x} = \binom{200}{3} .025^3 .975^{197} = 0.1399995$$

By the Poisson approximation we have

$$c = (200)(.025)$$

and

$$p(x) = \frac{e^{-c}c^x}{x!} = \frac{e^{-5}5^x}{3!} = 0.13403739$$

7.2.4 The inspection unit

Before the control chart parameters are defined there is one more definition: *the inspection unit.* We shall count the number of defects that occur in a so-called inspection unit. More often than not, an inspection unit is a single unit or item of product; for example, a wafer. However, sometimes the inspection unit could consist of five wafers, or ten wafers and so on. The size of the inspection units may depend on the recording facility, measuring equipment, operators, etc.

Suppose that defects occur in a given inspection unit according to the Poisson distribution, with parameter c (often denoted by np or the Greek letter λ). In other words

Control charts for counts, using the Poisson distribution

$$p(x) = \frac{e^{-c}c^x}{x!}$$

where x is the number of defects and $c > 0$ is the parameter of the Poisson distribution. It is known that both the mean and the variance of this distribution are equal to c. Then the k-sigma control chart is

$$\text{UCL} = c + k\sqrt{c}$$

$$\text{Center Line} = c$$

$$\text{LCL} = c - k\sqrt{c}$$

If the LCL comes out negative, then there is no lower control limit. This control scheme assumes that a standard value for c is available. If this is not the case then c may be estimated as the average of the number of defects in a preliminary sample of inspection units, call it $\bar{c}$. Usually k is set to 3 by many practioners.

7.2.5 Control chart example using counts

An example may help to illustrate the construction of control limits for counts data. We are inspecting 25 successive wafers, each containing 100 chips. Here the wafer is the inspection unit. The observed number of defects are

Wafer Number	Number of Defects	Wafer Number	Number of Defects
1	16	14	16
2	14	15	15
3	28	16	13
4	16	17	14
5	12	18	16
6	20	19	11

7	10	20	20
8	12	21	11
9	10	22	19
10	17	23	16
11	19	24	31
12	17	25	13
13	14		

From this table we have

$$\bar{c} = \frac{\text{total number of defects}}{\text{total number of samples}} = \frac{400}{25} = 16$$

$$\text{UCL} = \bar{c} + 3\sqrt{\bar{c}} = 16 + 2\sqrt{16} = 28$$

$$\text{LCL} = \bar{c} - k\sqrt{\bar{c}}$$

7.2.6 Sample counts control chart

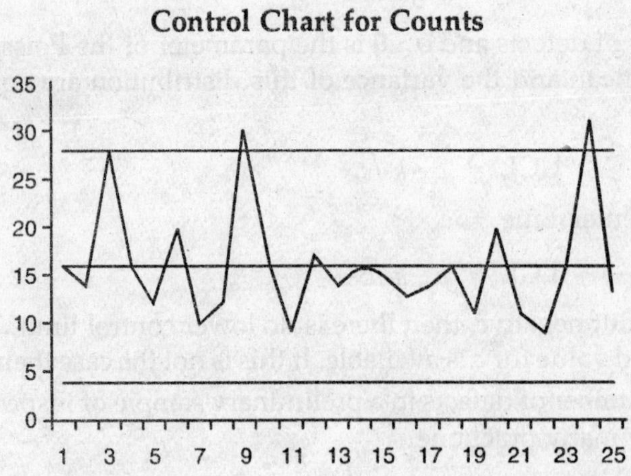

7.2.7 Transforming Poisson Data

Normal approximation to Poisson is adequate when the mean of the Poisson is at least 5

We have seen that the 3-sigma limits for a c chart, where crepresents the number of nonconformities, are given by

$$\bar{c} \pm 3\sqrt{\bar{c}}$$

where it is assumed that the normal approximation to the Poisson distribution holds, hence the symmetry of the control limits. It is shown in the literature that the normal approximation to the Poisson is adequate when the mean of the Poisson is at least 5. When applied to the c chart this implies that the mean of the defects should be at least 5. This requirement will often be met in practice, but still, when the mean is smaller than 9 (solving the above equation) there will be no lower control limit.

Let the mean be 10. Then the lower control limit = 0.513. However, $P(c = 0) = .000045$, using the Poisson formula. This is only 1/30 of the assumed area of .00135. So one has to raise the lower limit so as to get as close as possible to .00135. From Poisson tables or computer software we find that $P(1) = .0005$ and $P(2) = .0027$, so the lower limit should actually be 2 or 3.

7.2.8 Transforming count data into approximately normal data

To avoid this type of problem, we may resort to a transformation that makes the transformed data match the normal distribution better. One such transformation described by Ryan (2000) is

$$Y = 2\sqrt{c}$$

which is, for a large sample, approximately normally distributed with mean = $2\sqrt{\lambda}$ and variace = 1, where λ is the mean of the Poisson distribution.

Similar transformations have been proposed by Anscombe (1948) and Freeman and Tukey (1950). When applied to a *c*chart these are

$$y_1 = 2\sqrt{c+3/8} \quad \text{and} \quad y_2 = \sqrt{c} + \sqrt{c+1}$$

The repspective control limits are

$$\bar{y} \pm 3, \quad \bar{y}_1 \pm 3 \quad \text{and} \quad \bar{y}_2 \pm 3$$

While using transformations may result in meaningful control limits, one has to bear in mind that the user is now working with data on a different scale than the original measurements. There is another way to remedy the problem of symmetric limits applied to non symmetric cases, and that is to use *probability*limits. These can be obtained from tables given by Molina (1973). This allows the user to work with data on the original scale, but they require special tables to obtain the limits. Of course, software might be used instead.

7.2.9 Warning for highly skewed distributions

Note: In general, it is not a good idea to use 3-sigma limits for distributions that are highly skewed (see Ryan and Schwertman(1997) for more about the possibly extreme consequences of doing this).

7.3 PROPORTIONS CONTROL CHARTS

7.3.1 p is the fraction defective in a lot or population

The proportion or fraction nonconforming (defective) in a population is defined as the ratio of the number of nonconforming items in the population to the total number of items in that population. The item under consideration may have one or more quality characteristics that are inspected simultaneously. If at least one of the characteristics does not conform to standard, the item is classified as nonconforming.

The fraction or proportion can be expressed as a decimal, or, when multiplied by 100, as a percent. The underlying statistical principles for a control chart for proportion nonconforming are based on the binomial distribution.

Let us suppose that the production process operates in a stable manner, such that the probability that a given unit will not conform to specifications is *p*. Furthermore, we assume that successive units produced are independent. Under these conditions, each unit that is produced is a realization of a Bernoulli random variable with parameter *p*. If a random sample of *n* units of product is selected and if *D* is the number of units that are nonconforming, the *D*follows a binomial distribution with parameters *n* and *p*

7.3.2 The binomial distribution model for number of defectives in a sample

The mean of *D* is *np* and the variance is *np(1 – p)*. The *sample*proportion nonconforming is the ratio of the number of nonconforming units in the sample, *D*, to the sample size *n*,

The mean and variance of this estimator are and

This background is sufficient to develop the control chart for proportion or fraction nonconforming. The chart is called the *p*-chart.

7.3.3 p control charts for lot proportion defective

If the true fraction conforming *p* is known (or a standard value is given), then the center line and control limits of the fraction nonconforming control chart is

$$\text{UCL} = p + 3\sqrt{\frac{p(1-p)}{n}}$$

$$\text{Centre Line} = p$$

$$\text{LCL} = p - 3\sqrt{\frac{p(1-p)}{n}}$$

When the process fraction (proportion) *p* is not known, it must be estimated from the available data. This is accomplished by selecting *m* preliminary samples, each of size *n*. If there are D_i defectives in sample *i*, the fraction nonconforming in sample *i* is

$$\hat{p}_i = \frac{D_i}{n} \qquad i = 1, 2, \ldots, m$$

and the average of these individuals sample fractions is

$$\bar{p} = \frac{\Sigma_{i=1}^{m} D_i}{mn} = \frac{\Sigma_{i=1}^{m} \hat{p}_i}{m}$$

The $\bar{p}$ is used instead of *p* in the control chart setup.

7.3.4 Example of a *p*-chart

A numerical example will now be given to illustrate the above mentioned principles. The location of chips on a wafer is measured on 30 wafers.

On each wafer 50 chips are measured and a defective is defined whenever a mis registration, in terms of horizontal and/or vertical distances from the center, is recorded. The results are

Sample Number	Fraction Defectives	Sample Number	Fraction Defectives	Sample Number	Fraction Defectives
1	.24	11	.10	21	.40
2	.30	12	.12	22	.36
3	.16	13	.34	23	.48
4	.20	14	.24	24	.30
5	.08	15	.44	25	.18
6	.14	16	.16	26	.24
7	.32	17	.20	27	.14
8	.18	18	.10	28	.28
9	.19	19	.26	29	.18
10	.20	20	.22	30	.12

7.3.5 Sample proportions control chart

The corresponding control chart is given below:

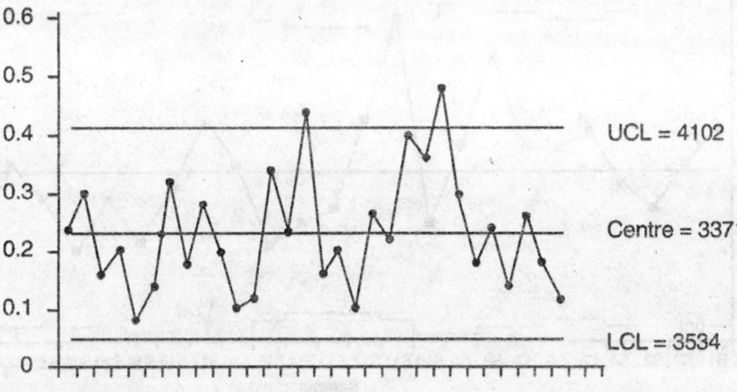

7.3.6 Control Chart Example - Product Specifications

The most common type of control chart used to monitor a product specification is an "X" chart: XmR, XbarR or XbarS chart.

7.3.7 XmR Chart - Individuals and Moving Range

In this control chart example.we're measuring an individual piston ring diameter using an XmR chart. The XmR or Individuals and Moving Range chart has two charts: one shows individual measurements over time and the other monitors the range (i.e., difference) between measurements.

In this control chart example, while the X chart appears to be in control, the range chart shows a potentially unstable condition: too many points in a row hugging the center line. The QI Macros SPC Software for Excel highlights all potentially unstable (i.e., out of control) points in read.

Most manufacturing applications measure five or more samples at a time to form a single subgroup. The five are then averaged to create a XbarR charts orXbarS charts.

7.3.8 X bar R - Average and Range Chart

Using five samples per subgroup in this control chart example, the variation in range shows that it's in control.

With five samples per subgroup, you could also use the X bar S Chart - Average and Standard Deviation.

7.3.9 X bar S - Average and Standard Deviation Chart

7.3.10 Control Chart Example - Defects

Another common type of control chart involves measuring defects and defect rates.

P Chart - Fraction Defective

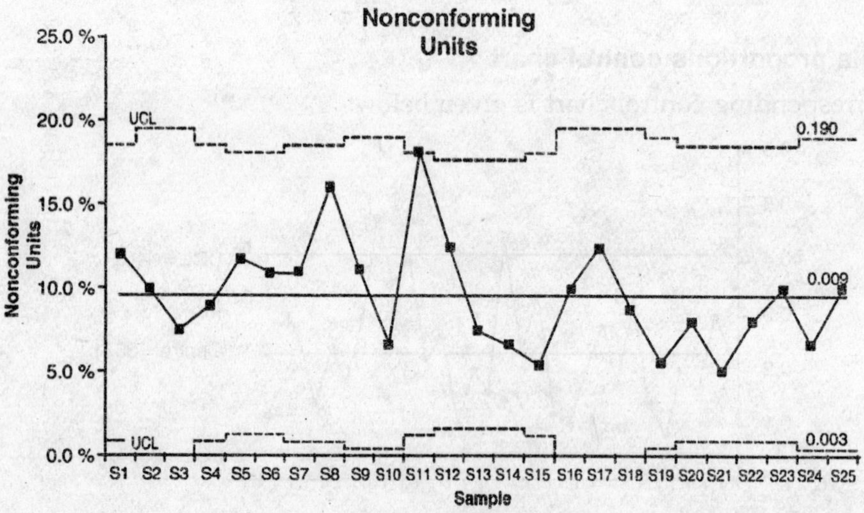

U Chart - Number Defective

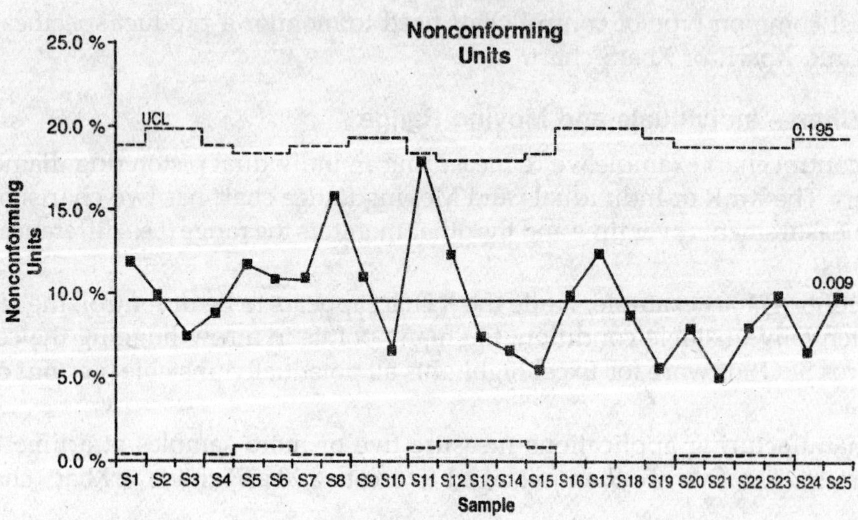

C Chart - Number Defective

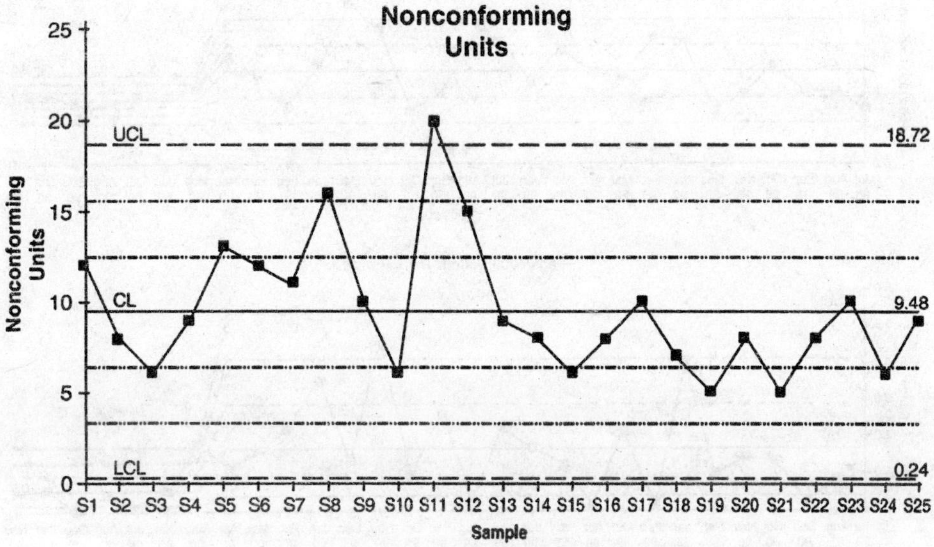

NP Chart - Number Defective

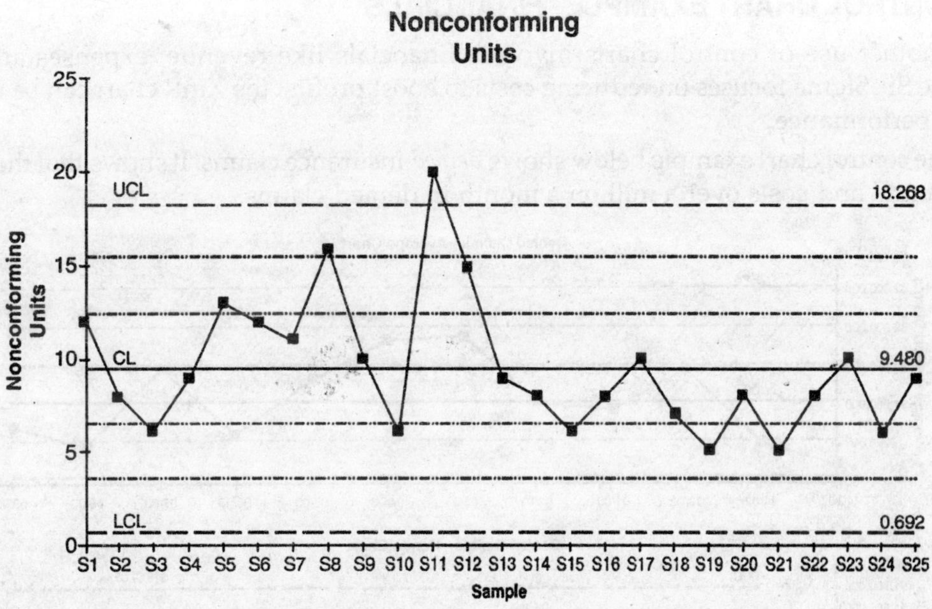

7.3.11 XmR Individual Moving Range Chart - Defect Rate

In the control chart example below, the XmR chart shows patient falls per 1000 patient days. The downward trend (red below) was caused by an improvement project. The limits were changed to reflect the new process performance: less variation and lower falls rate.

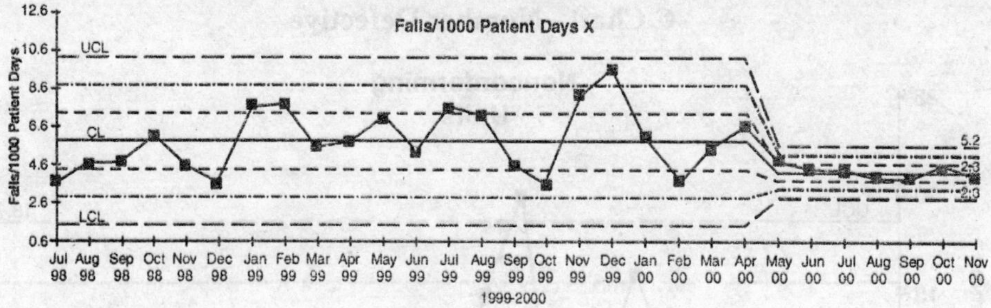

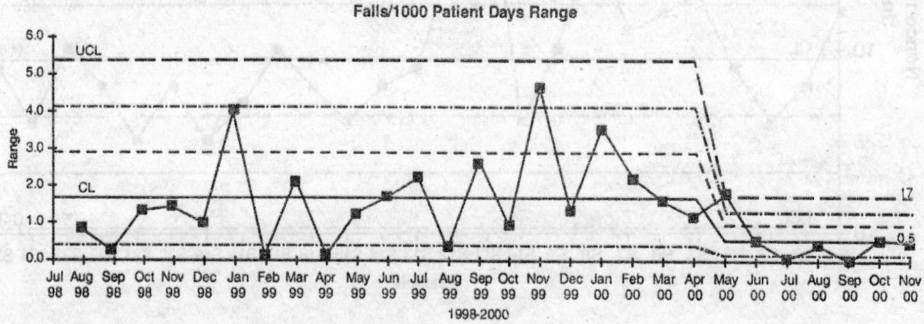

7.4 CONTROL CHART EXAMPLE - FINANCIALS

Another use of control charts involves financials like revenue, expenses and costs. Because Six Sigma focuses on reducing costs to boost profits, the XmR chart can be useful to detect performance.

The control chart example below shows *denied* insurance claims. It shows that the process is in control and costs over a million a month in denied claims.

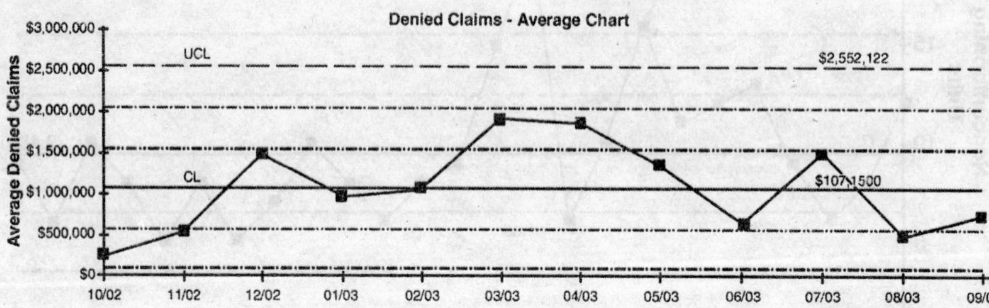

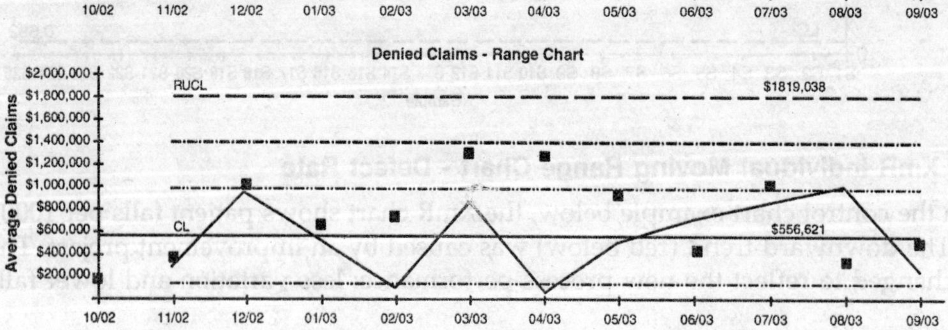

7.5 AN APPLICATION OF CONTROL CHARTS IN MANUFACTURING INDUSTRY

The range control chart and the X bar control chart are the well known and the most popular tools for detecting out- of-control signals in the Statistical Quality Control (SQC). The control charts has shown his worth in the manufacturing industry. In this study we have applied the range and the X bar control charts to a product of Swat Pharmaceutical Company. The variables under study were weight/ml, Ph, Citrate % and the amount of fill. Besides the X bar control chart, the exponentially weighted moving average control chart and the multivariate Hotelling'sT2 control chart were applied to the same data.

n this study we have applied the control chart approach to the data collected from Swat Pharmaceutical Company. The variables under study were X1 = weight/ml, X2 = Ph, X3 = Citrate% and X4 = Amount of fill.

SUMMARY

Control charts dealing with the *proportion* or *fraction* of defective product are called *p* charts (for proportion).There is another chart which handles *defects per unit*, called the*u* chart (for unit). This applies when we wish to work with the average number of nonconformities per unit of product.

Exercise Question

1. What is process capability and process capability index?
2. What is the standard deviation and the average for the normal curve shown below?
3. What are x and R charts?
4. Upper limit and lower limit are +4σ and - 4σ respectively and the process capability is ± 3σ, what is the process capability index C_p?
6. What does a negative C_{pk} mean?
7. What is an attribute?
8. What are p charts and np charts?
9. Write down the difference between a defect and defective.
10. What is six sigma?
11. List any two merits of six sigma.
12. What is relationship diagram?

□

Defect Diagnosis

8

A defect is defined as a nonconformance of a quality characteristic (e.g., strength, width response time) to its specification. DPMO is stated in opportunities per million units for convenience: Processes that are considered highly-capable (e.g., processes of Six Sigmaquality) are those that experience only a handful of defects per million units produced (or services provided).

Note that DPMO differs from reporting defective parts per million (PPM) in that it comprehends the possibility that a unit under inspection may be found to have multiple defects of the same type or may have multiple types of defects. Identifying specific opportunities for defects (and therefore how to count and categorize defects) is an art, but generally organizations consider the following when defining the number of opportunities per unit:

- Knowledge of the process under study
- Industry standards
- When studying multiple types of defects, knowledge of the relative importance of each defect type in determining customer satisfaction
- The time, effort, and cost to count and categorize defects in process output

Other measures of process performance include:

- Process capability indices such as C_{pk}
- Natural tolerance limit or sigma level
- PPM defective
- Process performance indices such as P_{pk}
- Quality costs or cost of poor quality (COPQ)

In process improvement efforts, **defects per million opportunities** or **DPMO** (or **nonconformities per million opportunities(NPMO)**) is a measure of process performance. It is defined as

$$\text{DPMO} = \frac{1{,}00{,}000 \times \text{number of defects}}{\text{number of units} \times \text{number of opportunities per unit}}$$

Six Sigma is a set of tools and techniques/strategies for process improvement originally developed by Motorola in 1985. Six Sigma became well known after Jack Welch made it a central focus of his business strategy at General Electric in 1995, and today it is used in different sectors of industry.[4]

Six Sigma seeks to improve the quality of process outputs by identifying and removing the causes of defects (errors) and minimizing variability in manufacturing and business processes.[5] It uses a set of quality management methods, including statistical methods, and creates a special infrastructure of people within the organization ("Champions", "Black Belts", "Green Belts", "Yellow Belts", etc.) who are experts in the methods. Each Six Sigma project carried out within an organization follows a defined sequence of steps and has quantified value targets, for example; process cycle time reduction, customer satisfaction, reduction in pollution, cost reduction and/or profit increase.

The term *Six Sigma* originated from terminology associated with **manufacturing**, specifically terms associated with statistical modeling of manufacturing processes. The maturity of a manufacturing process can be described by a *sigma* rating indicating its yield or the percentage of defect-free products it creates.

8.1 DEFECT TYPES

Before we look at test quality, it is important to understand the types of defects we are trying to find. For diagnostic purposes, defects can be divided into two types.

The first type is a defect such as a short, open, missing, or nonfunctioning device that stops the PCB from working correctly. These normally are easy to verify by a diagnostic and repair technician because they are absolute defects that affect the performance of the board. If the test system cannot detect this type of defect, then it is straightforward to understand why.

The classic example of an electrical test system not finding a clear defect is a missing capacitor when it is used for decoupling power on the board. One capacitor missing from a large number of parallel devices cannot be measured because it is well within the tolerance of the total capacitance used to decouple the board.

The second type of defect is a subjective defect, which may or may not cause a PCB to work correctly or cause a failure in the future. These are defects whose measurement by the test system is close to the limits of the test of a particular device. With electrical test, these limits normally are the tolerance limits from the device manufacturer but actually should be the limits required for the PCB design to work correctly.

Another example of a subjective electrical defect is the capacitance measurement from a test technique like FrameScan or TestJet/VTEP (for testing open pins on connectors or devices) that is learned using a known-good board. In electrical test, these subjective measurements can be moved to quality absolute limits using signal measurement algorithms to eliminate the effects of noise. These tools improve measurement reliability and reduce the false failure possibilities associated with subjective defects.

This is in contrast to image inspection systems where the number of subjective measurements generates a high degree of false failures and false passes. Component position, solder-joint shape, and color are simple examples of defects that can be classed as subjective and generate the significant number of false failures common with imaging systems.

8.2 PREVENTION OF DEFECT

Defect Management Process

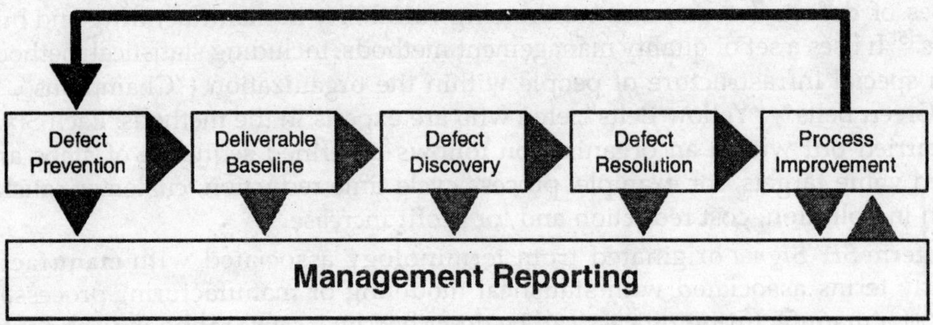

Without a doubt, the best approach to defects is to eliminate them altogether. While that would be ideal, it is virtually impossible given current technology. In the meantime, developers need strategies to find defects quickly and minimize their impact. Identifying and implementing the best defect prevention techniques (which is a large part of identifying the best software development processes) should be a high priority activity in any defect management program

Defect prevention should begin with an assessment of the critical risks associated with the system. Getting the critical risks defined allows people to know the types of defects that are most likely to occur and the ones that can have the greatest system impact. Strategies can then be developed to prevent them. The major steps for defect prevention are as follows:

Defect Prevention Process

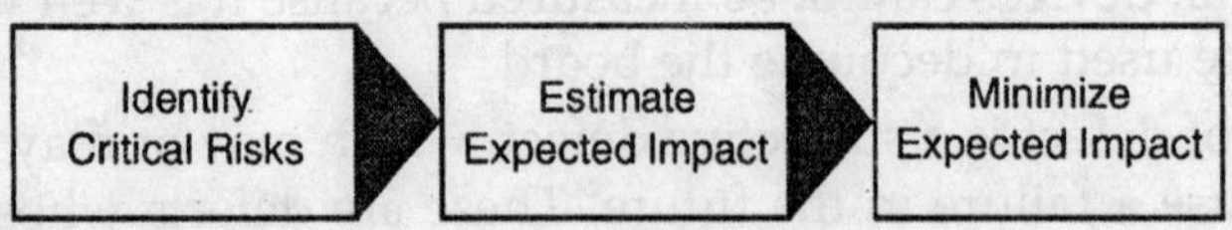

Click on the following links to read more about these steps:

- **Identify Critical Risks.** Identify the critical risks facing the project or system. These are the types of defects that could jeopardize the successful construction, delivery and/or operation of the system.
- **Estimate Expected Impact.** For each critical risk, make an assessment of the financial impact if the risk becomes a problem.
- **Minimize Expected Impact.** Once the most important risks are identified try to eliminate each risk. For risks that cannot be eliminated, reduce the probability that the risk will become a problem and the financial impact should that happen.

8.3 DEFECT MANAGEMENT PROCESS

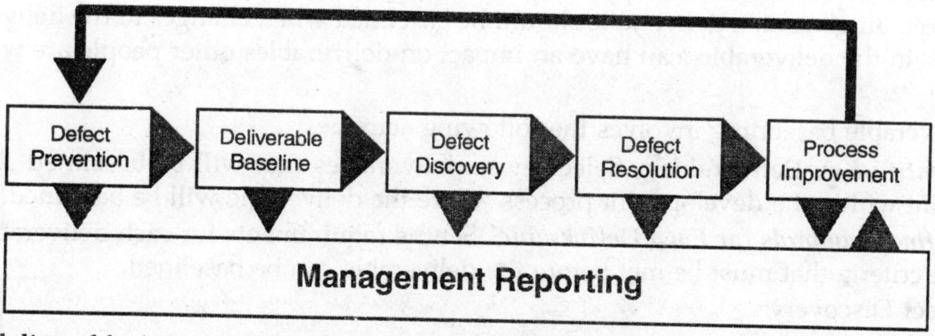

A deliverable (e.g. work product) is ***baselined*** when it reaches a predefined milestone in its development. This milestone involves transferring the product from one stage of development to the next. As a work product moves from one milestone to the next, defects in the deliverable have a much larger impact on the rest of the system, and making changes becomes much more expensive. A deliverable is subject to configuration management (e.g., change control) once it is "baselined."

For purposes of this model, a defect is defined as an instance of one or more ***baselined*** product components not satisfying their given set of requirements. Thus errors caught before a deliverable is baselined would not be considered defects. For example, if a programmer had responsibility for both the programming and the unit testing of a module, the program would not become baselined until after the program was unit tested. Therefore a bug discovered during unit testing would not be considered a defect. If, on the other hand, an organization decided to separate the coding and unit testing, it might decide to baseline the program after it was coded, but before it was unit tested. In this case, a bug discovered during unit testing would be considered a defect (See Figure below).

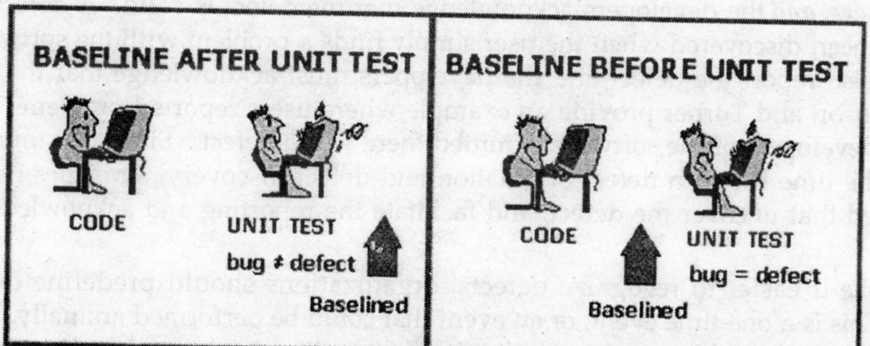

Even for organizations that do not recognize this concept, a deliverable is, for practical purposes, baselined when the deliverable passes to the next stage of development. For example, developers should consider a program specification baselined when a programmer uses it as the basis to code a program. A program should be considered baselined when developers pass it on for integration testing. Finally, developers should consider a requirements specification baselined if it is being used as the basis for a technical design.

The concept of baselining is important because it requires an organization to decide both the level of formality that is appropriate, and the point in the process when the formality takes effect. In general, a deliverable should be baselined when changes to the deliverable, or defects in the deliverable, can have an impact on deliverables other people are working on.

Deliverable baselining involves the following activities:

- ***Identify Key Deliverables***: Select those deliverables that will be baselined and the point within the development process where the deliverable will be baselined.
- ***Define Standards for Each Deliverable***: Set the requirements for each deliverable and the criteria that must be met before the deliverable can be baselined.

Defect Discovery

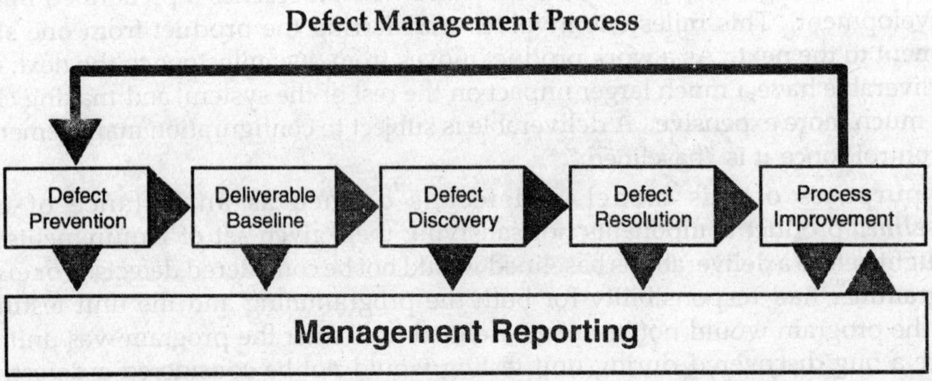

If technology can not guarantee that defects will not be created, then defects should be found quickly before the cost-to-fix becomes expensive. For purposes of this model, a defect has been discovered when the defect has been formally brought to the attention of the developers, *and* the developers acknowledge that the defect is valid. A defect has not necessarily been discovered when the user simply finds a problem with the software. The user must also report the defect and the developers must acknowledge that the defect is valid. Levinson and Turner provide an example where users reported problems for years before the developers of the software admitted there was a defect . Since it is important to minimize the time between defect origination and defect discovery, strategies need to be implemented that uncover the defect, and facilitate the reporting and acknowledge of the defect.

To make it easier to recognize defects, organizations should predefine defects by category. This is a one-time event, or an event that could be performed annually. It would involve the knowledgeable, respected individuals from all major areas of the IS organization. The group should be run by a facilitator. The objective is to identify the errors/problems that occur most frequently in the IS organization and then get agreement that they are, in fact, defects. A name should be attached to each category of defect. The objective of this activity is to minimize conflicts over the validity of defects. For example, developers may not want to acknowledge that a missing requirement is a defect, but if it has been previously defined as a defect category then that conflict can be avoided.

The steps involved in defect discovery are as follows:

Defect Discovery Process

Click on the following links to read more about these steps:

- **Find Defect.** Discover defects before they become major problems.
- **Report Defect.** Report defects to developers so that they can be resolved.
- **Acknowledge Defect.** Obtain development acknowledgement that the defect is valid and should be addressed

8.4 FIND DEFECT

Defect Discovery Process

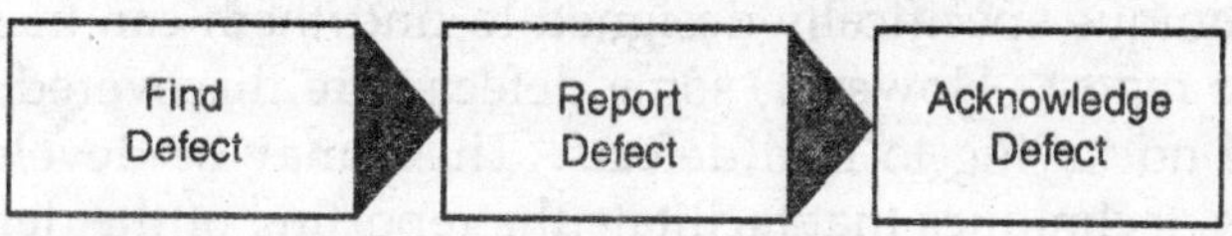

Defects are found either by preplanned activities specifically intended to uncover defects (e.g., quality control activities such as inspections, testing, etc.) or by accident (e.g., users in production).

Techniques to find defects can be divided into three categories:

- ***Static techniques***: Testing that is done without physically executing a program or system. A code review is an example of a static testing technique.
- ***Dynamic techniques***: Testing in which system components are physically executed to identify defects. Execution of test cases is an example of a dynamic testing technique.
- ***Operational techniques***: An operational system produces a deliverable containing a defect found by users, customers, or control personnel — i.e., the defect is found as a result of a failure.

While it is beyond the scope of this study to compare and contrast the various static, dynamic, and operational techniques, the research did arrive at the following conclusions:

- Both static and dynamic techniques are required for an effective defect management program. In each category, the more formally the techniques were integrated into the development process, the more effective they were.
- Since static techniques will generally find defects earlier in the process, they are more efficient at finding defects.

When Shell Oil followed the inspection process, they recorded the following results:

- For each staff-hour spent in the inspection process, ten hours were saved!
- More informal (and less effective) reviews saved as much time as they cost. In other words, worst case (informal reviews) — no extra cost, best case (formal inspections) — a 10-1 savings.
- Their defect removal efficiency with inspections was 95-97% versus roughly 60% for systems that did not use inspections.

Shell Oil also emphasized the more intangible, yet very significant, benefits of inspections. They found that if the standards for producing a deliverable were vague or ambiguous (or nonexistent), the group would attempt to define a best practice and develop a standard for the deliverable. Once the standard became well defined, checklists would be developed. (NASA also makes extensive use of checklists and cross references defects to the checklist item that should have caught the defect). Inspections were a good way to train new staff in both best practices and the functioning of the system being inspected

8.5 REPORT DEFECT

Defect Discovery Process

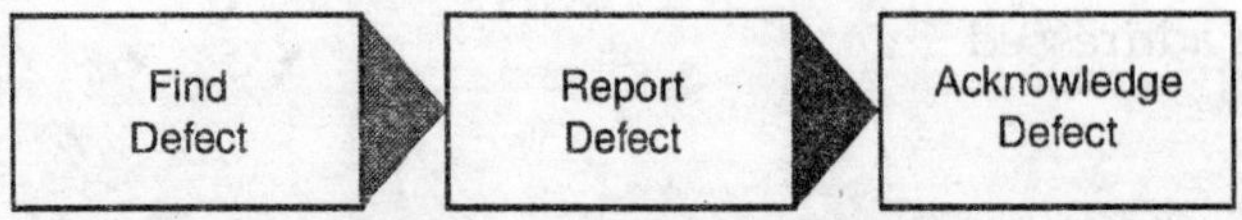

Once discovered, defects must be brought to the developers' attention. Defects discovered by a technique specifically designed to find them can be reported by a simple written or electronic report. However, some defects, are discovered more by accident — i.e., people who are not trying to find defects. These may be development personnel or users. In these cases, techniques that facilitate the reporting of the defect may significantly shorten the defect discovery time. As software becomes more complex and more widely used, these techniques become more valuable. These techniques include computer forums, email, help desks, etc.

It should also be noted that there are some human factors/cultural issues involved with the defect discovery process. When a defect is initially uncovered, it may be very unclear whether it is a defect, a change, user error, or a misunderstanding. Developers may resist calling something a defect because that implies "bad work" and may not reflect well on the development team. Users may resist calling something a "change" because that implies that the developers can charge them more money. Some organizations have skirted this issue by initially labeling everything by a different name — e.g., "incidents" or "issues." From a defect management perspective, what they are called is not an important issue. What is important is that the defect be quickly brought to the developers' attention and formally controlled.

8.6 ACKNOWLEDGE DEFECT

Defect Discovery Process

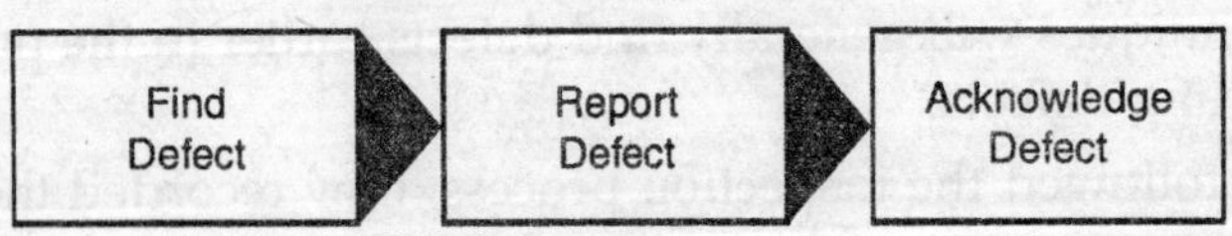

Once a defect has been brought to the attention of the developer, the developer must decide whether or not the defect is valid. Delays in acknowledging defects can be very costly. The primary cause of delays in acknowledging a defect appears to be an inability to reproduce the defect. When the defect is not reproducible and appears to be an isolated event ("no one else has reported anything like that"), there will be an increased tendency for the developer to assume the defect is invalid — that the defect is caused by user error or misunderstanding. Moreover, with very little information to go on, the developer may feel that there is nothing he or she can do anyway. Unfortunately, as technology becomes more complex, defects which are difficult to reproduce will become more and more common. Software developers must develop strategies to more quickly pinpoint the cause of a defect.

8.7 STRATEGIES TO PINPOINT CAUSE OF DEFECT

One strategy to pinpoint the cause of a defect is to instrument code to trap the state of the environment when anomalous conditions occur. Microsoft's Dr. Watson concept would be an example of this technique. In the Beta release of Windows 3.1, Microsoft included features (i.e., Dr. Watson) to trap the state of the system when a significant problem occurred. This information was then available to Microsoft when the problem was reported and helped them analyze the problem.

Writing code to check the validity of the system is another way to pinpoint the cause of a defect. This is actually a very common technique for hardware manufacturers. Unfortunately diagnostics may give a false sense of security — they can find defects, but they cannot show the absence of defects. Virus checkers would be an example of this strategy.

Finally, analyzing reported defects to discover the cause of a defect is very effective. While a given defect may not be reproducible, quite often it will appear again (and again) perhaps in different guises. Eventually patterns may be noticed which will help in resolving the defect. If the defect is not logged, or if it is closed prematurely, then valuable information can be lost. In one instance reported to the research team, a development team was having difficulty reproducing a problem. Finally, during a visit to the location, they discovered how to reproduce the problem. The problem was caused when one of the users fell asleep with her finger on the enter key. In order to protect the user, the circumstances surrounding the problem were not reported to the developers until the on-site visit.

A resolution process needs to be established for use in the event there is a dispute regarding a defect. For example, if the group uncovering the defect believes it is a defect but the developers do not, a quick-resolution process must be in place. While many approaches can address this situation, the two most effective are:

- Arbitration by the software owner — the customer using the software determines whether or not the problem is a defect.
- Arbitration by a software development manager — a senior manager of the software development department will be selected to resolve the dispute

8.8 DEFECT RESOLUTION

Defect Management Process

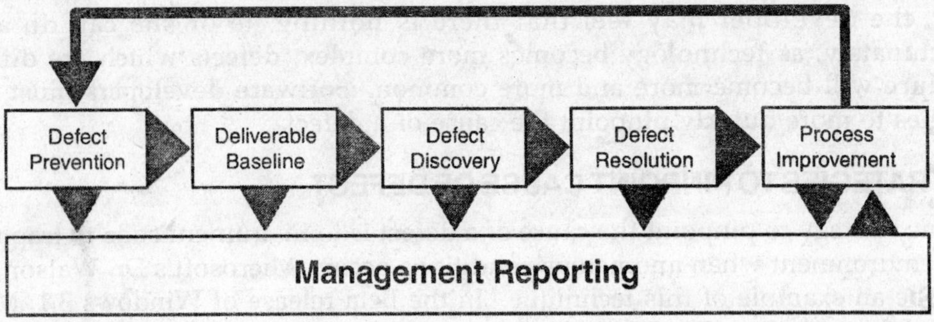

Once the developers have acknowledged a valid defect, the resolution process begins. The steps involved in defect resolution are as follows:

Defect Resolution Process

Click on the following links to read more about these steps:

- **Prioritize Risk.** Developers determine the importance of fixing a particular defect.
- **Schedule Fix and Fix Defect.** Developers schedule when to fix a defect. Then developers should fix defects in order of importance.
- **Report Resolution.** Developers notify all relevant parties how and when the defect was repaired.

Defect Resolution Process

- **Prioritize Risk.** Developers determine the importance of fixing a particular defect.
- **Schedule Fix and Fix Defect.** Developers schedule when to fix a defect. Then developers should fix defects in order of importance.
- **Report Resolution.** Developers notify all relevant parties how and when the defect was repaired.

Defect Resolution Process

The purpose of this step is to answer the following questions and initiate any immediate action that might be required:

- Is this a previously reported defect, or is it new?
- What priority should be given to fixing this defect?
- What steps should be taken to minimize the impact of the defect prior to a fix? For example, should other users be notified of the problem? Is there a work-around for the defect?

A suggested prioritization method is a three-level method, as follows:

- **Critical.** Would cause the software to stop.
- **Major.** Would cause an output of the software to be incorrect.
- **Minor:** Something wrong, but it does not directly affect the user of the system, such as a documentation error or cosmetic GUI error.

8.9 SCHEDULE AND FIX DEFECT

Defect Resolution Process

8.9.1 Schedule Fix

Based on the priority of the defect, the fix should be scheduled. It should be noted that some organizations treat lower priority defects as changes. All defects are not created equal from the perspective of how quickly they need to be fixed.

8.9.2 Fix Defect

This step involves correcting and verifying one or more deliverables (e.g., programs, documentation) required to remove the defect from the system. In addition, test data, checklists, etc. should be reviewed, and perhaps enhanced, so that in the future this defect would be caught earlier.

Defect Resolution Process

Once the defect has been fixed and the fix verified, appropriate developers, users, and testers must be notified that the defect has been fixed along with other pertinent information such as:

- The nature of the fix,
- When the fix will be released, and
- How the fix will be released.

As in many aspects of defect management, this is an area where automation of the process can help. Most defect management tools capture information on who found and reported the problem, and therefore provide an initial list of who needs to be notified.

The figure below illustrates this process. The developer identifies and fixes problems that caused the defects. Then the developer must record resolution information with the defects. The resolution information is then passed back to impacted parties. Computer forums and electronic mail can help notify users of widely distributed software.

Report Resolution

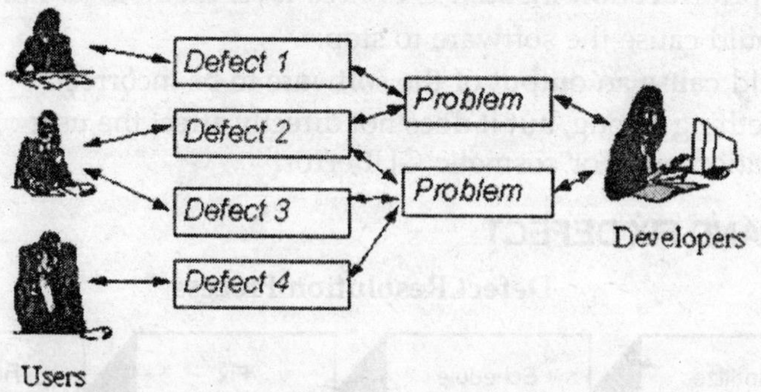

8.10 PROCESS IMPROVEMENT

Defect Management Process

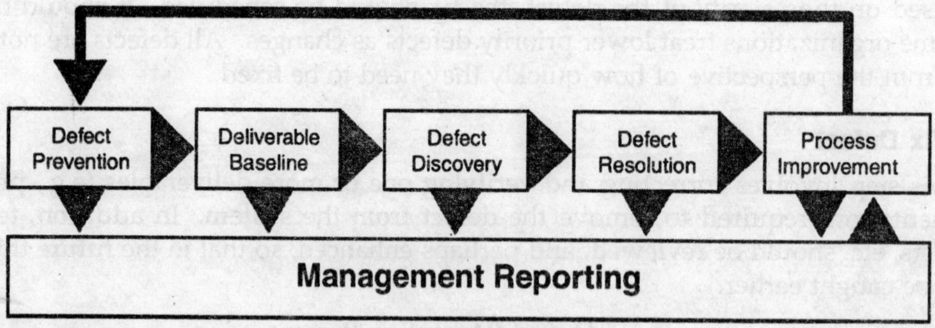

This is perhaps the activity that is most ignored by organizations today, but offers one of the greatest areas of payback. NASA emphasizes the point that any defect represents a weakness in the process. Seemingly unimportant defects are, from a process perspective, no different than critical defects. It is only the developer's good luck that prevents a defect from causing a major failure. Even minor defects therefore represent an opportunity to learn how to improve the process and prevent potentially major failures. While the defect itself may not be a big deal, the fact that there was a defect *is* a big deal.

Based on the study's findings, participants should go back to the process that originated the defect to understand what caused the defect. Then they should go back to the validation process that should have caught the defect earlier in the process. Not only can valuable insight be gained as to how to strengthen the review process, this step serves to make everyone involved in these activities take them more seriously. This human factors dimension alone, according to some of the people the research team interviewed, can have a very large impact on the effectiveness of the review process.

NASA, takes an additional step of asking the question: If this defect could have gotten this far into the process before it was captured, what other defects may be present that have not been discovered. Thus not only is the process strengthened to prevent defects, it is strengthened to find defects that have been created, but not yet discovered. This aggressiveness should be mandatory on life critical systems. The well-known "Thearc-25" case of a radiation machine that kept issuing "Malfunction 25" messages is one example where problems might have been caught earlier if this step had been pursued

8.11 MANAGEMENT REPORTING

Defect Management Process

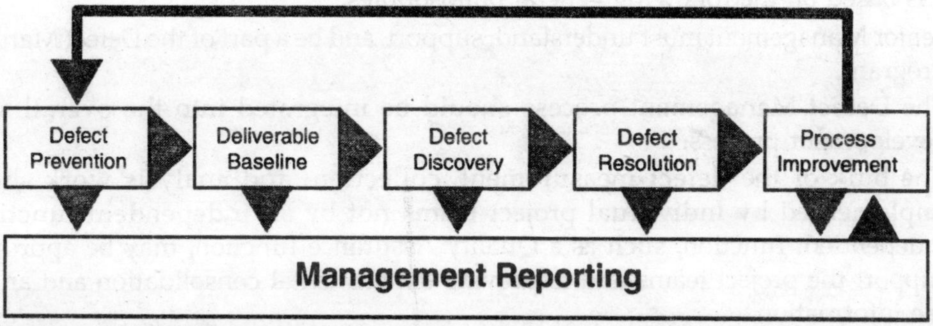

It is important that the defect information, which is a natural by-product of the defect management process, be analyzed and communicated to both project management and senior management. This could take the form of defect rates, defect trends, types of defects, failure costs, etc. From a tactical perspective, defect arrival rate (rate at which new defects are being discovered) is a very useful metric that provides insight into a project's likelihood of making its target date objectives. Defect removal efficiency is also considered to be one of the most useful metrics, however it can not be calculated until the system is installed. Defect removal efficiency is the ratio of defects found prior to product operation divided by the total number of defects found in the application.

Information collected during the defect management process has a number of purposes:

- To report on the status of individual defects.
- To provide tactical information and metrics to help project management make more informed decisions — e.g., redesign of error prone modules, the need for more testing, etc.
- To provide strategic information and metrics to senior management — defect trends, problem systems, etc.
- To provide insight into areas where the process could be improved to either prevent defects or minimize their impact.
- To provide insight into the likelihood that target dates and cost estimates will be achieved.

Management reporting is a necessary and critically important aspect of the defect management process, but it is also important to avoid overkill and ensure that the reports that are produced have a purpose and advance the defect management process.

The basis for management reporting should be the information collected on individual defects by the project teams. Thus the information collected during the defect management process and the classification of individual defects needs to be considered by each organization.

8.12 IMPLEMENTING THE PROCESS

Since the model we developed represents a cultural change for most organizations, the manner in which the process is implemented is critically important to the overall success of the program. As such, the purpose of this section is to provide a framework for establishing an effective Defect Management Program. The implementation approach presented in this section is based on the following general philosophies:

- Senior Management must understand, support, and be a part of the Defect Management Program.
- The Defect Management process should be integrated into the overall software development process.
- The bulk of the defect measurement, collection, and analysis work should be implemented by individual project teams not by an independent function. An independent function, such as a Quality Assurance function, may be appropriate to support the project teams and to provide departmental consolidation and analysis of the information.
- To the extent practical, the process should be repeatable and automated.
- Specific development approaches (e.g., testing, inspections, etc.) should be chosen based on project objectives and risks that must be addressed.
- Process improvement efforts should be driven by the measurement process.

It should be noted, the process does not require a significant investment, yet will likely result in significant payback.

The basic steps to establish a defect management program are as follows:

8.13 PROCESS IMPLEMENTATION

Define Critical Metrics
↳ Identify Critical Risks
↳ Identify Process Improvements
↳ Develop Defect Management Plan
↳ Pilot the Defect Management Process

- **Define Critical Defect Metrics.** The first step in establishing a defect management program is to understand the organization's objectives. These objectives should point to the defect measures that are most important to the organization.
- **Identify Critical Risks.** The next step is to understand the critical risks the organization faces when developing and maintaining software.

- **Identify Process Improvements.** Once the critical metrics have been defined and the critical risks have been identified, one can identify the areas where process improvements are needed.
- **Develop Defect Management Plan.** The Defect Management Plan documents the results of the earlier steps and defines the implementation strategy for the Defect Management Program.
- **Pilot the Defect Management Process.** The concept of a pilot project is designed to implement the program in a controlled manner so that issues and obstacles to successful implementation can be identified and resolved quickly.

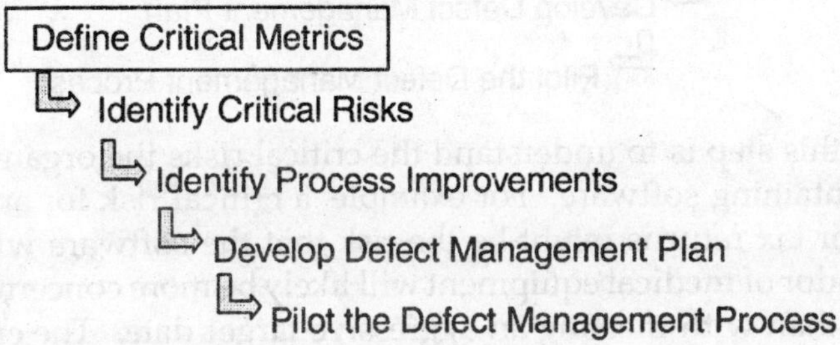

The first step in establishing a defect management program is to understand the organization's objectives. These objectives should point to the defect measures that are most important to the organization. While the measurement data will actually be collected and reported in a bottom-up manner, the actual requirements for measurement data should be defined in a top-down manner as follows:

- ***Identify Senior Management Sponsors***: By definition, the Critical Metrics are those metrics which senior management deems critical to the successful operation of the organization. Therefore the Critical Metrics should be chosen by senior management. Ideally senior management from user areas as well as IT management would be involved.
- ***Educate Senior Management***: Before they are asked to define the Critical Metrics, senior management should be given an overview of the proposed defect management process as well as relevant quality and measurement concepts.
- ***Critical Metrics Joint Definition Session***: The Critical Metrics should be chosen by the senior managers as a group decision. This is best accomplished in a group meeting so that each senior manager understands that even if his or her favorite metric was not chosen for the Critical Metrics Set, the Critical Metrics reflect a group consensus of the metrics important to the organization. Normally the Critical Metrics Set consists of 5-7 metrics of which 2-3 are defect related.

This step is designed not only to understand what metrics are most important, but also to get senior management involvement and commitment, and set the stage for ongoing interest in the Defect Management Program.

Because the Critical Metrics Set is highly situational, we can only provide examples of defect related Critical Metrics. Such examples are as follows:

- Failure index (failure cost/IT budget)
- Defect removal efficiency
- Mean time to failure of critical systems
- Defect arrival rate for critical development projects

Define Critical Metrics
↳ **Identify Critical Risks**
↳ Identify Process Improvements
↳ Develop Defect Management Plan
↳ Pilot the Defect Management Process

The purpose of this step is to understand the critical risks the organization faces when developing and maintaining software. For example, a critical risk for an organization that develops software for tax returns might be the risk that the software will not be available for tax season. A vendor of medical equipment will likely be more concerned with delivering a defect free system than with meeting an aggressive target date. The critical risks should be those risks which can negatively impact the Critical Metrics Set. If they are not, then the Critical Metrics Set, or the critical risks should be reexamined.

There are a wealth of techniques that can reduce risk. Which ones can do the best job depends on what the risks are. Moreover as the business changes and as technology changes, the risks will also change. Some of the factors that will influence the risk profile include:

- Regulated business vs. highly competitive
- Development vs. maintenance
- Many users vs. few users
- Stable mature technology vs. new technology
- Centralized system vs. distributed system
- Technical platform
- Large integrated system vs. small stand-alone system
- Tight target dates
- Limited budget
- Rapidly changing business environment
- Life critical product

The risk profile should heavily influence the priorities in the Defect Management Plan

Define Critical Metrics
↳ Identify Critical Risks
↳ **Identify Process Improvements**
↳ Develop Defect Management Plan
↳ Pilot the Defect Management Process

Once the critical metrics have been defined and the critical risks have been identified, one can identify the areas where process improvements are needed. Process improvements will tend to address two areas:

- More reliable calculation of the critical metrics.
- Improvements in the critical metrics.

There are many techniques that can lower risk and improve defect levels. The challenge is to choose the techniques that best address the risk profile and critical metrics defined in the earlier steps. As much as possible, this step should build upon existing methodology and procedures. The figure below illustrates this concept by cross referencing various techniques with the defect management objectives they are most effective in addressing. Some techniques tend to be very effective across a broad array of objectives and should receive high priority in the Defect Management Plan.

Technique Vs. Objective Matrix

Technique/ Objective	Prevention		Discovery			Resolution			Management Reporting	Process Improvement
	Reduce Probability	Reduce Impact	Find	Report	Acknowledge	Prioritize	Schedule	Fix Report		
Inspections	X		X	X	X					
Testing			X	X	X					
Early Test										
Planning	X		X	X	X					
Defensive										
Design	X		X	X	X					
Assertions	X		X	X	X					
Help Desk			X	X						
Contingency Planning		X								
Defect Reporting				X		X	X	X	X	X
Defect Classification										X
Disaster										
Recovery										
Planning		X								

The following areas should be viewed as prerequisites to process improvement:

- ***Documented Process.*** The process used to develop and maintain software should be documented.
- ***Deliverable Definitions.*** The process must define the required content of deliverables, the point in the development process where each deliverable is produced, and the point in the process where each deliverable is baselined. This step is required to define and identify defects.
- ***Defect Reporting System.*** Procedures should be established to formally and concisely report defects and gather the data required to compute the critical metrics. The bulk of this work should be the responsibility of individual project teams. A quality assurance function or other group should be responsible for consolidating and reporting information across projects.

Once the above areas are in place, defect information should be collected and analyzed. This information should be used to guide the ongoing process improvement activities.

IBM has done some very interesting work on a concept called Orthogonal Defect Classification (ODC), which can guide process improvement activities. ODC attempts to exploit the relationship between the cause of the defect and the type of defect. Defects are categorized into classes that are related to the part of the process that needs attention. Defect types are mapped into the process to provide the relation between the defect and the process. The figure below illustrates this association.

The assumption is that the distribution of defect types provides insight into status of a product. If for example, there are many defects associated with edit/validation rules found during system testing, then the distribution of defects would indicate that unit testing was inadequate and that the product was rushed prematurely into system test.

Defect Type and Process Associations

Defect Type	Process Association
Function	Requirements
Interface	Design
Edit/Validation Checking	Program Specification/Coding/Unit Test
Algorithm	Design/Program Specification

IBM is also researching the concept of a **defect trigger**. A defect trigger is a condition that allows a defect to be discovered. Unlike defect types, defect triggers can potentially be identified early in the life cycle of a defect. Like the defect type attribute, the defect trigger distribution can provide insight into the development process. It can also, however, provide insight into the verification process. Ideally, for example, the distribution of defects found in production should be similar to the distribution found during system testing. Significant differences in the two distributions would indicate weaknesses in the system testing.

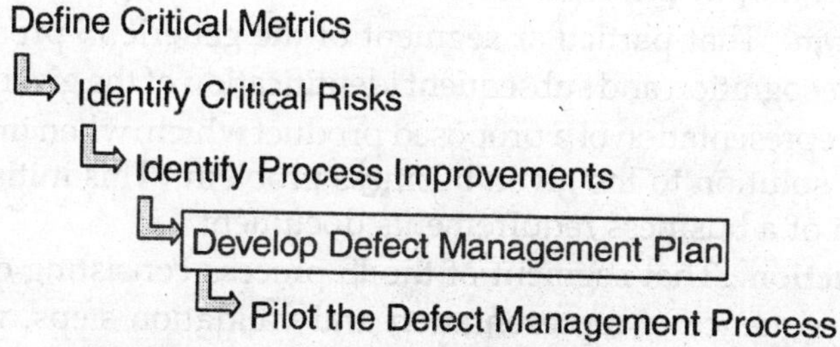

The Defect Management Plan documents the results of the earlier steps and defines the implementation strategy for the Defect Management Program. A sample table of contents of this document is given in the figure below.

Defect Management Plan

1. Introduction and Management Summary
- **1.1 Objectives**
- **1.2 Critical Risk Profile**

2. Critical Defect Procedures
- **2.1 Calculation Procedures**

3. Process Improvement
- **3.1 Existing Process and Procedures**
- **3.2 Planned Process Improvements**

4. Pilot Project Implementation Approach
- **4.1 Project Manager's Metrics**
- **4.2 Training**

5. Management Reporting

6. Work Plan For Next Phase

The Defect Management Plan must integrate process improvement, training, pilot project implementation into a workable implementation plan

So we can say that—

- **DEFECT.** An instance of one or more ***baselined*** product components not satisfying their given set of requirements. A product is ***baselined*** when it reaches a predefined milestone in its development and is placed under change control. Defects are identified during product construction as the result of the verification portion of the refinement process, or they are identified as a result of failures during product operation, or as the result of unplanned discoveries. A defect is ***discovered*** when the defect has been formally brought to the attention of the developers, **and** the developers acknowledge the defect is valid.
- **Business Environment**. The external system of people, procedures, and machines organized to supply a given set of products and services to its customers and internal users.
- **Business Problem**. An opportunity or legal requirement to reduce costs, increase value, and generally improve some specific subset of the business environment.

- **Change**. An alteration in the business environment or the given business problem.
- **Product Definition**. That particular segment of the generic IS process consisting of:
  - The initial recognition and subsequent identification of the given business problem.
  - The initial representation of a proposed product which, when implemented, would provided a solution to the given business problem. This initial representation is in the form of a business requirements document.
- **Product Construction**. That segment of the IS process consisting of:
  - A specific sequence of representation and validation steps, which successively translate the original representation of the business problem into lower and lower levels of refinement until a set of software, administrative procedures, documentation, and hardware components are realized, i.e. the product.
  - A disciplined set of management, organizational, technical, and administrative methodologies and tools, which are designed to ensure that the sequence of representation and validation steps are applied in a reliable and predictable manner to produce a product that will represent a solution to the original business problem.
- **Product Operation**. That segment of the IS process consisting of:
  - Installing the product into a given hardware, operating, procedural, and data environment.
  - Operating the product so that it properly alters the original business environment and thus represents an implementation of the solution of the given business problem.

8.14 DEFECT PREVENTION: REDUCING COSTS AND ENHANCING QUALITY

Prevention is better than cure" applies to defects in the software development life cycle as well as illnesses in medical science. Defects, as defined by software developers, are variances from a desired attribute. These attributes include complete and correct requirements and specifications as drawn from the desires of potential customers. Thus, defects cause software to fail to meet requirements and make customers unhappy.

And when a defect gets through during the development process, the earlier it is diagnosed, the easier and cheaper is the rectification of the defect. The end result in prevention or early detection is a product with zero or minimal defects.

How serious are defects in software development? In the United States, up to 60 percent of software developers are involved in fixing errors, *Computer Finance Magazine* reported in 1998. This fact alone, without consideration of providing the quality needed to please customers, shows the value of preventing software defects.

8.15 ADVANTAGEOFEARL Y DEFECT DETECTION

Data to support the need for early fixes of software defects is supplied by several reports. The National Institute of Standard Technology (NIST) published a study in 2002 noting that the cost of fixing one bug found in the production stage of software is 15 hours compared to five hours of effort if the same bug were found in the coding stage.

The Systems Sciences Institute at IBM has reported that the cost to fix an error found after product release was four to five times as much as one uncovered during design, and up to 100 times more than one identified in the maintenance phase (Figure 1).

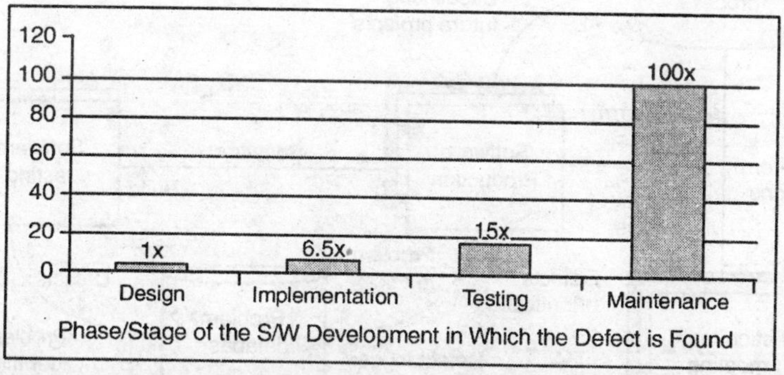

Fig. 1. Relative Costs to Fix Software Defects (Source: IBM Systems Sciences Institute)

Can software defects be prevented by simply logging them into some "defect tracking tool/system," documenting them and providing fixes for them? The obvious answer is no, though this is the first step toward defect prevention.

Defect prevention involves a structured problem-solving methodology to identify, analyze and prevent the occurrence of defects. Defect prevention is a framework and ongoing process of collecting the defect data, doing root cause analysis, determining and implementing the corrective actions and sharing the lessons learned to avoid future defects.

8.16 PRINCIPLES OF DEFECT PREVENTION

How does a defect prevention mechanism work? The answer is in a defect prevention cycle (Figure 2). The integral part of the defect prevention process begins with requirement analysis – translating the customer requirements into product specifications without introducing additional errors. Software architecture is designed, code review and testing are done to find out the defects, followed by defect logging and documentation.

The blocks and processes in the gray-colored block represent the handling of defects within the existing philosophy of most of the software industry – defect detection, tracking/documenting and analysis of defects for arriving at quick, short-term solutions.

The processes that form the integral part of the defect prevention methodology are on the white background. The vital process of the defect prevention methodology is to analyze defects to get their root causes, to determine a quick solution and preventive action. These preventive measures, after consent and commitments from team members, are embedded into the organization as a baseline for future projects. The methodology is aimed at providing the organization a long-term solution and the maturity to learn from mistakes.

Most of the activities of the defect prevention methodology require a facilitator. The facilitator can be the software development project leader (wearing another hat of responsibility) or any member of the team. The designated defect prevention coordinator is actively involved in leading defect prevention efforts, facilitating meetings and communication among team and management, and consolidating the defect prevention measures/guidelines.

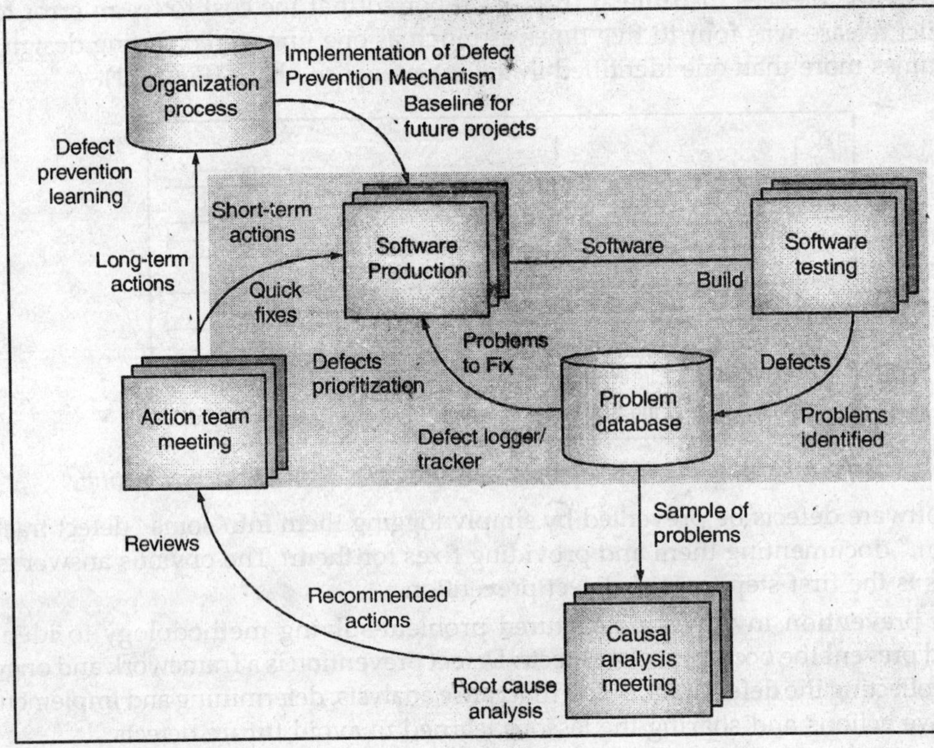

Fig. 2. Defect Prevention Cycle (Source: 1998 IEEE Software Productivity Consortium)

The five general activities of defect prevention are:

1. Software Requirements Analysis

Table 1. Division of Defects Introduced into Software by Phase

Software Development Phases	Percent of Defects Introduced
Requirements	20 Perecent
Design	25 Percent
Coding	35 Percent
User Manuals	12 Percent
Bad Fixes	8 Percent

Source: *Computer Finance Magazine*

Errors in software requirements and software design documents are more frequent than errors in the source code itself, according to *Computer Finance Magazine*. Defects introduced during the requirements and design phase are not only more probable but also are more severe and more difficult to remove. Front-end errors in requirements and design cannot be found and removed via testing, but instead need pre-test reviews and inspections. Table 1 shows the defects introduced during different phases of the software development life cycle.

From the studies made by various software development communities, it is evident that most failures in software products are due to errors in the requirements and design phases – as high as 64 percent of total defect costs (Figure 3), according to *Crosstalk, the Journal of Defense Software Engineering*.

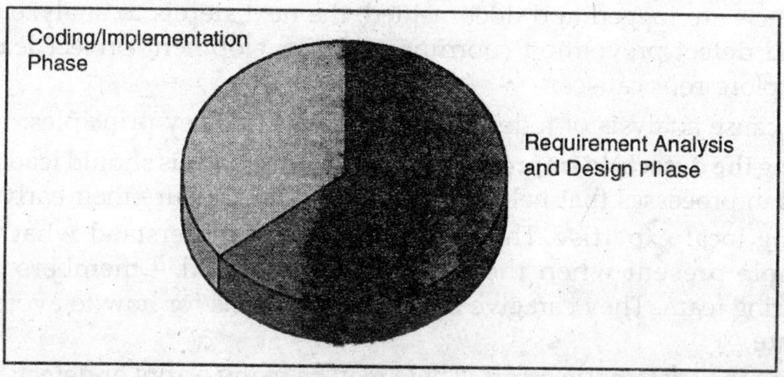

Fig. 3. Origin of Software Defects (Source: Crosstalk, the Journal of Defense Software Engineering)

Hence, it is important to have a proper process of analyzing the requirements in place to ensure that the customer needs are correctly translated into product specifications. Perhaps two or three iteration of interactive sessions with the customer can be of great help in verifying the understanding of the developer about actual requirements.

2. Reviews: Self-Review and Peer Review

Self-review is one of the most effective activites in uncovering the defects which may later be discovered by a testing team or directly by a customer. The majority of the software organizations are now making this a part of "coding best practices" and are really increasing their product quality.

Often, a self-review of the code helps reduce the defects related to algorithm implementations, incorrect logic or certain missing conditions. Once the developer feels they are ready with the module code, a glance through the code and understanding what it does compared to what it is supposed to do, would complete the self-review.

Peer review is similar to self-review in terms of the objective – the only difference is that it is a peer (someone who understands the functionality of the code very well) who reviews the code. The advantage is that of a "fresh pair of eyes."

3. Defect Logging and Documentation

Effective defect tracking begins with a systematic process. A structured tracking process begins with initially logging the defects, investigating the defects, then providing the structure to resolve them. Defect analysis and reporting offer a powerful means to manage defects and defect depletion trends, hence, costs.

A defect logging tool should document certain vital information regarding the defect such as:

- Correct and complete description of the defect – so that everyone on the development team understands what it is and how to reproduce it.
- Phase at which it is found – so that preventive measures can be taken and propagation of the defect to next phase (software build) is avoided.

- Further description of the defect by screenshots.
- Names of those who uncover defects – so everyone knows who to contact for a better understanding of the defect.

4. Root Cause Analysis and Preventive Measures Determination

After defects are logged and documented, the next step is to analyze them. Generally the designated defect prevention coordinator or development project leader facilitates a meeting to explore root causes.

The root cause analysis of a defect is driven by three key principles:

- **Reducing the defects to improve the quality.** The analysis should lead to implementing changes in processes that help prevent defects and ensure their early detection.
- **Applying local expertise.** The people who really understand what went wrong are the people present when the defects were inserted – members of the software engineering team. They can give the best suggestions for how to avoid such defects in the future.
- **Targeting the systematic errors.** There may be many errors or defects to be handled in such an analysis forum; however, some mistakes tend to be repeated. These systematic errors account for a large portion of the defects found in the typical software project. Identifying and preventing systematic errors can have a big impact on quality (in terms of defects) for a relatively small investment.

With these guidelines, defects are analyzed to determine their origins. A collection of such causes will help in doing the root cause analysis. The defects are classified based on their types. A Pareto chart is prepared to show the defect category with the highest frequency of occurrence – the target. An example of defect classification in a Pareto chart is shown in Figure 4.

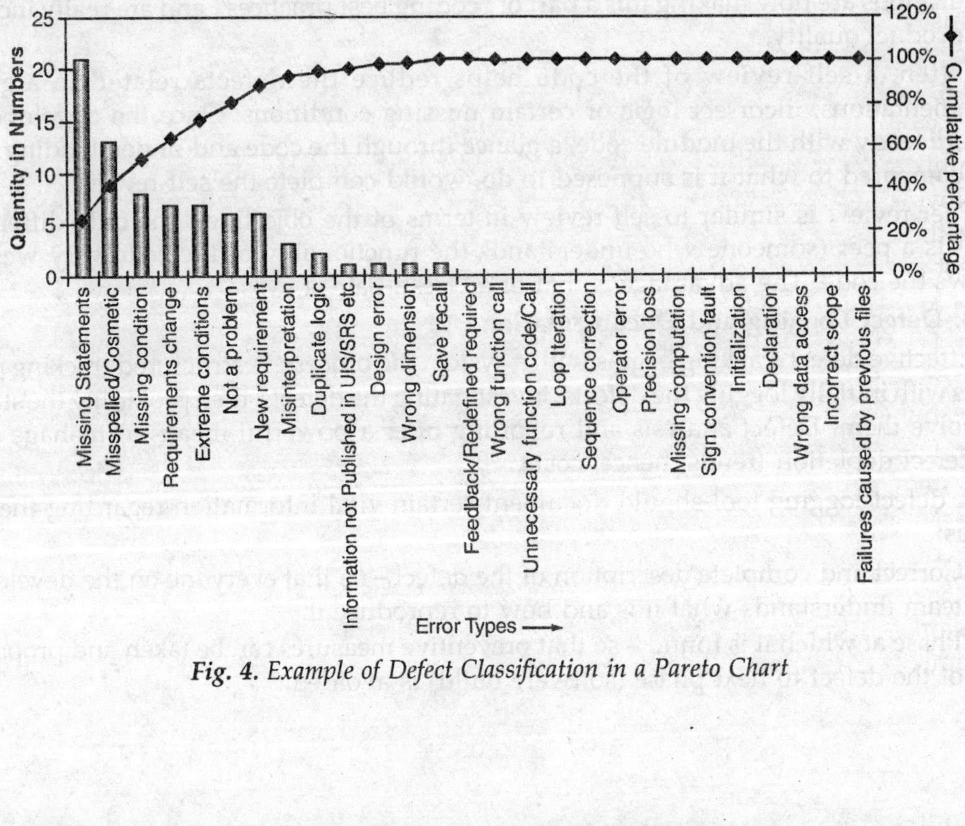

Fig. 4. Example of Defect Classification in a Pareto Chart

Root cause analysis is the process of finding and eliminating the cause, which would prevent the problem from recurring. Finding the causes and eliminating them are equally important.

Each defect category and the causes making those defects happen can be represented using a cause-and-effect diagram, as shown in Figure 5.

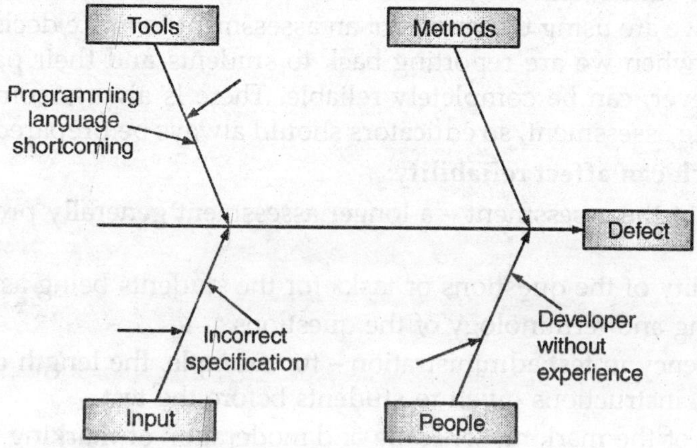

Fig. 5. Cause-and-Effect Diagram for a Defect

The cause-and-effect diagram, also known as a fishbone diagram, is a simple graphical technique for sorting and relating factors that contribute to a given situation. A team usually develops the cause-and-effect diagram in a facilitated brainstorming session. Once the root causes are documented, finding ways to eliminate them requires another round of brainstorming. The object is to determine what changes should be incorporated in the processes so that recurrence of the defects can be minimized.

5. Embedding Procedures into Software Development Process

Implementation is the toughest of all activities of defect prevention. It requires total commitment from the development team and management. A plan of action is made for deployment of the modification of the existing processes or introduction of the new ones with the consent of management and the team. Some of the other activities in this phase of defect prevention are:

- Monthly status of the team should mention the severe defects and their analyses.
- Fortnightly or monthly (based on the project schedule) meetings to make the team aware of the systematic errors/defects, their symptoms and solutions.
- Embedding the defect prevention measures in software development life cycle processes.
- Learning from the previous project's root cause analysis of defects should be used as the baseline for future projects.
- Monitoring the defect prevention progress. Is the number of defects decreasing? Is the development team learning from past mistakes?

Finally, defect prevention is not an individual exercise but a team effort. The software development team should be striving to improve its process by identifying defects early, minimizing resolution time and therefore reducing project costs.

8.17 FACTORS AFFECTING RELIABILITY

The **reliability** of an assessment is the extent to which it consistently and accurately measures learning.

When the results of an assessment are reliable, we can be con?dent that repeated or equivalent assessments will provide consistent results. This puts us in a better position to make generalised statements about a student's level of achievement, which is especially important when we are using the results of an assessment to make decisions about teaching and learning, or when we are reporting back to students and their parents or caregivers. No results, however, can be completely reliable. There is always some random variation that may affect the assessment, so educators should always be prepared to question results.

Factors which can affect reliability:

- The length of the assessment – a longer assessment generally produces more reliable results.
- The suitability of the questions or tasks for the students being assessed.
- The phrasing and terminology of the questions.
- The consistency in test administration – for example, the length of time given for the assessment, instructions given to students before the test.
- The design of the marking schedule and moderation of marking procedures.
- The readiness of students for the assessment – for example, a hot afternoon or straight after physical activity might not be the best time for students to be assessed.

8.18 MTTF

Reliability is "the probability that a part will last at least a specified time under specified experimental conditions".

Mean time to failure (MTTF) is the length of time a device or other product is expected to last in operation. MTTF is one of many ways to evaluate the reliability of pieces of hardware or other technology.

Mean time to failure is extremely similar to another related term, mean time between failures (MTBF). The difference between these terms is that while MTBF is used for products than that can be repaired and returned to use, MTTF is used for non-repairable products. When MTTF is used as a measure, repair is not an option. As a metric, MTTF represents how long a product can reasonably be expected to perform in the field based on specific testing. It's important to note, however, that the mean time to failure metrics provided by companies regarding specific products or components may not have been collected by running one unit continuously until failure. Instead, MTTF data is often collected by running many units, even many thousands of units, for a specific number of hours.

One of the main situations where terms like MTTF are extremely important is when hardware pieces or other products are used in mission-critical systems. Here it becomes valuable to know about general reliability for these items. For non-repairable items, MTTF is a statistic that is of great interest to engineers and others assessing these pieces as parts of larger systems.

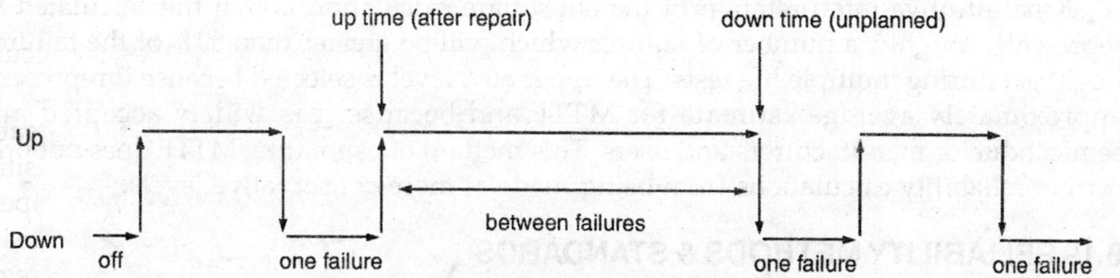

Time Between Failures = {down time - up time}

MTTF is the mean time to the first failure under specified experimental conditions. It is calculated by dividing the total number of device • hours by the number of failures. It is important to note, at this time, that the dimensions of MTTF are not hours per failure, but rather, device • hours per failure. If each part has a 0.1% chance of failure before 1 hour then 10 parts have a 1% chance experiencing a failure by that time. The MTTF will be the same in both cases. 1 failure in 10 hours on 1 part or 1 failure in 1 hour on 10 parts both produce an MTTF of 10 device • hours.

Failure rate is the conditional probability that a device will fail per unit of time. The conditional probability is the probability that a device will fail during a certain interval given that it survived at the start of the interval.(5) When failure rate is used to describe the frequency with which failures are expected to occur, the time units are typically device • hours.

FITS is simply failure rate scaled from failures per device • hour to failures per billion device • hours.

In the definition section MTTF is defined as the average time, in device • hours, per failure observed under specific experimental conditions such as a life test. Here at BurrBrown we use a slightly modified formula for MTTF. We calculate 2 times the total device • hours, Tdh, divided by the upper 60% confidence limit of a chi-square distribution with 2 times the observed number of failures + 2 degrees of freedom, X2

(2f + 2). Our formula is

$$MTTF = 2Tdh/\chi 2\,(2f+2)$$

Since both time and failures are doubled, these definitions are roughly equivalent. Some explanation is in order.

If multiple life tests are run on the same type of device, it is unlikely that all tests will have the same number of failures for the same number of device • hours. Rather there will be a distribution of failures. The minimum value must be 0 for no failures. The maximum value could correspond to 100% failures, but we can presume that we are running enough parts that this will not happen. Rather the distribution will taper off as the number of failures increases. Somewhere in between there will be a concentration of failures.

The chi-square calculation provides us with a tool for adjusting the actual number of failures from a limited life test to make it more accurately reflect what we might expect from the population as a whole. For example, applying a confidence level of 60% to a chi-square distribution with 8 degrees of freedom will return a value into the denominator of the MTTF calculation which is greater than or equal to 60% of the values in a chi-square distribution with a mean of 8.

One intuitive interpretation of the chi-square calculation is that the calculated value represents, roughly, a number of failures which will be greater than 60% of the failures we might get during multiple life tests. The upper 60% level is selected because it represents an approximately average estimate for MTTF and because it is widely accepted among semiconductor manufacturers and users. This method of estimating MTTF does not prevent further reliability calculations from being made at more conservative levels.

8.19 RELIABILITY METHODS & STANDARDS

Reliability methods such as MTTR, MTTF and FIT apply to products or to speci?c components. However, MTBF remains a basic measure of a systems' reliability for most products. It is often debated, sometimes even rejected as no longer relevant, and overall, widely misunderstood. It is still regarded as a useful tool when considering the purchase and installation of a product. Remember, along with obtaining an MTBF value, ask questions regarding how current that information is and on what standards it is based on to ensure choosing the most appropriate product for your installation.

Several prediction methods over time have been developed to determine reliability, but the two standards most often used when compiling reliability data for media converters

8.20 MTBF

When the failure rate needs to be as low as possible, especially for mission critical systems, for example, utilizing MTBF data to ensure maximum uptime for an installation. It is a common misconception, however, that the MTBF value is equivalent to the expected number of operating hours before a product fails, or the "service life". There are several variables that can impact failures.

Aside from component failures, customer use/installation can also result in failure. For example, if a customer misuses a product and then it malfunctions, should that be considered a failure? If a product is delivered DOA because it was not properly packaged, is that a failure?

The MTBF is often calculated based on an algorithm that factors in all of a product's components to reach the sum life cycle in hours. In reality, depreciation modes of the product could limit the life of the product much earlier due to some of the variables listed above. It is very possible to have a product with an extremely high MTBF, but an average or more realistic expected service life.

$$MTBF = 1 / FR1 + FR2 + FR3 + \ldots\ldots\ldots\ldots FRn$$

where FR is the failure rate of each component of the system up to n components MTBF is not just a simple formula. A person certi?ed and educated in calculating MTBF is a good investment. That person must review the MTBF for every component as well as other factors such as operating temperature range, storage temperature range, etc.

Beyond the MTBF calculation, Quality Assurance Managers should track all reported ?eld failures as well as the root cause of those product failures to produce a true snapshot of a product's service life. Since this process takes time, the MTBF and other predictions of reliability for a product are on-going. MTBF can be subject to change. For example, in 2006, RoHS (Restriction of Hazardous Substances) was mandated by the European Community. If a released product is re-developed in order to meet RoHS-compliancy, the entire calculation has to be performed again, since non-RoHS components may have a different life cycle than those that do meet the RoHS standard.

ISO-9001 can also effectively support MTBF. How? Companies that are ISO certi?ed agree to meet the goals of "zero defect" and "continue improvement". With processes in place, a product is developed and tested in numerous ways, including submissions to lab certi?cations appropriate for the product. The result is that before a product is ever introduced into the market, it is as ?awless and as functional as it was intended to be.

3 types of reliability analysis: 1. test-retest, 2. alternate forms, 3. internal consistency.

1. **Test-Retest** - one group takes the same test at two different times. They should score similarly both times relative to each other.
2. **Alternate Forms** - like test-retest, BUT, the questions are slightly different to eliminate "Carryover Effects" (having taken the test once affecting scores on the second administration)
3. **Internal Consistency** - one administration only, the test is split into two halves. If all items are drawn from the same domain, then the two halves should correlate highly with each other.

"X = T + E" - True Score (Reliability) Theory. Any raw score (X) is made up of True Score or "stable characteristics" (T) plus some Error (E).

"T / X" - Proportion test score representing differences in "stable characteristics."

"E / X" - Proportion test score representing "error."

We will never know the exact proportion for any one person, BUT, we can calculate it in general for a group of people.

Reliability Coefficient (r_{xx}) - most simply, the test correlated with itself using Pearson's r. Use meaningful subscripts like "r_{x1x2}" to keep things clear.

If the above is true then:

$\square^2_X = \square^2_T + \square^2_E$ and **rxx** $= \square^2_T / \square^2_X$

10 = 8 + 2 .8 = 8 / 10 (example with a reliable test)

8.21 FACTORS AFFECTING RELIABILITY (ACTUAL OR APPARENT)

A. **Inconsistent Performance** - (with test-retest or alternate forms) makes the test "appear" less reliable than it is.
   1. **True Score Change** - somehow actual knowledge has changed at second testing (carryover effect).
   2. **Error Score Change** - Something about the test situation (noisy?) or person (tired?) is different at second testing.

B. **Sampling Factors (item)** - number and nature of items affect reliability.
   1. **Test Length** - as the test gets longer, it gets more reliable.
   2. **Item Representativeness** - the more completely the items cover (capture) the domain AND not having items that don't really belong to the domain produce higher reliability.

C. Statistical Factors- characteristics of your samples (people)

1. **Range Restriction** - using a sample more "restricted" than the target audience of the test leading to an "underestimation" of the actual reliability.
2. **Range Extension (Expansion)** - using a sample "more varied" than the target audience of the test leading to an "overestimation" of the actual reliability.

8.22 TYPES OF RELIABILITY ANALYSIS—USING TWO SETS OF SCORES

1. **Test-Retest Reliability** - the same group takes the same test at two times (1 & 2), the two sets of scores are correlated using Pearson's r (means and SD formula).
2. **Alternate Forms Reliability** - the same group takes two different but equivalent versions of the same test at two times (1 & 2), the two sets of scores are correlated using Pearson's r (means and SD formula).
3. **Using One Set of Scores (Internal Consistency Reliability)** - tells us something different, the extent to which all items tap the same domain.

   A. Split Half Reliability - simplest method, the test (e.g., 100 items) is split into two halves (50 items each, often odd-even).

   Spearman Brown Prophecy Formula - when the "correction factor" (N) is set at "2," it corrects the split half reliability coefficient.

   Corrected $r_{oe} = (2)\ (r)\ /\ 1 + (2 - 1)\ (r)$

   B. Guttman Formula - Use of Pearson's r for split half reliability assumes the variances of the two halves are about equal. If not, do not use. The Guttman formula can be used instead.

   Guttman $r_{oe} = 2[1 - (\square O^2 - \square E^2)\ /\ \square X^2]$

   C. Cronbach's Alpha (and the two KR formulas) - "compare all possible split halves." Item variances ($\square^2 i$) are summed. This is for **LIKERT** (continuous) items.

   K = number of test items

   $alphar_{xx} = K\ /\ K - 1\ (1 - \square\square^2 i\ /\ \square^2 x)$

Negative Reliabilities - occasionally result when using one of the "alpha" formulas. It means the domain is not as well defined as it should be. If this happens, use regular split half reliability. Even more rarely, this happens with regular split half, then domain is really not well defined and r_{xx} cannot be calculated.

Which Reliability Formula to Use? - If we are measuring a single well focused domain such as a personality trait (shyness), then one of the "alpha" formulas will likely be superior. HOWEVER, if we are measuring a broader domain (a cumulative final exam) then simple split half may be the better way to go.

Standard Error of Measurement and Confidence Intervals - tell us how close we think we have come (and with what level of confidence) to identifying the person's "true score"

Standard Error of Measurement - the standard deviation of the hypothetical distribution of possible X scores a person might have obtained on a given testing.

$$SEM = \square x * SQRT(1 - r_{xx})$$

Confidence Interval - two values (upper and lower bounds) define an interval (centered on the score X). Tells us with what degree of certainty (e.g., 95%) we think the person's "true score" lies between the upper and lower bound values. Most IQ tests are reported in terms of this interval.

$$68\%\ CI = X + \text{or} - 1(SEM)$$

$$95\%\ CI = X + \text{or} - 1.96(SEM)$$

Factors Affecting CI Width:

1. We want our CIs to be "Narrow"
2. Higher levels of confidence (e.g., 95 vs. 90) means a wider interval
3. lower reliability means a wider interval
4. more variability (SD, look back at SEM formula) means a wider interval

8.23 EVALUATION OF MEASUREMENT INSTRUMENTS

- **Reliability** has to do with the consistency of the instrument.
- – **Internal Consistency** (Consistency of the items)
  – **Test-retest Reliability** (Consistency over time)
  – **Interrater Reliability** (Consistency between raters)
  – **Split-half Methods**
  – **Alternate Forms Methods**
- **Validity** of an instrument has to do with the ability to measure what it is supposed to measure and the extent to which it predicts outcomes.
  – **Face Validity**
  – **Construct & Content Validity**
  – **Convergent & Divergent Validity**
  – **Predictive Validity**
  – **Discriminant Validity**

Reliability is synonymous with consistency. It is the degree to which test scores for a an individual test taker or group of test takers are consistent over repeated applications.No psychological test is completely consistent, however, a measurement that is unreliable is worthless.

For Example

A student receives a score of 100 on one intelligence tests and 114 in another or imagine that every time you stepped on a scale it showed a different weight.

8.24 WOULD YOU KEEP USING THESE MEASUREMENT TOOLS

The consistency of test scores is critically important in determining whether a test can provide good measurement.

Because no unit of measurement is exact, any time you measure something (observed score), you are really measuring two things

True Score - the amount of observed score that truly represents what you are intending to measure.

Error Component - the amount of other variables that can impact the observed score

Observed Test Score = True Score + Errors of Measurement

For Example - if you weigh yourself today and weigh 140 lbs. and then weigh yourself tomorrow and weigh 142 lbs., is the 2 pound increase a true measure of your weight gain or could other variables be involvedOther variables may include: food intake, placement of scale, error in the scale itself.

8.25 MEASUREMENT ERROR

- Any fluctuation in test scores that results from factors related to the measurement process that are irrelevant to what is being measured.
- The difference between the observed score and the true score is called the error score.
  S true = S observed - S error
- Developing better tests with less random measurement error is better than simply documenting the amount of error.
  Measurement Error is Reduced By:
  - Writing items clearly
  - Making instructions easily understood
  - Adhering to proper test administration
  - Providing consistent scoring

8.26 DETERMINING RELIABILITY

- There are several ways that a measurements reliability can be determined, depending on the type of measurement the and the supporting data required. They include:
  - Internal Consistency
  - Test-retest Reliability
  - Interrater Reliability
  - Split-half Methods
  - Odd-even Reliability
  - Alternate Forms Methods

8.27 INTERNAL CONSISTENCY

- **Measures the reliability of a test solely on the number of items on the test and the intercorrelation among the items. Therefore, it compares each item to every other item.**
- **If a scale is measuring a construct, then overall the items on that scale should be highly correlated with one another.**
- **There are two common ways of measuring internal consistency ...**
  1. **Cronbach's Alpha:** .80 to .95 (Excellent)
     .70 to .80 (Very Good)
     .60 to .70 (Satisfactory) <.60 (Suspect)
  2. **Item-Total Correlations** - the correlation of the item with the remainder of the items (.30 is the minimum acceptable item-total correlation).

Internal consistency estimates are a function of:

The Number of Items - if we think that each test item is an observation of behaviour, high internal consistency strengthens the relationship — i.e., There is more of it to observe.

Average Intercorrelation - the extent to which each item represents the observation of the same thing observed.

The more you observe a construct, with greater consistency

= Reliability

8.28 SPLIT HALF & ODD-EVEN RELIABILITY

Split Half - refers to determining a correlation between the first half of the measurement and the second half of the measurement (i.e., we would expect answers to the first half to be similar to the second half).

Odd-Even - refers to the correlation between even items and odd items of a measurement tool.

- In this sense, we are using a single test to create two tests, eliminating the need for additional items and multiple administrations.
- Since in both of these types only 1 administration is needed and the groups are determined by the internal componentsof the test, it is referred to as an internal consistency measure.

8.29 SPLIT HALF & ODD-EVEN RELIABILITY WITH ADVANTAGES AND DISADVANTAGES

Possible Advantages

- Simplest method - easy to perform
- Time and Cost Effective

Possible Disadvantages

- Many was of splitting
- Each split yields a somewhat different reliability estimate

Which is the real reliability of the test

8.30 TEST-RETEST RELIABILITY

- Test-retest reliability is usually measured by computing the correlation coefficient between scores of two administrations.

8.31 INTERRATER RELIABILITY

Whenever you use humans as a part of your measurement procedure, you have to worry about whether the results you get are reliable or consistent. People are notorious for their inconsistency. We are easily distractible. We get tired of doing repetitive tasks. We daydream. We misinterpret.

- **For some scales it is important to assess interrater reliability.**
- **Interrater reliability means that if two different raters scored the scale using the scoring rules, they should attain the same result.**

- **Interrater reliability is usually measured by computing the correlation coefficient between the scores of two raters for the set of respondents.**
- **Here the criterion of acceptability is pretty high (e.g., a correlation of at least .9), but what is considered acceptable will vary from situation to situation.**

8.32 Factors Affecting Reliability

- **Administrator Factors**
- **Number of Items on the instrument**
- **The Instrument Taker**
- **Heterogeneity of the Items**
- **Heterogeneity of the Group Members**
- **Length of Time between Test and Retest**

8.33 Administrator Factors

- Poor or unclear directions given during administration or inaccurate scoring can affect reliability.

  For Example - say you were told that your scores on being social determined your promotion. The result is more likely to be what you think they want than what your behavior is.

8.34 Number of Items on the Instrument

- The larger the number of items, the greater the chance for high reliability.

  For Example - it makes sense when you ponder that twenty questions on your leadership style is more likely to get a consistent result than four questions.
- **Remedy: Use longer tests or accumulate scores from short tests.**

8.35 The Test Taker

For Example -If you took an instrument in August when you had a terrible flu and then in December when you were feeling quite good, we might see a difference in your response consistency. If you were under considerable stress of some sort or if you were interrupted while answering the instrument questions, you might give different responses.

8.36 Heterogeneity

Heterogeneity of the Items. The greater the heterogeneity (differences in the kind of questions or difficulty of the question) of the items, the greater the chance for high reliability correlation coefficients.

Heterogeneity of the Group Members. The greater the heterogeneity of the group members in the preferences, skills or behaviors being tested, the greater the chance for high reliability correlation coefficients.

Length of Time between Test and Retest

- The shorter the time, the greater the chance for high reliability correlation coefficients.
- As we have experiences, we tend to adjust our views a little from time to time. Therefore,

the time interval between the first time we took an instrument and the second time is really an "experience" interval.

- Experience happens, and it influences how we see things. Because internal consistency has no time lapse, one can expect it to have the highest reliability correlation coefficient.

8.37 How High Should Reliability Be

- A highly reliable test is always preferable to a test with lower reliability.
  .80 > greater (Excellent)
  .70 to .80 (Very Good)
  .60 to .70 (Satisfactory) <.60 (Suspect)

A reliability coefficient of .80 indicates that 20% of the variability in test scores is due to measurement error.

Generalizability Theory

Theory of measurement that attempts to determine the sources of consistency and inconsistency

- Allows for the evaluation of interaction effects from different types of error sources.
- It is necessary to obtain multiple observations for the sample group of individuals on all the variables that might contribute to causing measurement error (e.g., scores across occasions, across scorers, across alternative forms).
- Allows for the evaluation of interaction effects from different types of error sources.
- **Useful when associated with complex methods:**
  1. The conditions of measurement affect test scores.
  2. Test scores are used for several different purposes.

  For Example - measurement involving subjectivity (e.g., interviews, rating scales) involve bias. Therefore, human judgement could be considered "conditions of measurement"
- If feasible, it is a more thorough procedure for identifying the error component that may enter scores.

8.38 Standard Error of Measurement (SEM)

- SEM is a statistic that obtains the confidence interval for many obtained scores. It represents the hypothetical distribution we would have if someone took a test an infinite # of times.
- A measure that allows one to predict the range of fluctuation that is likely to occur in a single individual's score because of irrelevant, chance factors. This measurement is used in analyzing the reliability of the test in obtaining the "true" score.
- Indicates how much variability in test scores can be expected as a result of measurement error.
- SEM is a function of two factors: reliability of test & variability of test scores. Formula for SEM is :

SM = SD(Sq root of 1 minus reliability)

- The most common use of the SEM is the production of the confidence intervals. The SEM is an estimate of how much error there is in a test.
- The SEM can be looked at in the same way as Standard Deviations. Sixty eight percent of the time the true score would be between plus one SEM and minus one SEM. We could be 68% sure that the students true score would be between +/- one SEM. Between +/- two SEM the true score would be found 96% of the time (e.g., SEM x +/- two SEM)
- Or, if the student took the test 100 times, 64 times the true score would fall between +/ - one SEM.

8.39 Calculation of Reliability

A lot of time has been spent on developing procedures for estimating reliability of electronic equipment. There are generally two categories: (1) predictions based on individual failure rates, and (2) demonstrated reliability based on operation of equipment over time. Prediction methods are based on component data from a variety of sources:failure analysis, life test data, and device physics. For some calculations (e.g. militaryapplication) MIL-HDBK-217 is used, which is considered to be the standard reliabilityprediction method. Vicor also performs calculations using Telcordia Technical ReferenceTR-332 "Reliability Prediction Procedure for Electronic Equipment." Both of theseprediction methods have several assumptions in common, e.g. constant failure rate, theuse of thermal and stress acceleration factors, quality factors, use conditions. The table below highlights the difference in the two methods of calculation.

8.40 Reliability Demonstration Methods

When predicting and demonstrating the reliability of a product, the exact failure time can never be know. Not withstanding this fact, we are required to hypothesize regarding our confidence in the integrity of our numbers. The Chi2distribution is often used in this case because it is a probability distribution that relates the observed to the expected values.

The relationship between failure rate and the Chi2 distribution is as follows:

((100 – CL)/100 CL (Confidence Level) = 60%, 90%.

Degrees of freedom = 2 * number of failures + 2

AF = Acceleration factor, as determined by one of the methods discussed earlier When estimating failure rates, Vicor uses acceleration factors to determine use failure rates based on lab failure rates.

8.41 Calculating Reliability using FIT & MTTF

Establish a method for calculating the standard reliability values *Failure Rate* (λ), *Failures in Time* (FIT) and *Mean Time to Failure* (MTTF) using the Arrhenius *High Temperature Operating Life* (HTOL) model. The focus of this topic is to present the applicable equations, terms and definitions along with an example of an Excel driven reliability calculator used to perform these calculations.

Reliability is defined as the probability that a component or system will continue to perform its intended function under stated operating conditions over a specified period of time.

The reliability level is derived by monitoring the functional stability of a number of representative subjects operating under elevated stress conditions resulting in a statistical prediction of reliability.

Two approaches to establishing a reliability level is to evaluate either the *probability of survival* or the *probability of failure.* Either method is equally effective, but the most common method is to calculate the *probability of failure* or *Rate of Failure* (λ). The values most commonly used when calculating the level of reliability are *FIT (Failures in Time)* and *MTTF (Mean Time to Failure)* or *MTBF (Mean Time between Failures)* depending on type of component or system being evaluated.

8.42 Equations & Calculations

- **Failure Rate (λ)** in this model is calculated by dividing the total number of failures or rejects by the cumulative time of operation. In the HTOL model, the cumulative time of operation is referred to as Equivalent Device Hours (EDH):

$$EDH = D*H*A_F$$

where: **D** = Number of Devices Tested

H = Test Hours per Device

Af = Acceleration Factor derived from the Arrhenius equation

The *Failure Rate (λ) per hour* is shown by:

$$\lambda_{hour} = R/D*H*A_{f=r/EDH}$$

where: **r** = number of failures or reject

- **Acceleration Factor (Af)** is the test time multiplier derived from the Arrhenius equation. This equation calculates the time acceleration value that results from operating a device at an elevated temperature. The test type used to achieve this is generally referred to as *High Temperature Operating Life* (HTOL) or *Burn-in.* More specific terms for these tests depend on the type of technology under test. Tests such as *High Temperature Reverse Bias* (HTRB), *DC Burn-in* and *Alternating Current Operating Life* (ACOL) are technology specific tests within the HTOL category.

Activation energy (Ea) is an empirical value that is the minimum energy required to initiate a specific type of failure mode that can occur within a technology type. Oxide defects, bulk silicon defects, mask defects, electro-migration and contamination are some examples of such failure modes, each with an unique associated Ea. In lieu of using empirical data for each individual failure mode, it is generally accepted that a standard single value of **Ea = 0.7 eV**provides a reasonably accurate average Eavalue for diode type semiconductors.

- To derive a more statistically accurate calculation for *Failure Rate (λ)*, the *number of rejects* (r) is replaced with the probability function using *Chi-squared* (χ_2).

8.43 BUILDING RELIABILITY IN THE PRODUCT

We have established a development management system that covers the entire lifecycle of a product, from the initial market research phase up to when the product is phased out. We build design quality into the development process by breaking the design phase down into detailed processes, in each of which the work details and the conditions for moving to the next process are standardized. In this way, the design quality of the entire product can be assured.

Design for Reliability (DFR) is not a new concept, but it has begun to receive a great deal of attention in recent years. What is DFR? What are the ingredients for designing for reliability, and what is involved in implementing DFR? Should DFR be part of a Design for Six Sigma (DFSS) program, and is DFR the same as DFSS? In this article, we will try to answer these questions and, at the same time, we will propose a general DFR process that can be adopted and deployed with a few modifications across different industries in a way that will fit well into the overall Product Development Process.

Design for Reliability, however, is more specific than these general ideas. It is actually a process. Specifically, DFR describes the entire set of tools that support product and process design (typically from early in the concept stage all the way through to product obsolescence) to ensure that customer expectations for reliability are fully met throughout the life of the product with low overall life-cycle costs. In other words, DFR is a systematic, streamlined, concurrent engineering program in which reliability engineering is weaved into the total development cycle. It relies on an array of reliability engineering tools along with a proper understanding of when and how to use these tools throughout the design cycle. This process encompasses a variety of tools and practices and describes the overall order of deployment that an organization needs to follow in order to design reliability into its products.

he development management system

The major development processes and the system used to manage them

The figure below shows the processes we use to develop a semiconductor. Products are developed under the control of our development management system starting from when we carry out market research in the target area and first plan a product. At all major points in the development process, that is, when we determine the target specifications, when we develop and evaluate a prototype, and when we start mass-producing a product, we implement a decision check point (DCP). The development management system also extends beyond product launch, covering the entire lifecycle of the product up until end-of-life. This is how we can ensure total product quality.

8.44 DEVELOPMENT PROCESSES AND DCPS

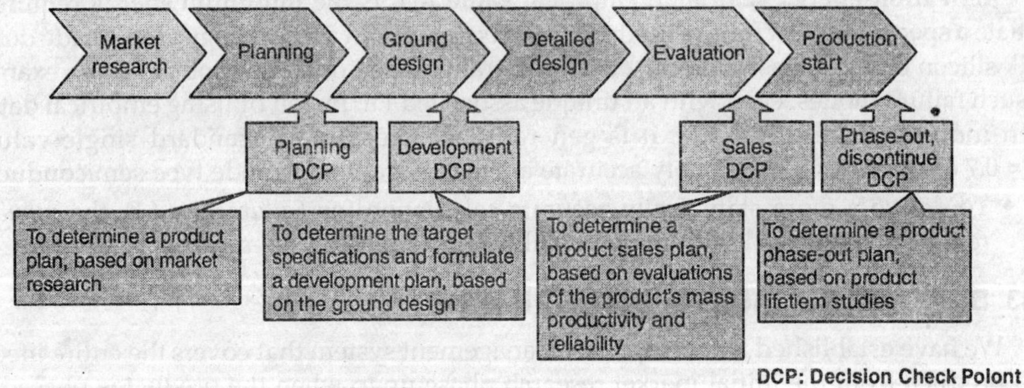

Building quality into each development process

The major development processes

The figure below shows the major development processes and specific design phases.

Development processes and specific design phases

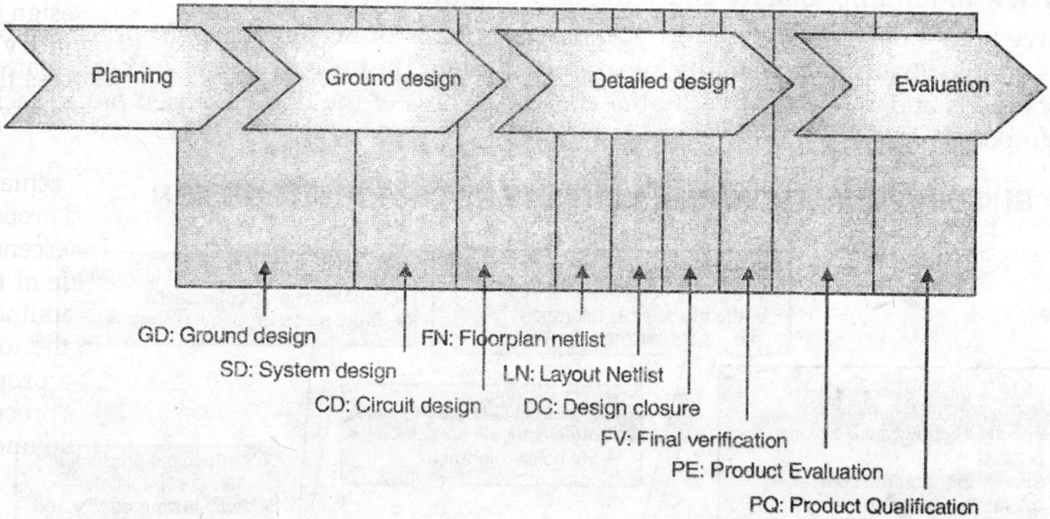

8.45 DIFFERENCES IN DEVELOPMENT PROCESSES USED FOR EACH SEMICONDUCTOR PRODUCT GROUP

The development processes we use are optimized to suit the characteristics of each semiconductor product group.

We handle a large variety of semiconductor products. The design phases required for each type will therefore differ. When designing ASICs, for example, the functional specifications are usually designed by the customer, and we design the rest. The figure below shows the design phases used for each of our semiconductor product groups.

8.46 DESIGN PHASES OPTIMIZED FOR EACH PRODUCT GROUP

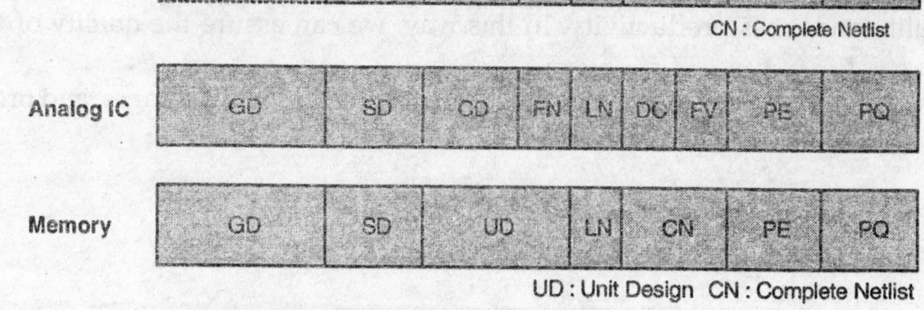

* ASSP : Application Specific Standard Product
ASCP : Application Specific Custom Product

Overview of building quality and reliability into product design

We hold a design review (DR) at the major points of all development processes in order to build quality and reliability into product design. The design reviews are participated in by experts and are used to verify the appropriateness of the design carried out in each design phase.

8.47 BUILDING QUALITY AND RELIABILITY INTO PRODUCT DESIGN

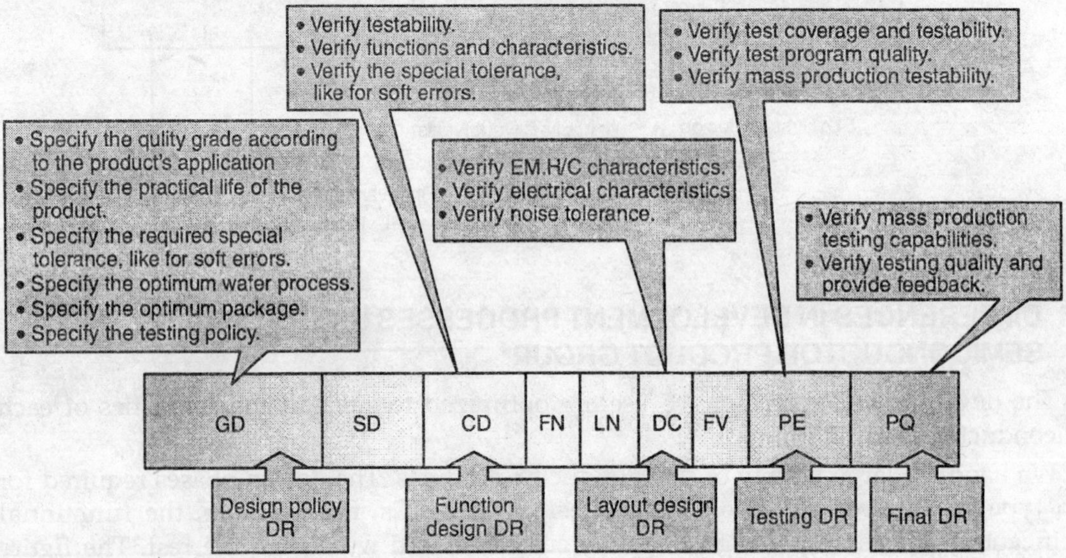

8.48 INTERPRETATION OFTEST RESULT

The figure below shows the system we use to evaluate prototypes created during semiconductor development. Generally, we determine the wafer and assembly (packaging) processes to be used before we start developing a new semiconductor. If the wafer and packaging processes themselves are also new, we will plan the process technologies required for each in conjunction with product development. We then model and evaluate these new processes to verify features such as performance, quality, and reliability. Next, we create a prototype of the new semiconductor to be supplied to the customer using these verified processes. This prototype is then evaluated to verify its functions and performance, as well as its reliability and mass productivity. In this way, we can assure the quality of the new product.

Overview of system used to evaluate new wafer processes, new packages, and prototypes

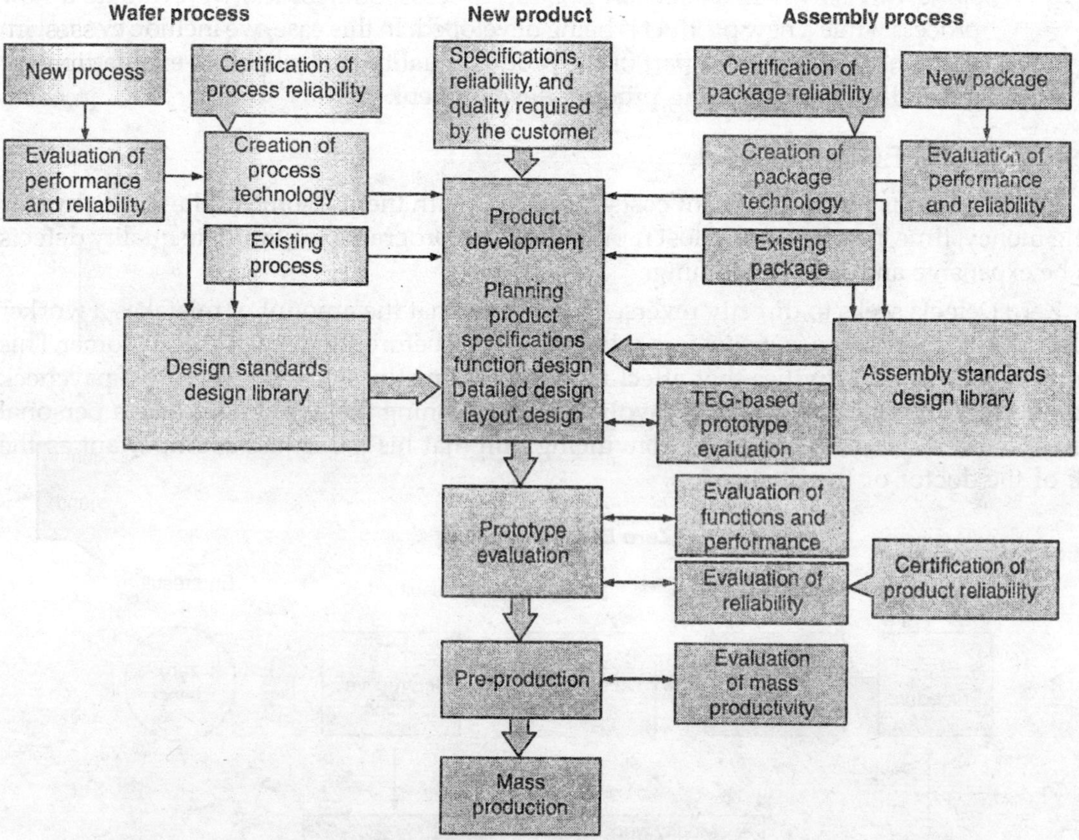

The objectives of each area of evaluation and the items evaluated are outlined below.

- Evaluation of functions and performance
  - The functions and performance of the prototype are evaluated to check that they meet the required specifications. We also check for any variations in the process that could affect mass production capability.
- Evaluation of reliability
  - The reliability of the prototype is evaluated to check that it satisfies the required level of quality and reliability. We also check for any variations in the process to be used for mass production and evaluate the environment in which the product is to be used. If an existing wafer or assembly process is to be used and the quality and reliability of that process has already been verified, the reliability evaluation will focus on the quality and reliability of the product itself.
- New process evaluation
  - If a new wafer or assembly process is to be used, the technology required for that process is created before product development starts. The performance, quality, and reliability of each process is evaluated and verified using a TEG (test element group: a dedicated evaluation chip) or a typical product. After the new process has been verified, we start developing the semiconductor product in the

same way as when we use an existing process. Sometimes, we evaluate a new process while a new product is being developed. In this case, we include evaluation of the new process as a part of the product quality and reliability evaluations we generally conduct during product development.

8.49 ZERO DEFECTS – MODEL

Quality defects have significant costs associated with them – some of the most obvious being money, time, resources, and lost reputation. And programs to eliminate quality defects can be expensive and time consuming.

Zero Defects seeks to directly reverse the attitude that the amount of mistakes a worker makes doesn't matter since inspectors will catch them before they reach the customer.This stands in contrast to activities that affect the worker directly, such as receiving a paycheck in the correct amount. Zero Defects involves reconditioning the worker "to take a personal interest in everything he does[,] by convincing him that his job is just as important as the task of the doctor or the dentist."

Zero Defects - Model

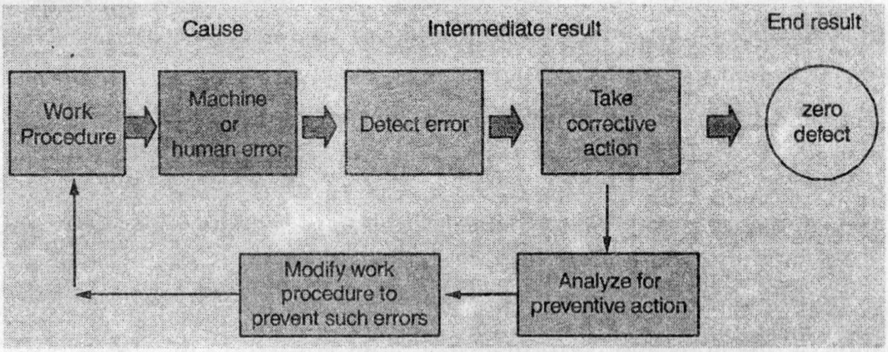

SUMMARY

A defect is defined as a nonconformance of a quality characteristic (e.g., strength, width response time) to its specification. DPMO is stated in opportunities per million units for convenience: Processes that are considered highly-capable (e.g., processes of Six Sigmaquality) are those that experience only a handful of defects per million units produced (or services provided).

Exercise Questions

1. What is BenchMarking?
2. What is product BenchMarking?
3. List any four objectives for benchmarking.
4. Why site visits are necessary in a benchmarking process?
5. What is house of quality?

6. What are the objectives of QFD?
7. List any three benefits of QFD.
8. What is target?
9. What is TPM?
10. What are the objectives of TPM?
11. What is meant by availability?
12. What is meant by performance efficiency?
13. Why TPM is required?
14. What are the objectives of FMEA?
15. What is down time?
16. What is FMEA?
17. Define risk priority number. Also state its significance.
18. Define reliability.
19. What is Quality function deployment?
20. What is meant by detection?
21. Define maintenance.
22. Define predictive maintenance.
23. List the types of maintenance.
24. Write down the philosophy of quality loss function.
25. What are the types of loss measurements in TPM?
26. Write the step by step procedure of implementing a benchmarking process in an organization.
27. (a) Discuss the different types of benchmarking.
    (b) List out the benefits of benchmarking.
28. List out the step by step procedure to build the house of quality.
29. What are the benefits of QFD?
30. Briefly explain the Taguchi's quality lost function with an illustration
31. Write the step by step procedure to develop a TPM programme in an organization.
32. Explain the different types of maintenance techniques in detail.
33. Write the step by step procedure for implementing a FMEA of a product.
34. (a) List out the benefits of the FMEA.
    (b) Discuss the different types of FMEA.
36. The specifications of a particular product are 25 ± 3 and the average repair cost is Rs.90. Determine the quality loss function and the loss when $X = 23$.

❑

ISO 9000

9

Based on ISO rules, all standards are to be reviewed every 5 years. The first revision of the ISO 9000 standard took place in 1994. However, because of inadequate experience in the usage of these standards, the 1994 revision of the standard was limited in character. The basic structure of the standards was retained and the revision was mainly intended to bring greater clarity in the requirements for ease of implementation

The ISO-9000 standards have been used by hundreds of thousands of companies of different types and sizes during the past decade. During its usage certain major inadequacies have been observed which are shown in subsequent headings.

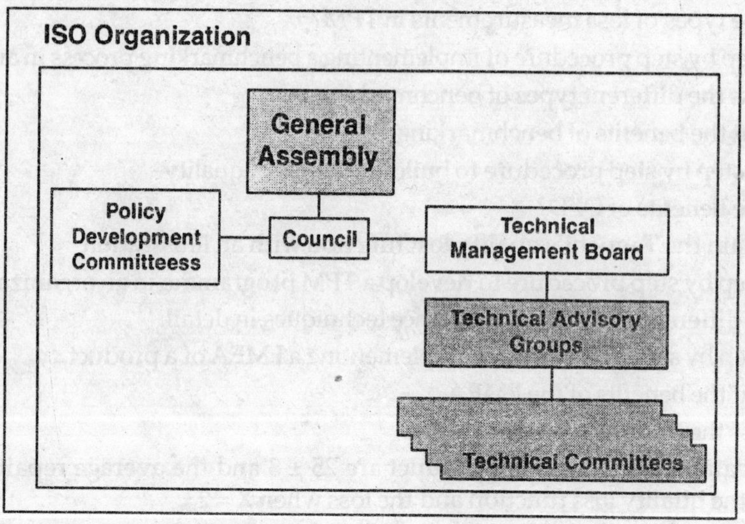

9.1 DEFINITION

ISO9000 is a series of standards, development and published by the ISO that define, establish and maintain an effective quality assurance system for manufacturing and service industries.

9.2 WHAT IS ISO

- ISO is a name used for the **International Organization for Standardization.**
- ISO is not an acronym.
- It was formed in 1947 in Geneva Switzerland.
- It is a federation of national standard bodies of 143 countries.

9.3 NEED

1. By implementing an organization can benefit many industries such as banking, health care, manufacturing etc.
2. The goal of this implementation is to achieve customer satisfaction at its highest value.
3. To compete in domestic markets.
4. To improve quality system.

9.4 OBJECTIVE

1. To promote development of standardization of facilitate international exchange of goods and services.
2. To promote cooperation in intellectual, scientific, technological and economic activity.

9.5 PRINCIPLE

PRINCIPLE

- **PLAN,**
- **DO,**
- **CHECK &**
- **ACT**

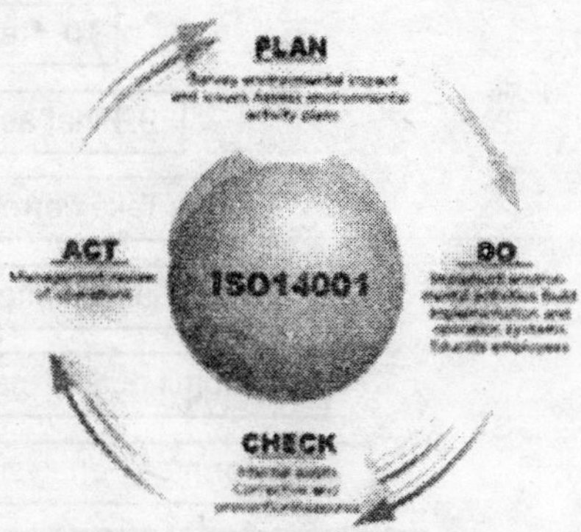

A The structure of ISO 9001:1994 was heavily oriented towards the manufacturing sector, making it difficult for application to the service sector and other types of organizations.

B It was a stand-alone document with no relationship to current quality management practices and business operations, causing confusion and conflict with existing quality control practices.

C Although higher-level standard in the shape of ISO-9004 already existed, there was no alignment between these two standards due to which the ISO-9004 standard was largely ignored by companies adopting ISO-9001.

D There was over-emphasis on documentation throughout almost all the requirements in the standard making it a bureaucratic system when implemented.

E Customer relationship management had been given inadequate attention and was limited to contract review. As a result, customers of most ISO- 9001 certified companies had not noticed any significant change after certification.

F Basically ISO-9001was a consistency standard at the existing level of quality. The need for continuous quality improvement has not been incorporated. This led to the adoption of additional quality improvement methodologies causing diffusion of quality management efforts.

G With the standard required various activities by different departments, but need for a proper vertical and horizontal communication system for proper coordination was not addressed.

H There were three certifiable standards in the form of ISO-9001, ISO-9002 and ISO-9003. For some businesses particularly in these services sector it was difficult to determine which standard would apply. ISO-9003 was literally ignored because it was focused only to inspection and testing, the concepts which had become obsolete in the light of the new quality philosophy.

I Although the standard called for the establishment of a documented quality system and its deployment in different areas no basis was provided against which the effectiveness of such a quality system could be assessed.

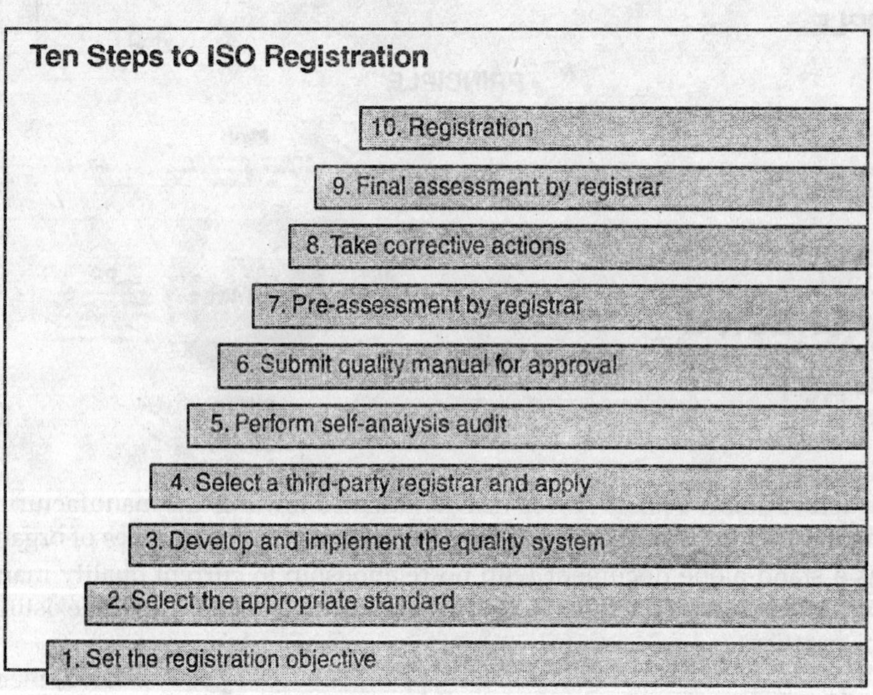

Six Essential Elements of a Successful Registration Effort

- Senior Management Commitment to the Effort
- Appropriate ISO 9000 Training
- An Effective Management Review Process
- Documentation of the Quality System
- An Effective Internal Auditing System
- An Effective Corrective Action Process

9.6 THE PHILOSOPHY BEHIND THE ISO9000 SERIES

The philosophy behind the ISO9000 series is that quality should be built into the systems and procedures of the organization, where the emphasis is on prevention rather than cure. To be able to meet the demands of ISO9000 an organization has to build quality in at each stage, from design through to delivery, assessment and evaluation, through a formal and rigorous management system to ensure conformity of the product or service to its specification. The aim is to produce a consistent level of product or service that is fit for purpose.

ISO9000 requires that all the activities necessary to produce the product or service be documented if the quality system is to conform to the standard. An educational establishment would, for example, need to document all the activity concerned with the delivery of its programmes, including selection, interviewing, induction, discipline, assessment, records of achievement, advice and guidance, etc. ISO9000 places a considerable discipline on those intending to use it. Putting a system in place is not easy or straightforward. It involves a large investment of resources and staff time. Everybody in the institution needs to understand its implications and to work to the systems and follow the procedures that have been put in place. Many teachers might consider the emphasis on following detailed written instructions stifling to initiative and excessively bureaucratic, although for or others they can provide useful guidance and direction Applying ISO9000:2000 to education The previous ISO9000 series gave problems to educational institutions because of the manufacturing origins of its language. It needed considerable translation for the educational context. It was based on the notion of conformity of product that was difficult to translate in an educational setting, especially if the product was defined as the student.

However, ISO9000:2000 is now about process and is far more accessible to service organizations and to educational establishments. The ISO9000:2000 series is based on eight principles that can be used by the management team of an organization to improve performance.

These principles are:

- **Customer focus**—this is the notion common to all quality processes that quality consists of meeting and exceeding the expectations of customers. Applying this principle could entail an organization researching customer needs and expectations and measuring how well they are performing against these expectations. In the educational context the customers could be the students, their parents, their future employers or other educational establishments.
- **Leadership**—a leader's ability to establish a vision and purpose is the key to a successful organization. Leaders inspire others, provide them with the resources to do their job, and ensure that the needs of all parties, staff, customers, the local communities and others are identified and met. Leadership has been shown to be the key variable in successful schools. The emphasis on leadership here works well and conforms to the research findings that are being generated on school improvement.
- **Involvement of people**—organizations need their people to use their abilities for the benefit of the organization. Ensuring that this happens is important for innovation and creativity. Without staff—both teachers and support staff—educational establishments could not function. Planning the needs of staff and ensuring that their talents are used to the full are key indicators of success.
- **Process approach**—this is about the efficiency and effectiveness of the organization's core activities and the importance of developing a systematic approach to their management. The establishment of clear roles and responsibilities and identifying key activities are some of the issues that are important in a process approach. The systematic management of the teaching and learning process is what is required to conform to the requirements of the process principle.
- Systems approach to management—this is about recognizing the interrelatedness of processes and aligning them to achieve the best results. It is about ensuring that there are clear systems in place and establishing clear targets and goals. Having clear indicators of performance and ensuring that there are management processes to meet those targets are key aspects of educational management.
- **Continuous improvement**—continuous improvement is the objective of all quality systems. It is about ensuring that people have the training and skills required to make improvements and ensures that there is an organization-wide approach to the improvement of performance. Schools and other educational establishments need to be as concerned with continuous improvement as any other organization. One of the key factors in this is the importance of staff training and development and the need to ensure that there is systematic approach to the development of staff and an adequate investment in their training.

Factual approach to decision making—this requires that decisions be made on the basis of information and data. It ensures that data is available and decisions are informed by available information. Data on students and their performance and on such things as the value added being given to them through the educational process is clearly important to good decision making in education.

- **Mutually beneficial supplier relationships**—any organization is in a mutually beneficial partnership with its suppliers that can create value for both parties. It is about clear and open communication, undertaking joint projects and pooling expertise. The importance of supplier relationships for educational establishments is clear. Senior schools have relationships with their feeder schools and universities have similar relationships in the school systems. Relationships with community groups also need to be considered under this heading.

9.7 MAJOR CHANGES IN THE NEW STANDARD

ISO-9000-2000 marks significant departure from the earlier versions of the standard. It has been developed abinitio in light of experience gained during the application of its predecessors for over ten years and after taking into account the needs of users of the standards and other stake holders.

9.8 CUSTOMER RELATIONSHIP

'Customer satisfaction' is recognized as the main driving force for any organization. Therefore, the new standard lays greater stress on interaction between the organization and its customers, before, during and after delivery of any product or service. This interaction helps to clearly understand customer requirements and monitor information about customer satisfaction as a measure of system performance.

One of the major complaints against the previous standard was that it required excessive documentation. The new standard has significantly reduced mandatory documented procedures. It has given greater flexibility to the organization to determine which procedures and instructions need to be documented, based on the nature of its activities, level of training and established work practices.

9.9 ADVANTAGES

9.9.1 For the customer

Increase satisfaction and growth in confidence.

9.9.2 For the company

1. Well defined organization and responsibilities.
   i.e., minimize grey areas and possible resources wastage.
2. Establishment of proper communication channel.
   - A greater degree of internal control
   - Greater productivity and cost reduction
   - Evidence of compliance
   - Recognition of standard achieved
   - Greater productivity and cost reduction

9.10 DISADVANTAGES

- Assessment and certification are costly.
- Need to change and accept new working practices may strain management.
- Unless carefully planned it becomes non cost effective and burdensome.
- ISO9001 only complements and supplements product quality standards.

9.11 STRUCTURE OF SERIES

Standard	Content	Application
ISO9000	Provides definition and concepts. Explain how to select other standards for a given business.	All industries including software development
ISO9001	Quality assurance in design. development, production, installation and servicing	Engineering and construction forms, manufacturers that design, develop, install and service products
ISO9002	Quality assurance in production and installation	Companies in the chemical process industries that are not involved in product design or after sales service.
ISO9003	Quality assurance in test and inspection	Small shops, divisions within a firm, equipment distribution that inspect and test supplied products.
ISO9004	Quality management and quality system elements	All industries

9.12 ISO9001:2000 REQUIREMENTS

1. Scope
2. Normative reference
3. Terms and definitions
4. Quality management system
5. Management responsibility
6. Resource management
7. Product realisation
8. Measurement, analysis and improvement

- **Scope.** The specified requirements are generic and applicable to all organizations, regardlessoft their type and size.
- **Normative Reference.**
- **Terms and Vocabulary.** Supplier, Organization, Customer.

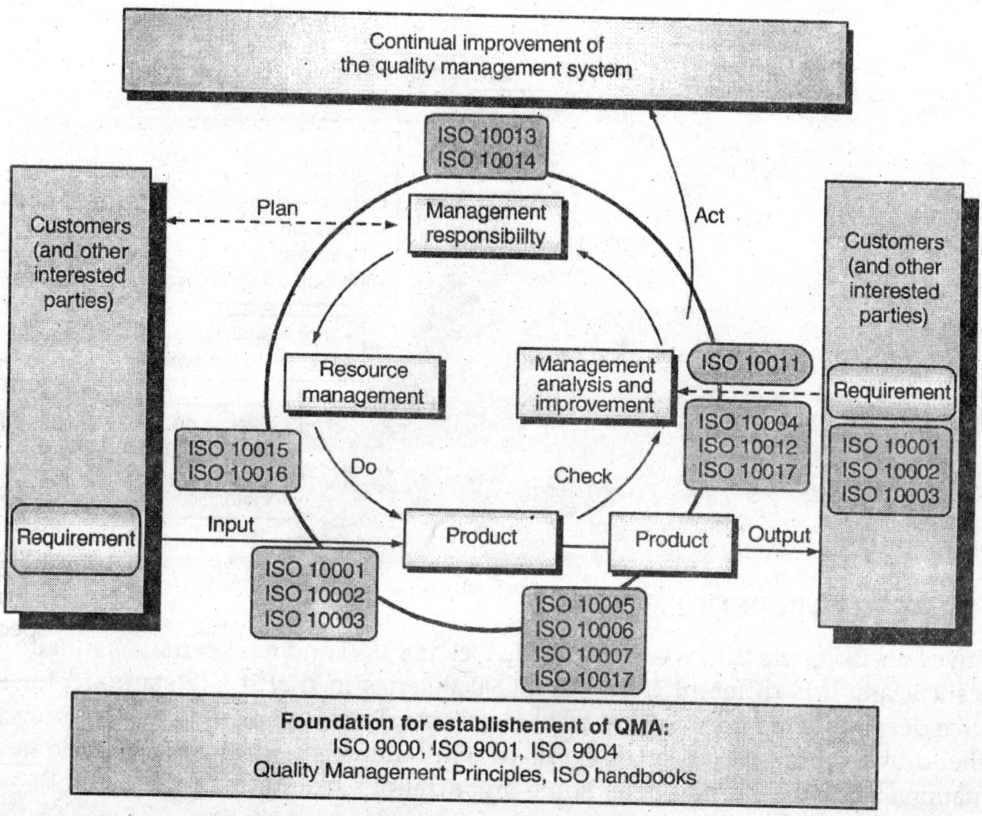

9.13 DOES ISO9000 GUARANTEE QUALITY

ISO9000 only sets the standard for the quality system. It does not set the standards that the institution or its learners should be achieving. The staff of the institution together with its customers and those to whom it is accountable are the arbitrators of standards of teaching and learning. What ISO9000 can do is to assure that there are systems in place to deliver those standards once they have been decided.

ISO9000 cannot guarantee consistency of standards between institutions. This is an important consideration because so much attention is given in British and other educational systems to the question of the consistency of standards between institutions.

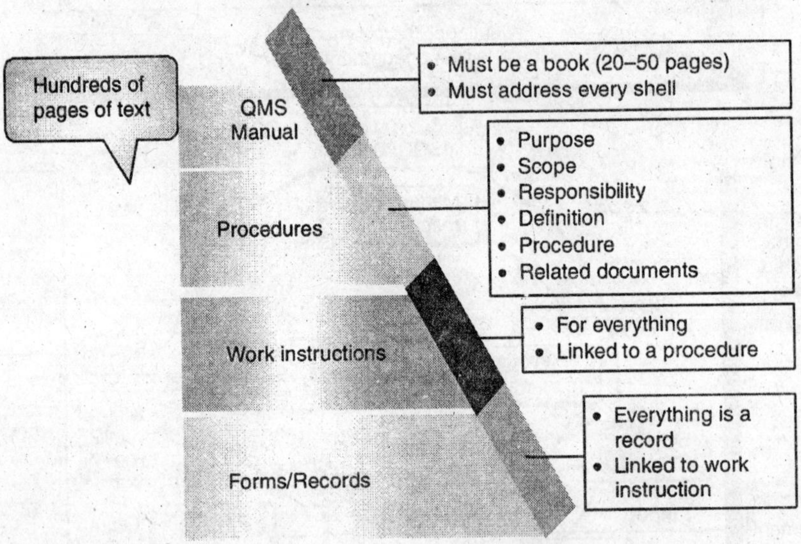

9.14 INVESTORS IN PEOPLE UK

Investors in People (IIP) was launched in October 1991 and has been substantially revised in recent years. It is different from the ISO9000 series in that it is a standard for human resource development and training, and as such is only one element in a TQM programme. Its other drawback is that it is a UK standard without international parallels, and its lack of international recognition may deter some organizations from pursuing it.

Investors in People is based on the experience of successful organizations in the UK that have recognized that a skilled and motivated workforce is crucial to their success. IIP provides a methodology for developing staff in ways that assist in the achievement of organization goals. The essential principles that have to be satisfied for an organization to become an Investor in People are:

- Commitment—an Investor in People is fully committed to developing its people in order to achieve its aims and objectives.
- Planning—an Investor in People is clear about its aims and objectives and what its people need to do to achieve them.
- Action—an Investor in People develops its people effectively effectively in order to improve its performance.
- Evaluation—an Investor of People understands the impact of its investment in people on its performance.

As with other quality standards, evidence is required by the external auditors who undertake the audit. It is a more flexible and less paperbased audit than that undertaken for ISO9000. The auditors gather their evidence largely by holding discussions with members of staff. The institution will need to demonstrate the spirit of IIP, not just the existence of a formal system to guarantee it.

Investors in People was developed for business but it is readily adaptable to education. A number of schools, colleges and universities have seen the possibilities in it for their quality development initiatives.

The process is one that appeals to many educational institutions who already have well-developed processes for staff development review.

Like ISO9000, Investors in People does not guarantee quality. However, it can be an important indication that the institution is developing a systematic management process to improve the effectiveness of its most valuable resource—its staff.

Various Logos of ISO9001

Various Logos used in p'industries

PS 9000 is an application of the standard for Pharmaceutical Packaging Materials.

high GMP conditions are mauntained

9.15 THE DEMING PRIZE (JAPAN)

The Deming Prize is the Japanese national prize for quality and it is not available internationally. The Union of Japanese Scientists and Engineers established it in 1950 to commemorate W Edwards Deming's contribution in Japan to total quality control.

Winning the Deming prize for mastering total quality control has been an obsession for many of the big names in Japanese business. There are a number of prize categories. Prizes are awarded to a large corporation, a division, a factory and to medium and small companies.

There is also a Deming prize for individuals who have made an outstanding contribution to statistical theory. In addition, there is the Japanese Quality Control Medal established in 1969, for which companies can compete five years after winning the Deming Prize. To qualify for a prize the top management of a company must make the application. Outside experts then carry out an exhaustive quality audit to determine the winner. Many of the household names of Japanese industry have won it, including Toshiba, Toyota and Komatsu.

Interestingly, while the prize criteria are exceptionally demanding, they do not require applicants to conform to a particular model of quality. Rather the applicants are expected to understand their own situation, establish their own themes and objectives and set their own improvement and transformational goals. The results and the processes used are scrutinized by the examiners, as are the future prospects of the organization. The examiners evaluate whether the applicant's processes were commensurate with their situation.

9.15.1 The Malcolm Baldrige National Quality Award(United States)

The Malcolm Baldrige National Quality Award is the US equivalent of the prestigious Japanese Deming Prize. The award was established by the US Congress in 1987 and was named in honour of former Secretary of State Malcolm Baldrige who was a keen proponent of quality management as the key to national prosperity. The US Commerce Department's National Institute of Standards and Technology manages the award.

The Malcolm Baldrige award is not a standard like ISO9000. Rather it is an annual competition. The award is designed to recognize US companies that excel in quality achievement and quality management. The awards are given annually in the following categories: manufacturing, service, and small businesses. In 1999, additional awards were introduced in health care and education. The award concentrates on:

- results and service;
- the involvement of a variety of trade and professional groups;
- innovative approaches to quality;
- human resources and a customer focus;
- the importance of sharing information.

The Malcolm Baldrige criteria fit extremely well with the Deming philosophy of quality. There is a strong emphasis on the non-procedural aspects of quality such as leadership, human resource management, including employee well-being and morale, and customer satisfaction.

Unlike ISO9000, which is about whether an organization complies with its own quality system, the Malcolm Baldridge award focuses on results and continuous improvement. Applications are examined against criteria that are regularly updated. Seven categories make up the award criteria. These are:

- Leadership—examines how senior executives guide the organization and how the organizations addresses its responsibilities to the public andpractises good citizenship.
- Strategic planning—examines how the organization sets strategic directions and how it determines key action plans.
- Customer and market focus—examines how the organization determines requirements and expectations of customers and markets.

- Information and analysis—examines the management, effective use, and analysis of data and information to support key organization processes and the organization's performance management system.
- Human resource focus—examines how the organization enables its workforce to develop its full potential and how the workforce is aligned with the organization's objectives.
- Process management—examines aspects of how key production/delivery and support processes are designed, managed and improved.
- Business results—examines the organization's performance and improvement in its key business areas: customer satisfaction, financial and market place performance, human resources, supplier and partner performance, and organizational performance. The category also examines how organizations perform relative to competitors.

9.16 GENICHITAGUCHI

Genichi Taguchi has developed methods for on-line & off-line quality control which formed the basis of his approach towards total quality assurance. His methods are primarily used by designers & engineers to optimize settings so that the products are robust. These methods are intended as problem solving tools in the early stages of product development cycle. His broad tenets are given on the following.

I. Minimize loss to the society

1. The aim of a good design is tominimize loss to the customer and the society .
2. **Sources of loss :** Product life , wear and tear, set up time etc.

II. Robust & simple design

A good design is the optimal trade off between cost and performance and must aim at *simplicity* . It is easier to make complicated designs , but it takes a genius to simplify the design. Costs are reduced as a result of :

1. Fast assembly & production
2. Robustness
3. Fewer suppliers & less administration.

III. Reduce Signal to noise ratio

A good design should aim at reducing ***Signal to noise ratio.***

Televisions emit both signal and noise. The signal consists of sound and picture. It is the desired part of transmission . The noise is the unwanted part of transmission.

9.17TAGUCHI - QUALITY IMPERATIVES

- Quality losses result from product failure after sale. Product 'robustness' is more a function of product design than on-line control, however stringent the manufacturing processes.
- Robust products deliver a strong 'signal' regardless of external 'noise' and with a minimum of internal 'noise'. Any strengthening of design, that is, any market increase in the signal-to-noise ratios of component parts, will simultaneously improve the robustness of the product as a whole.

- To set targets at maximum signal-to-noise ratios, develop a system of trials that allows you to analyze change in overall system performance according to the average effect of change in component parts, that is, when you subject parts to varying values, stresses and experimental conditions. In new products, average effects may be most efficiently discerned by means of 'orthogonal arrays'.
- To build robust products, set ideal target values for components and then minimize the average of the square of deviations for combined components, averaged over the various customer-user conditions.
- Before product go on to manufacturing, tolerances are set. Overall quality loss then increases by the square of deviation from the target value, that is, by the quadratic formula L = DC, where the constant C, is determined by the cost of the counter-measure that might be employed in the factory. This is the 'quality loss function'.
- Virtually nothing gained in shipping a product that just barely satisfies the corporate standard over a product that just fails. Get on target, don't just try to stay in spec.
- Work relentlessly to achieve designs that can be produced consistently: demand consistency from the factory. Catastrophic stack-up is more likely from scattered deviation within specifications than from consistent deviation outside. Where deviation from target is consistent, adjustment to the target is possible.
- A concerned effort to reduce product failure in the field will simultaneously reduce the number of defectives in the factory. Strive to reduce variances in the components of the product and variances will be reduced in the production system as a whole.
- Competing proposals for capital equipment or competing proposals for on-line interventions may be compared by adding the cost of each proposal to average quality loss, that is, the deviations expected from it.

9.18 JUST-IN-TIME (JIT)

ODAY manufacturing companies are becoming increasingly aware that excellence in manufacturing can provide a competitive weapon to compete in sophisticated worldwide markets. In order to compete effectively, companies must be capable of manufacturing innovative product of high quality at a low cost,and also provide a first class customer services. At the same time, they must have the flexibility to cope with short product life cycle, demands for greater product variety from more discriminating customers and increasing international competition. World-class manufacturing companies have responded to these competitive demandsby changing their traditional production system. To eliminate waste and improve quality, an innovation approachto inventory control called the Just-in-Time (JIT) system was developed by the Japanese-TaiichiOhno, but has gained popularity throughout the world.TaiichiOhno was considered to be the creator of the Toyota Productionsystem and the father of the JIT system. JIT production system means an organization purchases materialsand parts and produces components just when they are needed in the production process. Goods are not produceduntil it is time for them to be shipped to a customer. Many organizations adopt JIT systems to eliminate sources of manufacturing waste by producing the right part in the right place at the right time.

The goal is tohave minimum or zero inventories, because holding inventory is a non-value-added activity.

The main goals of JIT manufacturing system are eliminate non-value-adding activities, to increase the focusupon product quality throughout the production process, reduction of inventory level, space requirements, wastedmaterials, time and effort. Plants are design for maximizing efficiency which smoother production flow withfewer disruptions. Improve the organization's ability to compete with others and remain competitive over the long run.

9.19 RELATIONSHIPTO QUALITY

JIT cuts cost of quality ,JIT improves quality, Better quality means less inventory and better, easier-to-employ JIT system.

9.20 JIT IN PURCHASING

Management accounting are familiar with the use of Just-in –Time (JIT) in purchasing with the aim to reduce the finished goods inventory that a company has to keep and to overcome or avoid the delay of raw material at ordering, receiving and incoming inspection. This means that JIT purchasing enable the materials to be delivered in time once it is needed for production. JIT purchasing works well to reduce wastes in many forms such as

waste in raw materials, times, transaction process, etc. There are several goals of JIT purchasing: Firstly, to remove or eliminate inessential activities or process in the production. Secondly, to eliminate the carrying of stock inventory.Thirdly, to eliminate of transit inventory and finally to improve the quality and reliability of the suppliers.

However, to implement JIT program effectively, a series of changes needs to be made on to the production process. If these changes are not made, production will increase the level of work-in-process (WIP) inventory, which will result in higher cost of production. JIT also requires the plant to be balanced so that each task has the same output level to create transfer batches of equal size. JIT required fewer inventories, which led to reduction in manufacturing costs, better responsiveness to customer requirements, and the opportunity for better product quality. JIT results in lowering WIP inventories, which leads to lower investment in manufacturing costs. The most challenging area for most manufacturers in achieving JIT system can only be operated successfully when the material being fed into it are of sufficient quality and delivered on time. Therefore, unless the quality and delivery of purchased material does not create production issues, the purchasing function should begin to establish a JIT supplier base.

9.21 IMPROVED ORGANIZATIONAL EFFICIENCY

9.21.1 Why use JIT

Just in Time Inventory Control eliminates waste and improves quality, and in the process, improves all-around organizational efficiency. JIT improves organizational efficiency in five major ways:

- The Just in Time method entails sourcing the required raw material or item for processing on demand, and scheduling the work based on order or demand for the product. This synchronization of supply with production, and production with demand improves the flow of goods and reduces the need for storage facilities.

- JIT's focus on eliminating waste from the production process leads to redesign of the workspace to ensure a smooth flow of goods or processes, eliminating redundant tasks, and minimizing transportation of the product across the workspace.
- The traditional manufacturing process call for "batch" manufacturing or manufacturing of a particular component or model in a "lot" before moving on to another "batch" or "lot." JIT makes it possible to manufacture even single pieces or components without any delays.
- JIT's system of kanban or specific instructions for each worker eliminates all scope for mistakes in the workfloor.
- The relentless effort to eliminate waste and achieve zero-defects improves productivity, cuts down manufacturing time, and improves product quality.

9.22 REDUCED COSTS

Among the major benefits of JIT system is the elimination of raw material, inventory and product storage costs.

The traditional notion is to consider raw materials or inventory of finished goods as an asset. The JIT method turns this concept upside down and considers stock as waste or dead investment incurring opportunity costs.

The JIT system sources raw materials close to the manufacturing time, and ships out the product to the customer immediately without storage, leading to substantial savings resultant from not storing raw materials or stocking up finished goods. Deploying funds tied up in raw materials and inventories to generate additional revenue do wonders to the finances of the organization.

JIT's thrust on elimination of waste from the production process and improving product quality reduces damaged goods and saves on Human Resources costs considerably.

All these cost savings translate to a lower manufacturing price for the product.

Improved Supplier Relationships

The success of JIT depends on the ability of the supplier to produce raw materials on demand.The benefits of JIT extend to improved relationship with the suppliers on many counts:

JIT develops a system of effective communication with the supplier, specifying the exact product required in exact quantity and the specific time of delivery. This eliminates all scope of misunderstandings or miscommunication.

The success of JIT requires reliable suppliers and organizations takes the initiative to upgrade supplier competencies and establish a long-term relationship with the supplier to ensure compatibility and standardized products.

The exact nature of order and the long-term proactive relationship with suppliers eliminate the need for inspection of received goods

Facilitated Customization and Increased Customer Satisfaction

Just in Time Inventory adjusts production to demand, making possible the fulfillment of custom orders without any extra effort or extra time, leading to increased customer satisfaction.

A practical example in this aspect relates to McDonald's. The application of JIT principles has helped McDonald's cater to the order of any special type of burger with equal ease and in the same time as any other burger. Without JIT, the workforce would be geared to deliver fast-moving burgers fast, but a peak-hour order of a rare item on the menu or a special order would throw the kitchen out of gear.

9.23 JIT DEVELOPS HUMAN RESOURCES

Implementation of JIT requires workforce flexibility and a highly skilled and committed workforce. The advantages of Just in Time Inventory extend to the company's Human Resources in the following ways:

- Investment in training to develop existing skill and broaden skill sets.
- More effective usage of employees with multiple skills.
- Increased motivation through job rotation.
- Better productivity

The remarkable transformation made by organizations that have adopted JIT answers the question, why use JIT? The many JIT benefits make it one of the most successful management strategies ever.

SUMMARY

The ISO-9000 standards have been used by hundreds of thousands of companies of different types and sizes during the past decade.

When JIT manufacturing systems come across to accounting, the inventory costing system can be eliminated by the minimal inventory level at an optimal point in the JIT system. The firm can reduce the inventory costing system costs by improving the inventory control system. Furthermore, the change in the accounting system also influences the financial statement of the firms. After adopting the JIT manufacturing system, the inventory costing costs are eliminated and result in a low inventory holding costs. All these factors increase the profit of the firm, result in more attractive financial statement to the end users.

Exercise Questions

1. What is ISO-9000 explain its concept in terms of Quality Management.
2. Explain ISO-9000 series.
3. Explain Taguchi method.
4. Write Down JIT with details.

❑

MODEL TEST PAPER

QUALITY MANAGEMENT MODEL PAPER

Q.1. Define :

Quality

Quality control

Total quality

Total quality control

Total quality management

Q.2. What challenges Business / Industry has to face?

Q.3. What is ISO? What is ISO Quality System?

Q.4. What is the diff between ISO and TQM?

Q.5. What are Principles of TQM?

Q.6. What are the elements of TQM?

Q.7. What is the model for quality excellence?

Q.8. Write about a model for total quality?

Q.9. What are the characteristics of TQM?

Q.10. What is the need of TQM?

Q.11. What are the approaches to TQM?

Q.12. Write about Juran Trilogy?

Q.13. Write about Mckinsey TQM Model?

Q.14. What are the advantages of TQM? Q15 What are Quality Principles?

Q.16. What is Quality Management?

Q.17. What are the strategies for quality management?

Q.18. Write about quality characteristics?

Q.19. What is the role of top management in TQM?

Q.20. Write about quality process?

Q.21. Define quality control?

Q.22. What are the components of quality control?

Q.23. What are the objectives of quality control?

Q.24. What are the steps in quality control?

Q.25. Define: Total Quality Control

Q.26. How TQC can be implemented?
Q.27. What are the Benefits of TQC?
Q.28. What are the elements of TQC?
Q.29. Write about TQC Methology?
Q.30 Explain the concept of Quality?
Q.31. How does the concept of quality changed during recent years?
Q.32. Distinguish between Quality and Total Quality.
Q.33. What are the costs of quality?
Q.34. Explain the main elements of TQM .why is customer focuses so important in TQM?
Q. 35. What are the various conditions for excellence for Total quality?
Q. 36. Write down the salient features of TQC and TQMCUSTOMER.

❖❖❖❖❖

Q. 1. Who is Customer? Explain in Brief?
Q. 2. Write about customer panels?
Q. 3. Write about Customer Satisfaction?
Q. 4. How customer needs and expectations can be known?
Q. 5. Write about Customer surveys?
Q. 6. What are the customer complaints? What is the relevance of these complaints? How would you proceed for handling customer complaints?

PLANNING PROCESS

Q. 1. Explain the organizational structure for TQM implementation with the help of suitable block diagram .Also Explain the relation between functional structure and TQM work groups in org structure.
Q. 2. What do u mean by Hoshin Planning and Nichijo Planning?

JUST IN TIME & WASTE ELIMINATION

Q. 1. What do you understand by JIT?
Q. 2. Write down the objectives of JIT?
Q. 3. Explain the benefits of just in time manufacturing?
Q. 4. What do you understand by waste elimination?
Q. 5. What is waste?
Q. 6. How to find waste?
Q. 7. What are the major sources of waste?
Q. 8. What are the steps of waste elimination?
Q. 9. Write about Housekeeping.
Q. 10. Write about visual control.

Q. 11. Write about:

Andon.

Jidoka.

Poka yoke.

Q. 12. Write about material handling.

Q. 13. Write about setup time reduction.

Q. 14. Write about just in time.

Q. 15. Write about Kanban cards.

Q. 16. Write about total waste elimination planning and scheduling.

Q. 17. Discuss the benefits and drawbacks of MRP.

Q. 18. What is Kanban System? How does Kanban help in operationalisingJIT manufacturing? What are its advantages and disadvantages?

Q. 19. Compare MRP and JIT in detail also explain which one is more suitable to Indian companies?

PROCESS MANAGEMENT

Q. 1. What is quality function deployment?

Q. 2. Write about customer requirement planning matrix.

Q. 3. What are benefits of QFD?

Q. 4. What are the basic Principles of a QFD?

Q. 5. Explain the Methology of policy deployment?

Q. 6. What are the Pitfalls in implementing QFD?

Q. 7. How do you define a quality assurance?

Q. 8. Briefly describe quality plan.

Q. 9. Define quality assurance. What are the advantages of quality assurance?

Q. 10. What are Management Principles in QA?

Q. 11. Write about types of quality assurance.

Q. 12. What is the relation between quality assurance and top management?

Q. 13. Write about internal and external QA.

Q. 14. Write about hierarchical planning for QA.

Q. 15. Write notes on:

(1) QFD

(2) QC tools

Q. 16. What are the management principles in quality assurance?

Q. 17. What is daily management? How is it different from or similar to a Hoshin Plan? What are business fundamentals and related plans?

Q. 18. What is QFD? Describe the four phases (matrix) of QFD in detail?

Q. 19. Briefly explain various key processes involved in process management?

TOTAL EMPLOYEES INVOLVEMENT

Q. 1. How total employee involvement can be achieved?
Q. 2. Write about concepts about human beings.
Q. 3. What are the advantages and disadvantages of TEI?
Q. 4. What are employee involvement practices?
Q. 5. Write about force field analysis and force field diagram?
Q. 6. Write about decision making.
Q. 7. How problems can be solved?
Q. 8. Elaborate various types of cause and effect diagrams and their uses.
Q. 9. How do you define a quality circle? How does TEI increase through QC's? Explain.

PROBLEM SOLVING

Q. 1. Define problem. Write problem solving methodology for quality improvement.
Q. 2. Write structured problem solveng processes. What are Juran steps of problem solving?
Q. 3. What is Deming Cycle? Write about PDCA & SDAC cycles.
Q. 4. What are the various quality control tools for problem solving?

BENCHMARKING

Q. 1. Discuss the concept of Benchmarking.
Q. 2. Define Benchmarking? Why organizations are going for benchmarking?
Q. 3. Differentiate between various types of Benchmarking?
Q. 4. What are Benchmarking Metrics?
Q. 5. What do you Benchmark? Lists Processes.
Q. 6. Whom do you Benchmark with? What are the uses of output of Benchmarkinh?
Q. 7. Write about Benchmarking Model.
Q. 8. Write the process of Benchmarking.
Q. 9. What is the relation between Benchmarking and TQM?
Q. 10. What are the objectives of Benchmarking?
Q. 11. What are the advantages and limitations of Benchmarking?
Q. 12. Write about Benchmarking leadership and management process.
Q. 13. Write about training for Benchmarking.
Q. 14. How continuous improvement process can be related to Benchmarking?
Q. 15. What is the role of Benchmarking in TQM? Explain various approaches used for Benchmarking?
Q. 16. Define Benchmarking? What are different phases of Benchmarking process? Also Explain, what are the different Benchmarkers for TQC?

ADVANCED TECHNIQUES OF TQM

Q. 1. Write about Design of Experiments.

Q. 2. What are experimental design techniques?

Q. 3. What is contrast between the classical and modern methods of experimentation?

Q. 4. Write about statistical tests of significance.

Q. 5. Discuss one advanced technique of TQM.

Q. 6. List various weaknesses of Teguchi Method.

Q. 7. Write a short note on "Design of Excellence".

QUALITY SYSTEMS

Q. 1. What are the Elements of ISO 9000?

Q. 2. What do you understand by standards and what are the Benefits of ISO 9000 Series of standards?

Q. 3. What is the concept quality system standard?

Q. 4. What are the various elements and applications of ISO 9000?

❑❑❑

QUALITY MANAGEMENT –EOE-72

QUESTION BANK UNIT I

1. **Define the term quality.**

Ans. Quality is a dynamic state associated with products, services, people, processes, and environments that meets or exceeds expectations.

2. **What is total quality?**

Ans. Total quality is an approach to doing business that attempts to maximize the competitiveness of an organization through the continual improvement of the quality of its products, services, people, processes, and environments.

3. **List and explain the key elements of total quality.**

Ans. **Strategically-based**

Total quality organizations have a comprehensive strategic plan that contains at least the following elements: vision, mission, broad objectives, and activities that must be completed to accomplish the broad objectives. The strategic plan for a total quality organization is designed to give it a sustainable competitive advantage in the marketplace.

Customer Focus

In a total quality setting, the customer is the driver. This applies to both internal and external customers.

Obsession with Quality

This means all personnel at all levels approach all aspects of the job from the perspective of "How can we do this better?" When an organization is obsessed with quality, good enough is never good enough.

Scientific Approach

While it is true that people skills, involvement, and empowerment are important in a total quality setting, they represent only a part of the equation. Another important part of the equation is the use of the scientific approach in structuring work and in decision making and problem solving that relates to the work.

Long-Term Commitment

Organizations that implement management innovations after attending short-term seminars often fail in their initial attempt to adopt the total quality approach. This is because they approach total quality as just another management innovation rather than as a whole new way of doing business that requires a whole new corporate culture.

Teamwork

Internal competition tends to use energy that should be focused on improving quality, and, in turn, external competitiveness.

Continual Improvement of Systems

In order to continually improve the quality of products or services: which is a fundamental goal in a total quality setting. It is necessary to continually improve systems.

Continual Process Improvement

Products are developed and services are delivered by people using processes within environments (systems). To continually improve the quality of products and services—which is a fundamental goal in a total quality setting—it is necessary to continually improve the processes that make up the organization's systems.

Education and Training

Education and training are fundamental to total quality because they represent the best way to improve people on a continual basis. In a total quality organization, everyone is constantly learning.

Freedom through Control

Involving and empowering employees is fundamental to total quality as a way to simultaneously bring more minds to bear on the decision making process and increase the ownership employees feel in decisions that are made. The freedoms enjoyed in a total quality setting are actually the result of well-planned and carried out controls.

Unity of Purpose

In order to apply the total quality approach, organizations must have unity of purpose. Collective bargaining is about wages, benefits, and working conditions, not about corporate purpose and vision. Employees should feel more involved and empowered in a total quality setting than in a traditionally managed situation, but the goal of total quality is to enhance competitiveness not to eliminate unions.

Employee involvement

The basis for involving employees increases the likelihood of a good decision1 a better plan, or a more effective improvement by bring more minds to bear on the situation: not just any minds, but the minds of the people who are closest to the work in quest. It also promotes ownership of decisions by involving the people who will have to implement them. Empowerment means not just involving people but involving them in ways that give them a real voice.

Peak Performance

When effectively practiced, total quality allows every aspect of an organization to operate at peak levels. This means that personnel and processes operate at their best. Peak performance is essential to organizations that operate in a global environment where competition is intense, constant, and unforgiving.

4. Explain the rationale for the total quality approach to doing business.

Ans. Total quality is not just one individual concept. It is a number of related concepts pulled together to create a comprehensive approach to doing business. Many people contributed in meaningful ways to the development of the various concepts that are known collectively as total quality.

5. Why do some quality initiatives fail?

Ans. When organizations approach total quality as just another management innovation or, even worse, as a quick fix, their efforts are doomed to fail from the start.

6. Summarize the most common errors made when starting quality initiatives.

Ans. Senior management delegation and poor leadership

Team mania

Deployment process

Taking a narrow dogmatic approach

Confusion about the differences among education, awareness, inspiration, and skill building.

7. Explain the trends that are affecting the future of quality management are as follows:

Ans. Increasing global competition. Today's customers share two common characteristics: 1) they are part of regional trade alliances and 2) they expect both high quality and added value.

Increasing customer expectations. Customers want an excellent product or service from an organization that also provides accurate billing, reliable delivery, and after purchase support.

Opposing economic pressures. The global marketplace exerts enormous unrelenting pressure on organizations to continually improve quality while simultaneously reducing the prices they charge for goods and services.

New approaches to management. Companies that succeed in the global marketplace have learned that you manage budgets, but lead people.

8. Explain the relationship between quality and competitiveness.

Ans. Companies that used to compete only on a local, regional, or national level now find themselves competing against companies from throughout the world. Some of these companies find the competition to be more intense than any they have ever encountered. Those who are able to produce world-class quality can compete at this level.

9. Explain how the cost of poor quality can affect competitiveness.

Ans. The need to improve an organization's financial condition correlates directly with the process of making and measuring quality improvements. Lower deficiencies will lead to lower total costs. Improvements in product or service features can lead to higher market share at a better price, which means higher revenue.

10. Describe the evolution of the rebuilding effort undertaken by Japan and Germany following World War II.

Ans. As Japanese and German manufacturers rebuilt, two things became apparent to them: 1) In order to succeed, they would have to compete globally; and 2) In order to compete globally; they would have to produce goods of world-class quality. This meant producing better goods but at reasonable competitive prices.

11. Explain the actions of U.S. manufacturers during the same period on which Japan and Germany were rebuilding following World War II.

Ans. The U.S. came out of World War II as the only major industrialized nation with its manufacturing sector completely intact. A well-oiled manufacturing sector and the availability of abundant raw materials helped the U.S. become the world leader in the production and export of durable goods. This resulted in a period of unparalleled prosperity and one of the highest standards of living ever experienced by any country. While the U.S. was enjoying its position as the world's preeminent economic superpower, the other industrialized nations of the world, particularly Japan and Germany, were busy rebuilding their manufacturing sectors. The U.S. manufacturers were slow to catch on that the game had changed from mass production with acceptable levels of waste to quality production with things done right the first time every time. With foreign companies, through a combination of better people, better technology, and better management began to eat away at markets, U.S. companies, mistakenly seeing cost rather than quality as the issue, learned that quality was the key to success in the global marketplace, Japan, Germany, Taiwan, and Korea had made major inroads into global markets previously dominated by U.S. manufacturers (i.e., steel, automobiles, computers, and consumer electronics).

12. How does a nation's ability to compete affect its quality of life?

Ans. A nation's ability to compete in the global marketplace has a direct bearing on the quality of life of its citizens. Because the ability to compete translates into the ability to do a better job of producing quality goods, it is critical that nations and individual organizations within them focus their policies, systems, and resources in a coordinated way on continually improving both quality and competitiveness.

13. Explain how education-related factors can inhibit competitiveness.

Ans. The quality of a country's education system is a major determinant of the quality of its labor pool. The higher the quality of the labor pool, the higher the quality of entry-level employees. The higher the quality of entry-level employees, the faster they can become productive employees and contribute to the competitiveness of their employers. Consequently, a high-quality education system is an important component of the competitiveness equation. What all this means is that businesses in the U.S. are forced to spend money helping employees learn the basic skills of reading and writing while their competitors are able to devote their training dollars to developing advanced work-related skills. If international competition can be viewed as a footrace, this is the equivalent of forcing U.S. firms to start 100 yards behind the other competitor in a 200-yard race.

14. Compare investment and manufacturing productivity in the U.S with investment and manufacturing productivity in Japan.

Ans. Investment, from the perspective of global competitiveness, is the percent of gross national product spent on education, equipment, facilities, and research and development in the period of 1970-90, Japan led the list of competitive countries, with an investment level of approximately 30 percent. The U.S. invested just over 20 percent during this period. The other countries, taken as a group, invested slightly more than the U.S. when education is removed from the list of investments, the U.S. invested as much or more than all other countries except Canada. However, there is evidence that American dollars invested in education are not used as effectively as those invested by other competing nations. It should be noted also that Japanese investment in equipment began to decline in 1992. During the first three quarters of the twentieth century, the U.S. enjoyed the highest productivity levels in the world. For example, in 1972 U.S. manufacturing productivity was 56 percent better than that of Japan. By 1987, this lead had dwindled to just 6 percent. By 1993, Japan equaled the U.S. in productivity.

15. List and briefly explain the basic philosophical constructs underlying the human resource aspects of the competitiveness of Japan and Germany.

Ans. The basic philosophical constructs underlying the human-resource aspects of the competitiveness of both Japan and Germany are explained in the following list: Cooperation among business, labor, and government.

The term social partners is used in Japan just as it is in Germany. Prior to the war, this prevailing view among top business executives was very like that of the American rugged individualist. As in Germany, however, the crisis provoked by defeat shifted the balance toward those who believed that business must join with the other major economic actors in the task of rebuilding the society, tying its own goals with the larger interests of the nation as a whole.

16. What is strategic management?

Ans. Strategic management is management that bases all actions, activities, and decisions on what is most likely: within an ethical framework: to ensure successful performance in the marketplace. From the perspective of the strategic manager, resources are wasted unless they contribute to success in the marketplace, and the more direct the contribution, the better.

17. List the steps in the strategic planning process.

Ans. SWOT Analysis, Develop the Vision, Develop the Mission, Develop the Guiding Principles, Develop the Broad Strategic Objectives, and Develop the Specific Tactics

18. What is a core competency?

Ans. A core competency is anything an organization does so well that it can be viewed as a competitive advantage. An organization's core competencies might be based on its ability to achieve economy of scale, proprietary access to a given technology, expertise that is difficult to replicate, the ability to maintain world-class performance from critical processes, market proximity, a high-performance corporate culture, research and development expertise, the ability to respond rapidly to market research, or any other factor that contributes directly and significantly to the organization's ability to provide superior value consistently over time.

19. Explain why creative thinking is important in strategic planning and how to encourage it.

Ans. So as to ferret out things that are done the same way year after year just because that is the way they have always been done. This approach will not make an organization more competitive.

20. What is SWOT analysis?

Ans. SWOT is the acronym for Strengths, Weaknesses, Opportunities, and Threats. A SWOT analysis answers the following questions: What are this organization's strengths? What are this organization's weaknesses? What opportunities exist in this organization's business environment? What threats exist in this organization's business environment?

21. Write a sample vision for a hypothetical organization.

Ans. The Institute for Corporate Competitiveness will be recognized by its customers as the provider of choice for organizational development products that are the best in the world.

22. Write a mission statement for the hypothetical organization in Question21.

Ans. The Institute for Corporate Competitiveness (ICC) is a business-development company dedicated to helping organization's continually improve their ability to compete in the global marketplace. To this end, ICC provides high-quality competitiveness: enhancing products and services to an ever-increasing number of organizations in the United States.

23. Draft a set of guiding principles for the hypothetical organization in Question 6.

Ans. XYZ Company will uphold the highest ethical standards in all of its operations.

At XYZ Company, customer satisfaction is the highest priority. XYZ Company will make every effort to deliver the highest quality products and services in the business.

At XYZ Company, all stakeholders (customers, suppliers, and employees) will be treated as partners.

At XYZ Company, continued improvement of products, processes, and people will be the norm.

XYZ Company will provide employees with a safe and healthy work environment that is conducive to consistent peak performance.

XYZ Company will be a good corporate neighbor in all communities where its facilities are located.

XYZ Company will take all appropriate steps to protect the environment.

24. Establish two or three broad objectives for the hypothetical organization in Question 21.

Ans. 1. To produce organizational-development products of world-class quality that are improved continually.

2. To provide organizational-development services of world-class quality that is improved continually.
3. To establish and maintain a world-class workforce at all levels of the organization.
4. To continually increase the organizations market share for its existing products/services.
5. To continually introduce new products/services to meet emerging needs in the organizational development market.

25. Describe the steps you would apply in executing your strategic plan developed in Questions 21-24.

Ans. (A) Communicate; (B) Build capabilities; (C) Establish strategy-supportive stimuli; (D) Eliminate administrative barriers; (E) Identify advocates and resisters; (F) Exercise strategic leadership; (G) Be flexible and improvise; and H) Monitor and adjust as needed.

26. Define the term corporate social responsibility.

Ans. Corporate social responsibility is a balanced approach for organizations to address economic, social and environmental issues in a way that aims to benefit people, communities and society.

27. Define the term partnering.

Ans. The simplest way to understand the concept of partnering is to think of it as working together for mutual benefit. Those who work together may be suppliers, fellow employees, customers, and even businesses that are potential competitors. The creation of cooperation within an organization and between an organization and its suppliers and customers. Business partnering occurs through a pooling of resources in a trusting atmosphere focused on continual, mutual improvement.

28. What are the benefits of partnering?

Ans. The maximum benefits of partnering are realized when all parties in the chain of partners cooperate. Partnering can lead to continual improvements in such key areas as processes and products1 relationships between customers and suppliers, and customer satisfaction. Internal partnering can improve relationships among employees and between departments within an organization. When taken as a whole, these individual benefits add up to enhanced competitiveness.

29. Describe each step in the partnering model.

Ans. Develop a Partnering Briefing

Partnering is about creating cooperative alliances. Before trying to establish such an alliance, make sure everyone involved understands partnering as a concept.

Identify Potential Partners

Any external or internal supplier or customer is a potential partner. Choose partners in an order determined by how much value the partnership can have toward enhancing quality, productivity, and competitiveness.

Identify Key Decision Makers

In every organization (unit, department, etc.) there are key people whose support is needed to make an initiative involving their organization work. Identify these key decision makers in any organization considered a potential partner. Their support will have to be won if a successful partnership is to be formed.

Conduct a Partnering Briefing

Call a meeting of the decision makers in both organizations, yours and the potential partners. Present a briefing explaining the partnering concept, with time built in for discussion and questions. This briefing should answer such questions as 1) How can we mutually benefit from a partnership? and 2) What is expected of each partner?

Determine the Level of Commitment.

After the key decision makers have been briefed, gauge their level of commitment. Are they willing to commit to the partnership for the long term? Are they willing to make any and all procedural and/or philosophical changes that may be necessary in order for the partnership to work?

Decide If There is Sufficient Commitment

If the key decision makers show noticeable reluctance, they are not likely to make a full commitment to the partnership. There is no need to proceed any further with potential partners who seem reluctant. The better course of action in such a case is to break off further involvement and begin the process again with another external partner.Identify Key Operational Personnel

If the level of commitment is sufficient to proceed with the partnership, who are the key people from both organizations needed to put it into operation? Are personnel needed from Marketing? Purchasing? Engineering? Manufacturing? Receiving? Accounting? Identify the people needed to put into action the commitment made by executive-level decision makers.

Form the Partnership Team

The key people identified as necessary to putting the partnership into operation should be formed into a team. This means more than just naming them to the team. They must be given opportunities to get to know and trust each other. The success of the partnership will depend in great measure on the willingness and ability of these team members to work together.

Develop a Mission Statement

The partnership team needs a clear and concise mission statement so that everyone involved understands what the team is supposed to do. The mission statement should be developed by executive-level decision makers from both organizations.

Develop Objectives

The mission statement is written in general terms. It is translated into more specific terms by objectives. These objectives should be developed by the partners and ratified by the executive-level decision makers of both partnership organizations. Well-written objectives are stated in measurable terms.

Prioritize and Begin

It will typically take several objectives to completely translate the mission statement into measurable action. The importance of these objectives is relative. Although all are important, the objectives should be prioritized and listed in order from the most important to the least. After priorities have been established and confirmed by executive-level personnel, the work necessary to accomplish them begins Results should be monitored and appropriate action taken when problems arise.

30. Define the term internal partnering.

Ans. Internal partnering is creating an environment and establishing mechanisms within it that bring managers and employees, teams, and individual employees together in mutually supportive alliances that maximize the human resources of an organization.

31. What is partnering with suppliers?

Ans. True supplier partnering requires an understanding of each party's needs and capabilities to establish a clear vision for focusing the efforts of people who work for buyer and supplier. Necessary improvement can then be dedicated to those areas identified as requiring attention and improvement. If that focus is placed, as it has been in most cases, solely on the buyer's perceived needs, nothing happens to establish overall improvement to the buyer-seller network. Long-term commitments then become nebulous and difficult to achieve. Continual improvement is often reduced to a short-term project instead of an ongoing process.

32. Explain the mandatory requirements of supplier partnerships.

Ans. Supplier personnel should meet with buyer personnel beyond those in the purchasing office. It is particularly important for them to meet with personnel who actually use their products so that needed improvements can be identified and made.

The price only approach to buyer: supplier negotiations should be eliminated. Product features, quality, and delivery issues should also be part of the negotiations. The goal of the negotiations should be to achieve the optimum deal when price, features, quality, and delivery issues are all factored in.

The quality of supplier products should be guaranteed by the supplier's quality processes. The buyer should have no need to inspect the supplier's products.

The supplier should fully understand and be able to practice Just-In-Time/Lean (JIT/LEAN). Buyers should not need to maintain inventories.

Both partners should be capable of sharing information electronically so that the relationship is not inhibited by paperwork. Electronic data exchange is particularly important for successful JIT/LEAN.

33. List and explain the stages of development in supplier partnerships.

Ans. Uncertainty and Tentativeness

In the uncertainty and tentativeness stage, the buyer and seller are like two people on their first date. There is interest, but it is tentative and prefaced with uncertainty. Neither party knows exactly what to expect of the other. At this point, there is no trust between the partners.

Short-Term Pressures

The typical short-term business pressures that apply in a traditional business setting manifest themselves in this step. The buyer will be under the usual pressure to cut costs. The supplier will be under the usual pressure to increase sales volume. Both partners will be cautious and initial attempts to begin putting some substance to the partnership will be probing and vague.

Need for Approaches

In the need for approaches stage, traditional negotiations will inevitably occur. The buyer will press price discounts, better payment terms, freight allowances, and other concessions that save it money but cost the supplier. The supplier will press for higher concessions that save it money but cost the supplier. The supplier will press for higher volume to offset concessions made to the buyer. Then, if either partner has involved personnel who are total quality conscious, it will dawn on them that quality is not being served by this traditional negotiating. Both will begin to realize that a new approach is needed. If this awareness does not occur, the partnership will fail.

Adoption of New Paradigms

In the adoption of new paradigms state, both partners explore ways to move toward the concept of mutual benefit. The key is for both partners to accept the principle that absorbing costs within the partnership (either by the supplier or the buyer) gives neither an advantage. The best way to promote competitiveness is for both partners to work together to lower costs. This new way of thinking will give the partnership a competitive advantage over other organizations that produce the same product.

Awareness of PotentialIn the awareness of potential stage, both partners become fully aware of the potential benefits that can be realized from the partnership. The potential for a true-win-win relationship can now be seen. Rather than negotiating price concessions and volume increases, both partners realize that by working together they can exceed any short-term advantages that might have been realized from these traditional negotiating strategies.

Adoption of New Values

The adoption of new values stage, both partners adopt the new values inherent in a true supplier-buyer partnership. These values include trust, openness, and sharing. Each party trusts the other to protect the confidentiality of what they learn about one another. Both parties accept that the more information they share, including financial information, the better prepared they will be to help one another.

Mature Partnering

In the mature partnering stage, the partnership has solidified. A high level of trust and cooperation has been established between the partners. Continual interfacing between pertinent employees at all levels of both organizations exists as fact. Each partner has a strong self-interest in the success of the other partner.

34. Explain the rationale for partnering with customers.

Ans. The rationale for forming partnerships with customers in this context is simple. It is the best way to ensure customer satisfaction, which is, in turn, the best way to be competitive. No organization can possibly know better than its customers what the customers want. Customer-defined quality is a fundamental part of the total quality philosophy. Where it is best to guess what a customer wants or to ask is obvious. No organization can afford to squander its resources and, in turn, its competitive edge guessing what customers want Ask. Any organization that produces a product can benefit from observing how it is used by customers. By involving customers early in the product development cycle, a manufacturer can make changes inexpensively and with relative ease. The key to success in partnering with customers is to get them involved early in the product development cycle. Get their feedback at every stage in the product development cycle, and make any changes needed as soon as they are identified. When this approach is used, customer satisfaction surveys can solicit feedback from a broader audience to verily the input given earlier in the product development.

35. What is a manufacturing network?

Ans. A manufacturing network is a group of individual SMEs that cooperate in ways that increase their quality, productivity, and resultant competitiveness to levels beyond what the individual member companies could achieve by themselves.

36. What role does mutual need play in manufacturing networks?

Ans. What makes a network succeed are two concepts: interdependence of member companies and mutual need. The member companies depend on each other in developing mutual solutions to common problems. Manufacturing networks are characterized by relationships of collaboration or interdependence among firms. The interactions between participants are neither dominated by any one firm nor are they simple economic exchanges motivated by calculations of price and quantity. Firms in these networks are partners: they must rely on each other in order to accomplish their objectives.

37. List and explain the most widely practiced network activities.

Ans. **Production**

Networked SMEs are able to pursue production contracts larger than any individual member company could undertake alone. Through teaming arrangements, the work and the financing of it are divided among network members as appropriate.

Education and Training

Education and training are often a problem for SMEs. On the one hand, employees need ongoing education and training in order to continually improve quality, productivity, and competitiveness. On the other hand, they face the following problems because they have a limited employee base: a) Difficulty giving employees time off for education and training and still meeting production schedules; b) Difficulty convincing educational institutions that typically need 15-20 students in order to form a class to bring courses on-site; and c) high expenses for education because they do not get the substantial registration discounts large firms get when participating in training provided by private training firms. By partnering, SMEs can solve all three of these problems through economy of scale.

Marketing

Marketing is the most widely practiced joint activity among manufacturing networks of SMEs. Typically, the joint capabilities of the network are what are marketed. Member companies share the costs of producing marketing tools such as brochures, videos, and promotional materials; of attending trade shows; and of marketing personnel and related expenses such as travel.

Product Development

Developing new products can be too expensive an undertaking for SMEs. It typically involves such activities as research, design, market analysis, competition analysis, prototype production, performance testing, and test markets. The costs associated with these activities can be prohibitive for an individual SME. However, when the costs can be divided among network members, product development becomes a more feasible concept.

Technology Transfer Technology is the physical manifestation of knowledge. Technology transfer is the movement of technology from one arena to another. The form of technology transfer that is most readily and widely recognized is the transfer of a new technology from a research laboratory to a production setting. After it has been diffused, technology must be properly used in order to realize the potential benefits. Proper use of technology requires knowledge. Knowledge sharing is the approach networks use to promote effective technology.

Purchasing

One of the most productive applications of the economy of scale gained from networking is in purchasing. SMEs working alone are not able to enjoy the cost savings that large firms achieve by purchasing bulk quantities of expendable materials and other necessities such as insurance. However, by jointly purchasing necessities, networked SMEs can achieve similar cost savings.

1. **What types of service do educational institutions typically provide to business and industry partners?**

Ans. The need to continually improve employees' work skills is the primary driver behind business and education partnerships. Educational institutions provide on-site customized training, technical assistance, and consulting services to help organizations continually improve their people and their processes.

Why, in your own words, would an otherwise ethical person make an unethical decision?

THE TOTAL QUALITY APPROACH TO QUALITY MANAGEMENT

TRUE/FALSE: Place T or F in the space provided to the left of the statement.

1. Quality deals not only products and services but also includes people, processes, and environments.
2. Joseph M. Juran is best known for the Seven Deadly Diseases.
3. Today's consumers define quality as being flawless and having all of the attributes they want in just the way they want them.
4. According to the Three-Legged Stool of Total Quality, the seat of the stool is customer focus.
5. Quality management has o future in the 21st century.
6. Peak performance is essential to organizations that operate in a globally competitive environment.

MULTIPLE CHOICE: Circle the letter before the correct answer in each of the following questions.

1. The total quality approach has which of the following characteristics?
   - A. Teamwork
   - B. Obsession with quantity
   - C. Confusion and poor leadership
   - D. One employee in charge
2. Customers want an excellent product or service from an organization that also provides:
   - A. The Deming Cycle
   - B. Quick fixes
   - C. Reliable delivery and after purchase support
   - D. Stamps
3. Which of the following functions is part of the Juran Trilogy?
   - A. Pareto Principle
   - B. Quality planning
   - C. Unity of purpose
   - D. Six Sigma Program
4. Crosby's Quality Vaccine consists of three ingredients. Which of the following is not one of the three ingredients?
   - A. Teamwork
   - B. Education
   - C. Determination
   - D. Implementation
5. Which of the following is a trend that will shape the future of quality management?
   - A. The Deming Cycle.
   - B. The Juran Trilogy.
   - C. Global economy.
   - D. Increasing global competition.

6. Which of the following certifications is for managers who lead and champion continual-process improvement initiatives?
   A. Calibration technician
   B. Six Sigma Green Belt
   C. Manager of Quality/Organizational Excellence
   D. Quality Process Analyst

Test Key

True/False

1. T 2. F 3. T 4. T 5. F

Multiple Choice

1. A 2. C 3. B 4. A 5. D

QUALITY AND GLOBAL COMPETITIVENESS

TRUE OR FALSE: Place T or F in the space provided to the left of the statement.

1. U.S companies, mistakenly seeing quality as the issue, learned that quantity was the key to success in the global marketplace.
2. The need to improve an organization's financial condition correlated directly with the process of making and measuring quality improvements.
3. A nation's ability to compete in the global marketplace has a direct bearing on the quality of life of its citizens.
4. The only way the U.S. can overcome business-related inhibitors is for the government to enact policies that will reduce non-value-added costs to a minimum.
5. In order to be an exporter, a manufacturer must be able to outperform foreign competitors in terms of both quality and productivity.
6. Management-by-accounting encourages short-term cost cutting instead of long-term improvement.

MULTIPLE CHOICE:
Circle the letter before the correct answer in each of the following questions.

1. Of the trends listed below, which one increases the level of globalization in business?
   A. Growing irrelevance of distance.
   B. Shifts in the interest rates.
   C. Quality of the product.
   D. Rise of small towns.
2. Which of the following statements are considered true concerning the affects of global integration?
   A. It has helped fuel economic growth throughout the industrialized world.
   B. It can be the Achilles heel of economic growth.
   C. Downturns in one country can now have a ripple effect that quickly spreads to other countries.
   D. All of the above
3. Which of the following countries is the most competitive country in the world?
   A. Germany
   B. United States
   C. Japan
   D. Switzerland
4. When making comparisons among internationally competing countries, the following indicators are used:
   A. Standard of living and investment.
   B. Quality is the key to success.
   C. Government infrastructure.
   D. Ability to compete.

5. The most important key in maximizing competitiveness is:
   A. Education
   B. Human resources
   C. Teamwork
   D. Government
6. The most common college degree among American CEOs is the:
   A. Quality management
   B. MBA
   C. CFO
   D. Management and Leadership

Test Key

True/False

1. F 2. T 3. T 4. F 5. T 6. T

Multiple Choice

1. C 2. D 3. C 4. A 5. B 6. B

STRATEGIC MANAGEMENT: PLANNING AND EXECUTION FOR COMPETITIVE ADVANTAGE

TRUE OR FALSE: Place T or F in the space provided to the left of the statement.

1. In order to survive in a globally competitive environment, organizations must adopt a broad strategy that gives them a sustainable competitive advantage.
2. A core competency is something an organization does so well it can be viewed as a competitive advantage.
3. SWOT Analysis is the only step needed in the strategic planning process.
4. An organization's vision is a specific measurable goal it tries to achieve.
5. Change that is inflicted on employees will be resisted, but change that is engendered by employees who are involved in and prepared for it will be accepted and promoted.
6. Even the best plan can do no good until it is effectively executed.

MULTIPLE CHOICE: Circle the letter before the correct answer in each of the following questions.

1. Which of the following statements apply when developing a mission statement?
   A. The how-to statements.
   B. Describe the "who, what, and where" of the organization.
   C. Be brief, but comprehensive.
   D. Choose wording that is simple.
2. Which of the following statements best describe the acronym SWOT?
   A. Specific, Witness, Opportunities, and Time.
   B. Single, Weaknesses, Occasion, and Tactics.
   C. Strengths, Weaknesses, Opportunities, and Threats.
   D. Strategic, Weaknesses, Objectives, and Tactics.
3. Strategic management is
   A. Creative thinkers who look at their business environment from a different perspective.
   B. Expansive and wasteful.
   C. Constantly seeking gaps in the marketplace that their companies can fill.
   D. Management that bases decisions within an ethical framework.
4. Which of the following statements is true concerning strategies used to execute a strategic plan?

A. Organizations should communicate at all times.
B. Consult with only managers.
C. Adjust to administrative barriers.
D. Be flexible and improvise.

5. Which of the following strategies is important when executing a strategic plan?
A. Review the plan with customers.
B. Identify advocates and resisters.
C. Form an application task force.
D. Activate the steering committee.

6. To promote successful execution of strategies, organizations should undertake which of the following strategies?
A. Eliminate administrative barriers
B. Conduct a secondary SWOT analysis
C. Hold a stakeholder's gap analysis
D. Contract with an execution specialist

Test Key

True/False

1. T 2. T 3. F 4. F 5. T 6. T

Multiple Choice

1. A 2. C 3. D 4. A 5. B 6. A

TEAM BUILDING AND TEAMWORK

TRUE OR FALSE: Place T or F in the space provided to the left of the statement.

1. A team is a group of people with a common, collective goal.
2. A team must have a mission statement because it explains the team's reason for being.
3. Teams are not coached - they are bossed.
4. Coaches promote mutual respect among team members and promote cultural diversity.
5. Employees always work well together as a team just because it's the right thing to do.
6. People in teams will respond to change in the same ways.

MULTIPLE CHOICE: Circle the letter before the correct answer in each of the following questions.

1. Which of the following is not classified as a type of team according to Johnson, Katner, and Kikora?
A. Environmental improvement team
B. Departmental improvement team
C. Process improvement team
D. Task force

2. Which of the following strategies counter the negative influences of advisor and followers?
A. Personal identity of members
B. Looking for disagreement among advisors
C. Relationships among team members
D. Follower's identity within the organization

3. Which of the following strategies are applied in order to be a good team member?
A. Establish ground rules
B. Be well prepared and participate
C. Identify success criteria
D. None of the above

4. Which of the following character traits promote successful teamwork?
A. Honesty
B. Controlling
C. Impatience
D. Need to be in-charge (bossy)

5. Which of the following is a common structural inhibitor to teamwork in organizations?
A. Sensitivity
B. Honesty
C. Accountability to management
D. Tolerance

6. Which of the following is a personally negative response to conflict?
   - A. Filing a lawsuit
   - B. Going into denial
   - C. Filing a grievance
   - D. Submitting to mediation

Test Key

True/False

1. T	2. T	3. F	4. T	5. F	6. F

Multiple Choice

1. A	2. B	3. B	4. A	5. C	6. B

OVERCOMING POLITICS, NEGATIVITY, AND CONFLICT IN THE WORKPLACE

TRUE OR FALSE: Place T or F in the space provided to the left of the statement.

1. Internal politics consists of the games people play to promote decisions that are based on criteria other than merit.
2. Internal politics occurs when individuals put the organization's goals ahead of their own.
3. Power is the ability to exert influence.
4. There are certain organizational structures that tend to prevent internal politics.
5. Conflict management means resolving conflict whenever it is detrimental and initiating it when necessary to overcome stagnation in an organization.
6. One definition of corporate culture is the way things are done in an organization.

MULTIPLE CHOICE: Circle the letter before the correct answer in each of the following questions.

1. The Achilles Heel of the geographic structure with regard to internal politics is:
   - A. Individual goals of the division managers
   - B. The CEOs persona agenda
   - C. Distance
   - D. East/west and north/south conflict
2. A strategy used by internal politics that involves the sharing and/or selective withholding of information is:
   - A. Coalition building
   - B. Lobbying
   - C. Electioneering
   - D. Spreading of rumors and gossip
3. Bringing together people who have a common cause or goal is a strategy of internal politicians known as:
   - A. Electioneering
   - B. Lobbying
   - C. Coalition building
   - D. Rumor mongering
4. Which of the following is NOT typically an effect of internal politics in an organization?
   - A. Loss of morale
   - B. Counterproductive internal competition
   - C. Loss of quality, competitiveness, and customers
   - D. Enhanced competitiveness
5. Which of the following is NOT a strategy for preventing internal politics?
   - A. Explaining the strategic plan to all employees
   - B. Rewarding employees who win in internal competition situations
   - C. Leadership by example
   - D. Encouraging a customer focus

6. Which of the following situations indicates that conflict should be stimulated?
   A. When employees always agree and tell managers what they want to hear
   B. Employees willingly admit their mistakes
   C. The turnover rate is unusually high
   D. Employees avoid proposing new ideas

Test Key

True/False

1. T	2. F	3. T	4. F	5. T	6. T

Multiple Choice

1. C	2. B	3. C	4. D	5. B	6. A

ISO 9000 AND TOTAL QUALITY: THE RELATIONSHIP

TRUE OR FALSE: Place T or F in the space provided to the left of the statement.

1. ISO 9000 and total quality are interchangeable.
2. ISO 9000 is compatible with, and can be a subset of total quality.
3. ISO 9000 is never implemented in a non-total quality environment.
4. ISO 9000 can improve operations in a traditional environment.
5. ISO 9000 may be redundant in a mature total quality environment.
6. ISO 9001 is intentionally generic so it can be applied to any kind of organization.

MULTIPLE CHOICE: Circle the letter before the correct answer in each of the following questions.

1. Appropriate motives for adopting ISO 9000 include which of the following?
   A. To create a quality management system B. To improve operations
   C. To conform to the requirements of customers D. All of the above
2. Which of the following is a documentation requirement for the ISO 9000 quality system?
   A. A Quality Policy
   B. Statement of Customer Focus
   C. Statement of Management Commitment
   D. Declaration that Teamwork is to be employed in all areas
3. Which of the following statements outline the relationship factor?
   A. ISO 9000 and total quality are not in competition
   B. ISO 9000 and total quality are not interchangeable
   C. ISO 9000 is compatible with total quality
   D. All of the above
4. Characteristics of total quality include:
   A. Scientific approach to problem solving and decision making
   B. Concerned only with quality management procedures
   C. Unity of purpose - all employees, all levels
   D. Both A & C
5. Which of the following statements is true concerning the original aims of ISO 9000?
   A. To transform organizations into competitive players in the global marketplace.
   B. To create a universally recognized family of quality standards.

6. Which of the following is a basic principle of ISO 9000?
   A. Certification authority held by ISO
   B. Continual improvement of processes and products
   C. Management authority
   D. Periodic internal audits

Test Key

True/False

1. F	2. T	3. F	4. T	5. T	6. T

Multiple Choice

1. D	2. A	3. D	4. D	5. B	6. B

OVERVIEW OF TOTAL QUALITY TOOLS

TRUE OR FALSE: Place T or F in the space provided to the left of the statement.

1. A graphic representation of a process is called a Flowchart.
2. Attributes data are something resulting from measurement.
3. The diamond shaped symbol on a flowchart denotes an input or an output.
4. FMEA is a tool to deal with potential product failures.
5. Design of experiments is a very sophisticated method for experimenting with processes with the objective of optimizing them.

MULTIPLE CHOICE: Circle the letter before the correct answer in each of the following questions.

1. The purpose of the Pareto Chart is:
   A. To identify and isolate the causes of a problem
   B. To show where to apply resources by revealing the significant few from the trivial many
   C. To collect variables data
   D. To determine the correlation between two characteristics
2. Frequency Distribution Diagram is another name for a:
   A. Pareto Chart B. Fishbone Diagram
   C. Scatter Diagram D. Histogram
3. Which chart is often referred to as a trend chart?
   A. Control Chart B Run Chart
   C. Pareto Chart D. Scatter Diagram
4. Which of the following is used to show correlation of two variables?
   A. Run Charts B. Histograms
   C. Scatter Diagram D. Stratification
5. Which of the following reveals whether process variation is the result of a special cause?
   A. Control Chart B. Check Sheet
   C. Pareto Chart D. Run Chart

Test Key

True/False

1. T	2. F	3. F	4. T	5. T

Multiple Choice

1. B	2. D	3. B	4. C	5. A

PROBLEM SOLVING AND DECISION MAKING

TRUE OR FALSE: Place T or F in the space provided to the left of the statement.

1. When a problem solution returns a process to the state that existed before the problem occurred, a total quality organization would say that the problem was NOT resolved.
2. Dr. Juran's 85/15 rule holds that at least 85% of an organization's problems would be eliminated if employees did their jobs correctly.
3. The PDCA cycle is one model for continual improvement.
4. The Seven-Step Problem Solving process promoted by the authors was developed by Toyota.
5. The major problem with employee involvement in problem solving is time.
6. Repeatedly asking "why" related to the problem should eventually lead to a root cause.

MULTIPLE CHOICE: Circle the letter before the correct answer in each of the following questions.

1. There are two ways to evaluate decisions. One way is to:
   A. Examine the results
   B. Examine the input that is used in decision making
   C. Evaluate the process used in making the decision
   D. A or C
2. Objective information is:
   A. Not always factual
   B. Factual
   C. Open to interpretation
   D. Not reliable
3. Factors that inhibit problem solving creativity include:
   A. Failing to be concerned about risk
   B. Fear of looking foolish or being rejected
   C. Having more than 4-5 people on the team
   D. Allowing ambiguity
4. After defining a problem, the next step in the problem solving/decision making process should be:
   A. Institute a temporary fix to keep things moving
   B. Use Five-Why analysis
   C. Clarify the issue or problem in order to "grasp the situation"
   D. Define what the outcome should be
5. Which of the following is a strategy for helping people think creatively?
   A. Idea vending (or stirring the pot)
   B. Being risk averse
   C. Unwillingness to hear "over the top" ideas or input
   D. Looking for the one right answer

Test Key

True/False

1. T	2. T	3. F	4. T	5. T

Multiple Choice

1. D	2. B	3. B	4. C	5. A

CONTINUAL IMPROVEMENT METHODS WITH SIX SIGMA, LEAN, LEAN SIX SIGMA, AND MORE

TRUE OR FALSE: Place T or F in the space provided to the left of the statement.

1. As part of its leadership responsibility, management in an organization that practices total quality must be personally involved in continual improvement.

2. The only way a company can hope to compete in the modern marketplace is to improve its products, processes and people continually.
3. If there are 10 processes that might be improved, the processes that should be worked on first are those which will yield the most benefit if improved.
4. Six Sigma can only be achieved through process improvement.
5. When we combine the most important features of Lean with the best features of Six Sigma we have Lean Six Sigma.

MULTIPLE CHOICE: Circle the letter before the correct answer in each of the following questions.

1. In order for an organization to make continual improvement it must:
   A. Establish an organization-wide quality council
   B. Establish quality improvement goals with target dates
   C. Have top management commitment that is visible to all employees
   D. All of the above
2. Variation in processes
   A. Can be caused by include people, machines, material, and environment
   B. Is of three kinds
   C. Should not be of concern
   D. Must be eliminated if continual improvement is to happen
3. The Five-Step Plan that involves straightening up, putting things in order, cleaning up, standardizing, and discipline belongs to:
   A. Jidoka B. Kaizen
   C. CEDAC D. DMAIC
4. Lean is based on the manufacturing system that was developed by
   A. Motorola B. Toyota
   C. Goldratt D. IBM
5. Six Sigma process performance
   A. Represents a major advance in capability over the typical.
   B. Has yet to be achieved in actual practice
   C. Predicts 1 nonconformance in 500 million opportunities
   D. Is useful only in large scale manufacturing

Test Key

True/False

1. T 2. F 3. T 4. F 5. F

Multiple Choice

1. D 2. A 3. B 4. B 5. A

EFFECTIVE COMMUNICATION

TRUE OR FALSE: Place T or F in the space provided to the left of the statement.

1. Effective communication means receiving a message, correctly decoding it, and accurately perceiving what it means.
2. Company level communication is communication within a peer group.
3. When trying to communicate it is important that you do not use open-ended questions.

4. In order for employees and managers to function effectively in a total quality setting, they must have good interpersonal skills.
5. Interpersonal skills are those needed for people to work together in a positive manner that is conductive to both personal and corporate success.
6. One-way communication helps maintain a climate that is conducive to effective communication.

MULTIPLE CHOICE: Circle the letter before the correct answer in each of the following questions.

1. There are several components of communication. They are:
   A. The sender, the message, the receiver, verification
   B. The message, the medium, the sender, the customer
   C. The medium, the goals, the receiver, the message
   D. The message, the sender, the receiver, the medium
2. Which of the following is not a common inhibitor of communication?
   A. Lack of trust B. Lack of concentration
   C. Interference D. Inaccurate assumptions
3. Empathic listening means:
   A. Agreeing with what is being said
   B. Receiving the message, correctly decoding it, and accurately perceiving what is means
   C. Listening with the intent to understand D. Pretending to listen
4. Robert Luke offers four guidelines for enhancing the effectiveness of corrective feedback. They are:
   A. Be positive, be prepared, be realistic, and don't be completely negative
   B. Be positive, be prepared, be realistic, be accurate
   C. Be direct, be prepared, be realistic, be accurate
   D. Don't be completely negative, be positive, be brief, and be undersianding
5. Verbal communication is least effective when:
   A. Reprimanding an employee for poor performance
   B. Promoting a safety campaign
   C. Commending an employee for doing a good job
   D. Attempting to resolve conflict between or among employees
6. One of the highest levels of verbal communication occurs when speakers use what to make their points?
   A. Stories B. Facts
   C. Photographs D. Graphs and charts

Test Key

True/False

1. F 2. F 3. T 4. T 5. T 6. F

Multiple Choice

1. D 2. B 3. C 4. A 5. B 6. A

QUALITY MANAGEMENT, ETHICS, AND CORPORATE SOCIAL RESPONSIBILITY

TRUE OR FALSE: Place T or F in the space provided to the left of the statement.

1. Morality refers to the values that are subscribed to and fostered by society in general and by individuals within society.

2. Locus of control is a person's ability to undertake self-directed tasks and to cope with tense structure.
3. In a total quality setting, people are responsible for their actions and accountable for their performance.
4. Managers must establish ethical standards within their organization.
5. Corporate social responsibility is a balanced approach for organizations to address economic, social and environmental issues in a way that aims to benefit people, communities and society.
6. People in positions of authority are exempt from their organization's ethics standards.

MULTIPLE CHOICE: Circle the letter before the correct answer in each of the following questions.

1. The concepts of trust, integrity, and _______ are part of the value system of total quality.
   A. Morality B. Responsibility
   C. Trust D. Legality
2. Which of the following is not a value that leads to peak performance and excellence?
   A. Creativity B. Quality
   C. Dependability D. Opportunity
3. Managers have three main responsibilities in regard to ethics. Which of the following is NOT one of those?
   A. They are responsible for creating an internal environment that promotes, expects, and rewards ethical behavior.
   B. They are responsible for helping employees make ethical choices.
   C. They are responsible for setting an example of ethical behavior.
   D. They are responsible for helping employees follow through and exhibit ethical behavior after the appropriate choices have been made.
4. When handling an ethical dilemma, managers should select the option that will most likely:
   A. Pass the various ethics tests B. Build strength in the organization
   C. Set the best example for employees D. None of the above
5. When providing ethics training, it is important to:
   A. Facilitate, don't preach B. Stimulate discussion
   C. Highlight practical applications D. All of the above are important
6. An organization's responsibilities for ensuring ethical behavior include:
   A. Paying whistleblowers to speak up B. Creating and ethical environment
   C. Establishing in-house courts and juries D. Refusing to talk to the media

Test Key

True/False

1. T	2. F	3. T	4. F	5. T	6. F

Multiple Choice

1. B	2. C	3. A	4. A	5. D	6. B

PARTNERING AND STRATEGIC ALLIANCES

TRUE OR FALSE: Place T or F in the space provided to the left of the statement.

1. The overall purpose of internal partnering is to harness the full potential of the workforce and focus it on continual improvement of quality.

2. Any supplier would make a good partner.
3. If a manufacturer is not careful a customer-supplier partnership can be very costly, especially in the product development cycle.
4. The rationale for partnering with potential competitors is competitiveness.
5. Educational institutions provide on-site customized training, technical assistance, and consulting services to help organizations continually improve their people and their processes.
6. Government mandated partnerships are recommended when dealing with foreign countries.

MULTIPLE CHOICE: Circle the letter before the correct answer in each of the following questions.

1. The maximum benefits of partnering are realized when all parties in the chain of partners:
   A. Are satisfied B. Cooperate
   C. Get what they want D. Trust each other
2. Partnering can lead to continual improvements in such key areas as relationships between customers and suppliers, customer satisfaction, and
   A. Increased competitiveness B. Increased resources
   C. Processes and products D. Quality Control
3. Internal partnering occurs at three levels. Which of the following is NOT one of these levels?
   A. Team-to-team partnerships
   B. Management-to-management partnerships
   C. Management-to-employee partnerships
   D. Employee-to-employee partnerships
4. Successful supplier partnerships evolve in seven stages. They begin in the following order: Uncertainty and tentativeness; Short-term pressures; Need for new opportunity and ________.
   A. Adoption of new values B. Mature partnering
   C. Adoption of new paradigms D. Awareness of potential
5. Educational institutions provide which of the following services to help organizations continually improve their people and their processes.
   A. On-site customized training B. Technical assistance
   C. Consulting services D. All of the above
6. The rules for establishing global partnerships are the same as those for establishing domestic partnerships when:
   A. Partnerships are based on sound business principles rather than politics
   B. Governments agree to guarantee profits
   C. Governments are influenced
   D. Sound business principles are not allowed to inhibit partnerships

Test Key

True/False

1. T 2. F 3. F 4. T 5. T 6. F

Multiple Choice

1. B 2. C 3. B 4. C 5. D 6. A

QUALITY CULTURE: CHANGING HEARTS, MINDS, AND ATTITUDES

TRUE OR FALSE: Place T or F in the space provided to the left of the statement.

1. Expectations are important determinants of organizational culture.
2. If an organization begins to decline after moving to total quality it should return to its traditional approach.
3. The most effective way to implement changes is to make sure all employees have sufficient warning prior to the actual changes.
4. It might be necessary to change an organization's leadership to ensure needed cultural change.
5. The key people in an organization that is establishing a quality culture are those who can facilitate and those who can inhibit implementation of the change.
6. To maintain a quality culture organizations must recognize and reward behaviors that nurture quality.

MULTIPLE CHOICE: Circle the letter before the correct answer in each of the following questions.

1. There are several primary reasons why cultural change must either precede or at least parallel the implementation of total quality. Which of the following is NOT a primary reason?
   A. Moving to Total Quality takes time.
   B. Employees may not adapt to too many changes.
   C. It can be difficult to overcome the past
   D. Change cannot occur in a hostile environment
2. Which of the following is NOT a law of organizational change?
   A. Involve everyone affected by change in making it.
   B. Be prepared to listen and observe.
   C. Trust people and treat them with dignity and respect.
   D. Understand the history behind the current culture.
3. Which of the following strategies are needed for establishing a quality culture?
   A. Take a hearts and minds approach
   B. Put the planned changes in writing
   C. Support of management
   D. All the strategies above are needed for establishing a quality culture.
4. Advocates of change:
   A. Are often unaware of how a proposed change will be perceived by potential resisters.
   B. Fear a loss of control.
   C. Sometimes fear the unknown.
   D. Are patient with the concerns of resisters.
5. Strategies for establishing a quality culture include which of the following?
   A. Watching shocking videos
   B. Realization of the work effort
   C. Developing a plan for making the changes
   D. Rebuilding teams
6. Which of the following is a strategy for maintaining a quality culture?
   A. Increase the company's debt-to-assets ratio
   B. Streamline the RFP process
   C. Discourage initiative in favor of SOPs
   D. Keep employees involved

Test Key

True/False

1. T 2. F 3. F 4. T 5. T 6. T

Multiple Choice

1. B 2. C 3. D 4. A 5. C 6. D

CUSTOMER SATISFACTION, RETENTION, AND LOYALTY

TRUE OR FALSE: Place T or F in the space provided to the left of the statement.

1. The customer in a total quality setting defines quality.
2. It is important to acquire as many customers as an organization is able because customers are not reliable and an organization must always be replacing a lost customer.
3. Communication just happens.
4. Quality Function Deployment is a model for incorporating customer input and feedback into product development.
5. Meeting customer specifications does not produce customer satisfaction.
6. Satisfied customers will not migrate to a competitor.

MULTIPLE CHOICE: Circle the letter before the correct answer in each of the following questions.

1. In a total quality setting, quality is defined by:
   A. The employee B. The customer
   C. The management D. The organization
2. An organization with a customer focus is:
   A. Outward-looking B. Inward-looking
   C. Established D. Continually improving
3. Which of the following mechanisms can help improve communication?
   A. An internal customer
   B. Self-managed and cross-departmental teams
   C. Organization employees
   D. External customers
4. Which of the following statements are true concerning communication with customers?
   A. Must extend only to internal customers. B. Is never misunderstood.
   C. Is essential in a competitive marketplace D. Is not necessary in a small town
5. The customer loyalty model consists of which of the following components?
   A. Business performance
   B. Global perceptions
   C. Loyalty behaviors
   D. All of the above are components of the customer loyalty model
6. The best way to generate customer loyalty is to provide customers with:
   A. Rebates B. Discounts
   C. Superior value D. Uninhibited access

Test Key

True/False

1. T 2. F 3. F 4. T 5. T 6. F

Multiple Choice

1. B 2. A 3. B 4. C 5. D 6. C

EMPLOYEE EMPOWERMENT

TRUE OR FALSE: Place T or F in the space provided to the left of the statement.

1. Without empowerment, involvement is just another management tool that doesn't work.
2. Employee empowerment is a new name for participatory management.
3. A workforce that is ready for empowerment is accustomed to critical thinking.
4. A quality circle is a group of employees that meets regularly for the purpose of identifying, recommending, and making workplace improvement.
5. Employee enlistment means not simply empowering employees to participate in the decision-making process but expecting them to do so.
6. Fear of exclusion can cause managers to resist employee empowerment.

MULTIPLE CHOICE: Circle the letter before the correct answer in each of the following questions.

1. Employee empowerment is:
   A. Employee involvement in decision making.
   B. Power of the employee to make suggestions that will be reviewed by management
   C. Employee input that is heard, seriously considered, and followed up on whether it is accepted or not.
   D. Power of the employee to make a decision without management involvement.
2. The primary inhibitor of empowerment is:
   A. The Wohcao Syndrome
   B. Human nature's resistance to change.
   C. Resistance from employees and unions.
   D. Resistance from management.
3. The word that best describes management's role in employee empowerment is:
   A. Facilitation B. Leadership
   C. Commitment D. All of the above
4. Which of the following strategies will help organizations move beyond empowerment to enlistment?
   A. Set up a reward system.
   B. Make it clear to all employees that their ownership is not just wanted and needed but that it is expected.
   C. Make it clear to implement suggestions.
   D. Empower employees for suggestions that are implemented.
5. A workforce that is ready for empowerment:
   A. Is accustomed to critical thinking
   B. Understands the decision making process

C. Knows where it fits into the big picture

D. All of the above

6. Which of the following is an element of management's role in empowerment?

A. Commitment

B. Establishing quality circles

C. Establishing customer feedback mechanisms

D. Being impatient to earn employee buy-in

Test Key

True/False

1. T	2. F	3. T	4. T	5. T	6. T

Multiple Choice

1. C	2. B	3. D	4. B	5. D	6. A

Cooperation

Cooperation that was prompted by the devastation brought by war caught on and became the cornerstone of the competitiveness of both countries.

High-quality education and training

Germany and Japan take different routes, but they arrive at the same place regarding education and training. Germany uses a highly structured apprenticeship program that emphasizes both skills development and academic achievement. Japan relies on excellent primary and secondary education supplemented by industry-based training to prepare front-line employees.

Employee involvement and empowerment

In both Germany and Japan, employees are involved in functions traditionally viewed as management functions in the U.S. These functions include setting working hours, introducing new technologies, establishing compensation levels, human-resource planning, work design, and the provision of training.

Leadership at all levels

In both Germany and Japan, leadership occurs at all levels and leadership training is provided not just for managers but also for front-line employees. This is important in that it tends to improve the quality of employee involvement in continual improvement efforts.

Teamwork

In Germany and Japan, not only is work done by teams of employees, but the planning and designing of work, introduction of new technologies, and establishment of compensation levels are also done by teams that involve representatives from labor and management.

3. A workforce that is ready for empowerment is accustomed to critical thinking.
4. A quality circle is a group of employees that meets regularly for the purpose of identifying, recommending, and making workplace improvement.
5. Employee enlistment means not simply empowering employees to participate in the decision-making process but expecting them to do so.
6. Fear of exclusion can cause managers to resist employee empowerment.

MULTIPLE CHOICE: Circle the letter before the correct answer in each of the following questions.

1. Employee empowerment is:
   A. Employee involvement in decision making.
   B. Power of the employee to make suggestions that will be reviewed by management
   C. Employee input that is heard, seriously considered, and followed up on whether it is accepted or not.
   D. Power of the employee to make a decision without management involvement.
2. The primary inhibitor of empowerment is:
   A. The Wohcao Syndrome
   B. Human nature's resistance to change.
   C. Resistance from employees and unions.
   D. Resistance from management.
3. The word that best describes management's role in employee empowerment is:
   A. Facilitation B. Leadership
   C. Commitment D. All of the above
4. Which of the following strategies will help organizations move beyond empowerment to enlistment?
   A. Set up a reward system.
   B. Make it clear to all employees that their ownership is not just wanted and needed but that it is expected.
   C. Make it clear to implement suggestions.
   D. Empower employees for suggestions that are implemented.
5. A workforce that is ready for empowerment:
   A. Is accustomed to critical thinking
   B. Understands the decision making process
   C. Knows where it fits into the big picture
   D. All of the above
6. Which of the following is an element of management's role in empowerment?
   A. Commitment
   B. Establishing quality circles
   C. Establishing customer feedback mechanisms
   D. Being impatient to earn employee buy-in

Test Key

Multiple Choice

1. A 2. B 3. B 4. A 5. C 6. B

True/False

1. T 2. F 3. T 4. T 5. T 6. T

Multiple Choice

1. C 2. B 3. D 4. B 5. D 6. A

Cooperation

Cooperation that was prompted by the devastation brought by war caught on and became the cornerstone of the competitiveness of both countries.

High-quality education and training

Germany and Japan take different routes, but they arrive at the same place regarding education and training. Germany uses a highly structured apprenticeship program that emphasizes both skills development and academic achievement. Japan relies on excellent primary and secondary education supplemented by industry-based training to prepare front-line employees.

Employee involvement and empowerment

In both Germany and Japan, employees are involved in functions traditionally viewed as management functions in the U.S. These functions include setting working hours, introducing new technologies, establishing compensation levels, human-resource planning, work design, and the provision of training.

Leadership at all levels

In both Germany and Japan, leadership occurs at all levels and leadership training is provided not just for managers but also for front-line employees. This is important in that it tends to improve the quality of employee involvement in continual improvement efforts.

Teamwork

In Germany and Japan, not only is work done by teams of employees, but the planning and designing of work, introduction of new technologies, and establishment of compensation levels are also done by teams that involve representatives from labor and management.

OTHER USEFUL BOOKS

DATABASE MANAGEMENT SYSTEM

Salient Features

- Comprehensive coverage of theory and utilization of DBMS
- It is incredibly, robust, portable and adaptable
- This book coverage Solved examples
- Provide multiple-choice questions of PL/SQL
- Provides Lab Guide
- Includes model Paper
- Provides examination Questions
- Includes interview questions etc

Edition : Latest **ISBN : 9789381068267** **Pages (Approx.) : 488**

DATA STRUCTURES

Theory, Problems and Algorithms

Salient Features

- Comprehensive coverage of the syllabus
- Numerous illustrative examples with visual illustrations
- Development of algorithms in a lucid manner
- Attractive presentation and easy language
- Source code of all the data structures and algorithms in C language
- Glossary of terms for ready reference

Edition : Second **ISBN : 9789382609582** **Pages (Approx.) : 480**

DESIGN & ANALYSIS OF ALGORITHMS

Salient Features

- Asymptotic Notations
- Recurrences
- Sorting Algorithms
- Mathematical Formulae
- Linear Time Algorithms
- BST
- B Tree
- OBST
- AVL Tree
- Order Statistics Tree
- RB Tree
- Matrix Chain Multiplication
- LCS problem
- Knapsack problem
- Huffman Code Algorithm
- Amortization
- B-Trees
- Binomial Heaps
- Fibonacci Heap
- Disjoint Sets
- Backtracking
- Prim's Algorithm

Edition : Fourth **ISBN : 9789382609438** **Pages (Approx.) : 632**